The Struggle
for Pedagogies

The Struggle for Pedagogies

Critical and Feminist Discourses as Regimes of Truth

Jennifer M. Gore

ROUTLEDGE
New York   London

Published in 1993 by

Routledge
An imprint of Routledge, Chapman and Hall, Inc.
29 West 35 Street
New York, NY 10001

Published in Great Britain by

Routledge
11 New Fetter Lane
London ECAP 4EE

Copyright © 1993 by Routledge, Chapman and Hall, Inc.

Printed in the United States of America

Library of Congress Cataloging-in-Publication Data

Gore, Jennifer, 1959–
    The struggle for pedagogies : critical and feminist discourses as
regimes of truth / by Jennifer Mary Gore.
        p.   cm.
    Includes bibliographical references and index.
    ISBN 0-415-90563-X — ISBN 0-415-90564-8 (pbk.)
    1. Critical pedagogy.   2. Women—Education.   3. Feminism.
I. Title.
LC196.G67   1992
370.19—dc20   92-20918
                                                                          CIP

ISBN 0-415-90563-X (HB)
ISBN 0-415-90564-8 (PB)

To my parents
Jill Gore and Peter Gore

Contents

Acknowledgments

It is impossible to name all the individuals who have helped or in some way supported me in this endeavor. Some special people must be mentioned however because without them this book might never have been written and certainly would never have been completed.

This book was conceived and written as part of my Ph.D. studies at the University of Wisconsin-Madison, where I was very fortunate to have had the opportunity to work with other graduate students and faculty whose intellectual and political positions contributed profoundly to my own development. I am especially grateful to James Ladwig, Marie Brennan, Ken Zeichner, Elizabeth Ellsworth, Tom Popkewitz, Michael Apple, Bruce King, Ingolfur Johannesson, Ahmad Sultan, and Cameron McCarthy.

Those dear friends and colleagues who, in addition to the members of my committee, critically read the manuscript at various stages: Alison Dewar, Andrew Gitlin, Henry St. Maurice, Denise Meredyth, Annette Corrigan, Erica Southgate, Bernadette Baker, Terry Lovat, Helene O'Neill, and Ross Morrow deserve special thanks for their efforts and for the kindness of their responses which helped me find the courage to complete this project.

My former students have a special place in this work, especially Kelly Larsen, Bernadette Baker, Erica Southgate, and Chris Carley. For the ways in which our struggles have shaped this struggle, I am indebted.

Expressing enthusiastic support for my project from the beginning, Jayne Fargnoli at Routledge has provided boundless confidence and patience which have helped bring this project to fruition. Jennifer Allen, Jennifer Doyle, Terry Lovat and Pam Nilan, colleagues at The University of Newcastle, have been indispensable not only because they pushed my thinking but also because they made all kinds of concessions for my behavior during the final moments. I also appreciate my "cell-mates" in the Office Block (Out Back) building whose support kept me sane and smiling.

A special thanks is due to Erica Southgate, without whose entertaining and varied assistance sorting through the many details of this book during the final days and weeks of the project, the manuscript may still have been scattered across my desk and office floor. Rosalie Bunn, just beginning her postgraduate study while I was in the throes of completion, kindly helped where possible and proofread the entire manuscript. A research grant from The University of Newcastle's Research Management Committee partially supported the final stages of manuscript preparation.

Finally, I owe my greatest debt of thanks to James Ladwig, whose insightful and sensitive readings of endless drafts of this book helped me to articulate what I wanted to say. For his willingness to continue our struggles, with inordinate patience and understanding, my gratitude and my love.

Preface

Recently I received a research grant to follow up some of the ideas presented in this book. Amusingly, the formal grant offer had recorded my project as "Pedagogy and the disciplining of bofdies." While this was no doubt a simple typing error, it struck me that, to some people at least, whether it was bodies or bofdies, pedagogy or pedagogies, it was all a bit fuzzy. "Pedagogies," used in the title and throughout this book, (like "bofdies") does not even appear in my dictionary. However, I believe its use is important to signify the multiple approaches and practices that fall under the pedagogy umbrella. To rely upon the singular form is to imply greater unity and coherence than is warranted for a domain in which there is so much variation and contestation not only about meaning, but about function and goals.

Enormous obstacles are faced, and, indeed, created by those who seek (and seek to understand) new pedagogies. Many of these obstacles arise from the fundamental tension in pedagogy itself that requires of those who seek to change it their participation in it. My aim in this book is to begin to explore and explain the struggle that is pedagogy.

In particular, I focus on discourses of radical pedagogy and consider why my own efforts to teach in ways framed by those discourses so often felt like failures. As the postmodern condition is said to be diffusing the energies of even the most dogmatic of activists (within the sphere of the academy, at least); as many engaged in radical political projects perceive increased fracturing of their alliances; as the petty politics of institutions and personalities operate in ways such that individuals are marked as guilty by suspicion, the desire to participate in one's own failure seems not only an absurd recognition but an inescapable condition. Analyzing critical pedagogy and feminist pedagogy discourses through the lens of Foucault's notion, "regime of truth," has enabled me to identify ways to move within and beyond the paralysis that many have associated with postmodernism.

It will seem odd to some readers that I would focus on the marginalized discourses of critical and feminist pedagogies as regimes of truth. These discourses are grounded in particular, oppositional political and social movements. The pedagogies these discourses attempt to construct *are* radical (fundamental, extreme and iconoclastic). It is the project of *The Struggle for Pedagogies* to explore how it is that self-proclaimed emancipatory discourses, such as the named discourses of radical pedagogy, can have dominating effects.

Framed, as they so often are, within modernist concerns for universal explanations and for progress, I argue that these radical pedagogies are doomed to fail. However, this "failure" is not an ontological reality. Rather, it is constructed out of personal and collective frames (analytical, social, and political). That pedagogy is approached by critical and feminist discourses through modernist frames is hardly surprising, not the least because it is through action that there exists the potential to make some kind of difference. As a site of action in which there is an explicit and sanctioned attempt to exert influence, pedagogy is seductive. For critical and feminist pedagogues, pedagogy is a major site in which to attempt educational and societal change, to attempt to enact visions of different worlds. In this context, pedagogy's appeal is frequently coupled with the modernist temptation for structural and universal explanations and solutions. I argue that these seductions herald the failure of pedagogy on the very terms of its own construction.

While many associate the term pedagogy solely with the field of formal education, I argue that pedagogy is an activity integral to all learning, all knowledge production. Rather than distinguishing between pedagogy in the disciplinary field of education and elsewhere, I distinguish pedagogy that occurs within from that which occurs outside of formal educational institutions. I argue that the particular character of pedagogy within formal educational institutions has been largely neglected; yet, as the always-already-there for many of us who profess and practice radical pedagogies, its recognition and analysis offers possibilities for reconstructing and revisioning pedagogy.

Because of my own fundamental commitment to and deep passion for educational practice (I was one of those children who always wanted to teach), and given my concerns about the tendency for discourses of radical pedagogy to "resist" directly addressing practice, I will focus on bodies of literature which claim not only to be primarily concerned with pedagogy, but which also claim to be constructing pedagogies. My aim is not to map the whole field of radical pedagogy—such an aim would be impractical. Mine is not a modernist attempt to capture some extant reality of a field called radical pedagogy. Instead, through joint processes of inscription and description, I highlight tendencies of the discourses that I have analyzed. In focusing on selected discourses, my concern is to demonstrate through illustration some of the dangers and gaps in the ongoing struggles for radical pedagogies. I pursue this task for myself because of my own (differential) commitments to critical pedagogy and feminist pedagogy. Specifically, it was through critical pedagogy that I first found a language with which to name my frustrations with dominant approaches to education. Later, feminist pedagogy resonated both with my growing concerns about the work I was trying to do as a teacher educator in the name of critical pedagogy, and with my emerging feminist consciousness.

Although this book is situated in the specific domain of teacher education, and I address such pedagogical practices as journal keeping and action research, it is my contention that the major arguments presented in *The Struggle for Pedagogies* have implications beyond teacher education and beyond "radical" or oppositional endeavors. While I have consciously avoided the temptation to prescribe strategies for other pedagogues, having instead outlined specific strategies for my own work, my analysis does pose questions for practitioners of pedagogy across the spectrum of political and disciplinary affiliations. For instance, focusing on radical pedagogies, which are discursively positioned in opposition to traditional pedagogies, will accentuate the tensions within more traditional pedagogies. Similarly, by naming some of the historical consistencies of institutionalized pedagogy (such as its normative and regulative aspects), I highlight the cross-disciplinary implications of my work. From this perspective, the dynamics revealed at any micro level (such as teacher education) can be seen to speak more generally about institutionalized pedagogy. Thus, while teacher educators might find my analysis particularly pertinent, given the examples I provide from their field, it is my hope that pedagogical theorists and practitioners from a wide range of other contexts will seriously consider implications of those arguments that address the specificity of their own contexts.

I do not mean to claim or imply a monopoly on pedagogical discourse for the disciplinary field of Education. There has been some "cross-

fertilization" of ideas on pedagogy among disciplines, especially among
Women's Studies, Literary Studies, and Education (e.g., Culley and Portuges, 1985; Hill, 1990; Gabriel and Smithson, 1990; Spivak, 1992) and
even including such fields as Architecture (e.g., Dutton and Grant, 1991).
Clearly, there is room for much more. In this book, I have focused on
those discourses that have constructed radical pedagogy within Education
and, specifically, within teacher education. The reality is that much of
this work draws heavily, perhaps parochially, on other work in Education.
In partial defense of this practice, I would argue that education is an
important, unique site for the study of pedagogy and, as such, *ought* to
be prominent in any examination of pedagogy discourse. Some of the
most sophisticated work available on pedagogy comes from the field of
Education. The current limits of reciprocity among disciplines can be
attributed to institutional politics and disciplinary boundaries. It is my
hope that, despite focusing on educational discourses, my analysis will
provide openings for other disciplines.

The work presented in this book is clearly connected with other efforts
to re-examine and re-vision radical education (from a number of disciplinary perspectives) in the context of the recent ascendancy of postmodern and poststructural discourses in the academy (e.g., Aronowitz
and Giroux, 1991; Ball, 1990, Cherryholmes, 1988, Ellsworth, 1989;
Giroux, 1991; Henricksen and Morgan, 1990; Lather, 1991; Luke and
Gore, 1992; McLaren, 1991 ; Morton and Zavarzadeh, 1991; Wexler,
1987; Weiler, 1991). Furthermore, I position my work with other poststructuralist feminist challenges to critical pedagogy and attempts to construct pedagogies (e.g., Britzman, 1991; Ellsworth, 1989; Lather, 1991;
Luke and Gore, 1992).

I believe this book contributes to what I am calling "the struggle for
pedagogies" in a number of important ways. First, my focus on the
institutionalization of pedagogy points to a level and site of analysis that
has been largely neglected. Unlike those theorist/practitioners who have
reminded us that the power of the teacher is mediated by relations of
class, race, and gender (and other social formations), I emphasize the
power relations which operate through the fundamental and specific
relation of teacher and student. Previous "micro" level analyses of classrooms, more characteristic of traditional conceptions of pedagogy, have
tended to ignore the constitutive role of power in pedagogy. Radical
pedagogies, on the other hand, have tended to focus on the "macro"
level of ideologies and institutions while down-playing the instructional
act. My work fits between and responds to these discourses by focusing
on the "micro" functioning of power relations in pedagogy. In so doing,

I argue that the instructional act is an important site of investigation for radical educators—not investigation for the purpose of prescribing instructional practices, but investigation that seeks to identify specific practices that have made pedagogy what it is today.

Second, and related, it is my intention that the book function both as a poststructural critique of pedagogy and as a pedagogical demonstration of poststructural critique. As one effort to understand structural versus poststructural discourses, this book is consistent with major social theory debates over structural versus poststructural positions (those which find their grounding prior to the construction of discourses, for example, in the economy or in the category "woman," and those which reject such universalized and decontextualized notions and enter debates and critiques in specific contexts). As is consistent with other poststructural critiques, I demonstrate the universalizing, dominating tendencies of critical and feminist pedagogy discourses as regimes of truth. Here, I draw repeatedly on Foucault's notion that *everything* is dangerous, that "liberatory" and "emancipatory" discourses have no guaranteed effects. In order to make this critique I have attempted to step outside both the critical and feminist "regimes." Readings from within these regimes might not accept the perspective I propose, given that, as Cocks (1989) puts it, recognition of a regime must occur from "outside the pale" of that regime.

Insofar as this book functions as a poststructural critique, it also demonstrates aspects of such critique. Specifically, my analysis is grounded in the particular practices which generated the study rather than in philosophical debates. I have tried to avoid a rhetoric of solutions and pronouncements, having chosen instead to articulate local possibilities through an in-depth, systematic demonstration of my key arguments. Hence, it is my intention that there be congruence between what is argued for and the way it is argued.

Third, I believe this book points to ways out of the pessimism so often associated with poststructuralism and postmodernism. Perhaps it is in postmodern times that one can rest with the ongoing struggles of an endeavor that will never reach conclusion, that will never arrive at a final solution. I certainly find my ongoing struggle for pedagogies enabling in comparison with the failure inherent in the modernist framing of its own enterprise.

In the final chapter, I make specific suggestions for my own research and practice within teacher education that move beyond the kind of universalizing principles found even in some of the most recent attempts to re-construct radical pedagogies. Furthermore, through its suggestions for disrupting the regimes of critical and feminist pedagogies, and in its focus on reflexivity and re-assembling—working to understand "what we are today" and how we all participate in regimes of truth—the book provides strategic, but not prescriptive guidance for work in radical pedagogy, specifically, in teacher education. I argue that visions of different classrooms and different societies need not be rejected, just worked out locally. Hence, a different role for the intellectual is suggested—not a vanguard intellectual, leader of the masses, but one who is involved in local and specific struggles. This book addresses my specific struggles, as theorist and teacher, with critical and feminist pedagogies.

ONE

Introduction

I'm not into this regimented reflective stuff. (Scott, course journal, 1987).

This book has its origins in my attempts to practice radical pedagogy in teacher education. Despite my consistent struggles to feel confident that what I was doing in my classes was "right," Scott's journal entry was, and still is, a powerful statement of the inconsistencies and difficulties of radical pedagogical practice. My initial reaction to his comment was to view him as a recalcitrant student, unwilling to see the value of reflective journal keeping (see Gore, 1990a). At the same time, I questioned my understandings of radical pedagogy, assuming that I must have missed something, that I had not quite grasped what it meant to do radical pedagogy. I turned to the literature of radical pedagogy hoping to find "truth" there.

The direction and clarity I sought were not forthcoming. Rather, my recent immersion in critical and feminist pedagogy texts and my experiences as teacher and as student in classes framed by critical or feminist pedagogy "principles," helped me to see that the problem Scott highlighted was much larger than any recalcitrance on his part or ignorance on mine.

I would instead argue that there are many dimensions to what I call the struggle for pedagogies. In this study, I focus on discursive formations and discursive practices, on the construction of objects, statements, concepts, and strategies with sufficient regularity to enable the naming of discourses. In particular, this is an examination of the contemporary discourses of critical pedagogy and feminist pedagogy. I am using "discourse" in a poststructuralist sense where the concern is to answer such

1

questions as "How does discourse function?" "Where is it to be found?" "How does it get produced and regulated?" "What are its social effects?" In short, discourse in this sense is not a question of meaning or of method, but a description of function. My focus is therefore on practices within institutions and disciplines through which intellectuals participate in the formation and functioning of the discourses of critical and feminist pedagogy.[1]

There are four issues with which I want to introduce my analysis of critical and feminist pedagogy discourses: first, the ambiguities around "pedagogy" generally and around "critical pedagogy" and "feminist pedagogy," specifically; second, what I see as the fragmentation of these discourses; third, the institutional locations of these discourses both in the academy and in schools, that position critical and feminist pedagogy within broader discourses of social regulation and within a certain intellectual "will to truth"; fourth, what could be called the continuing marginality of critical and feminist pedagogy discourses as they seem only minimally to impact mainstream educational policy and practice, and teacher education. In this chapter, I introduce each of these issues and begin to situate them in social theoretical discussions about power and knowledge. I also outline the ways in which these issues will be carried through as themes and as direction for the remainder of the book.

While my own practice provided the impetus for this study, and is presented as its context, reasons for analyzing the internal relations of power and knowledge in the discourses of critical and feminist pedagogy extend beyond my own practical educational interests. I have become increasingly conscious of the marginal status of these radical pedagogies within the educational community at large, and within teacher education more specifically: it is clear their material impact on what takes place in the name of education in either schools or universities is limited. While it is possible to point to all kinds of external social and political conditions to explain the marginality (such as the predominance of neo-conservative politics in the 1980s), I have come to believe that reasons can also be found *within* the discourses of radical pedagogy. The reasons I consider internal to these discourses, which might be associated with their continued marginality, circulate around what I see as the discourses' dominating effects and their regimes of truth. Given these radical discourses' proclaimed allegiance to "empowerment" and "freedom," mainstream educators, it seems to me, would be justified in seeing these discourses as hypocritical or at least inconsistent. This situation, as it contributes to the struggle for radical pedagogies, is of concern to me. Therefore, this detailed exploration of contemporary discourses of critical and feminist pedagogy aims to strengthen the discourses both internally and in relation to other educational discourses. My concern about radical pedagogy discourses is similar to a concern articulated by the editors of *Telos* (1981–82) a decade ago: "critically theorizing about society, which once seemed so important because it would explain the world to itself . . . now appears to be only theory again since it reaches no 'material base' " (p. 115).

CONSTRUCTIONS OF "PEDAGOGY"

What is meant by the term "pedagogy"? Etymologically, the term refers to the science of teaching children. Some have called for a strict application of the term pedagogy to the teaching of *children*, which has led to the emergence of a body of educational literature on "andragogy," the science of teaching adults. Some feminist educators suggest the term "gynagogy" for the teaching of or by women, citing and rejecting the early usage of "pedagogue": "a man having the oversight of a child or youth . . . an attendant slave who led a boy to school . . . a schoolmaster" (Klein, 1987, p. 187). Klein (1987) "compromises" with the term "feminist teaching practice." While these constructions are based on whom is taught, most commonly "pedagogy" is used interchangeably with "teaching" or "instruction" referring, with various degrees of specificity, to the act or process of teaching. Frequently, as in my current institution's Department of Pedagogical Studies, "pedagogy" is linked with so-called positivistic approaches to educational science.[2]

Of specific interest here, when the term is attached to particular sociopolitical approaches, we find "progressive pedagogy," "radical pedagogy," "critical pedagogy," "feminist pedagogy," "socialist pedagogy," and others. These approaches have roots in particular political and theoretical movements and are variously constructed as oppositional to "mainstream" or "traditional" schooling practices and theories. In particular, a "critical social science" view of pedagogy has given rise to various critiques of, and alternatives to, "mainstream" pedagogy. Unlike approaches to pedagogy rooted in ostensibly positivistic and phenomenological thought, "critical" approaches focus on pedagogy as constitutive of power relations, making power a central category of their analysis. One strand of critical work has concerned itself with the development of theories of the pedagogical relation as a power relation (e.g., Bernstein, 1975, 1986, 1990; Bourdieu and Passeron, 1977). Another strand has focused on "pedagogy as possibility" and has been concerned with developing a discourse of "critical pedagogy" (e.g., Freire, 1973; Giroux,

1988a; McLaren, 1989; Shor, 1980; Simon, 1987). With roots in feminist political movements, some scholars have argued that schooling is patriarchal (e.g., Clarricoates, 1981; Grumet, 1988a, Kelly and Nihlen, 1982) and are working towards the articulation and practice of "feminist pedagogies" (e.g., Lewis, 1990a; Maher, 1985a; Morgan, 1987; Mumford, 1985; Schniedewind, 1985).

Unlike "mainstream" pedagogical discourses, the critical and feminist work on pedagogy has addressed "macro" issues in schooling, such as the institutions and ideologies within which pedagogy is situated. Beginning from the premise that schooling is not neutral, critical and feminist approaches to pedagogy emphasize their own social vision(s) for education and schooling, in an attempt to connect the macro and micro. While the dualisms created by such analytical oppositions as macro and micro, social vision and instruction, may be useful to begin to understand differences in arguments about pedagogy, they do not reflect the empirical realities of pedagogy. For instance, those approaches that emphasize instruction also contain within them a social vision, perhaps not an explicit vision, but often one that is based on notions of individual development and socialization. Hence, as Felman (1982) comments: "Every pedagogy has historically emerged as a critique of pedagogy" (p. 24); each pedagogy is never *only* a new set of instructional ideas.

While one could argue that the term "pedagogy" (indeed, any term) has no single meaning in and of itself, and that meaning is always struggled over and determined as it is constructed by particular discourses, I want to argue here for a particular, yet broad meaning for the term "pedagogy," which includes both instruction and social vision. In so doing, I enter into the struggle for meaning in a way which allows me to pose a particular critique of discourses of radical pedagogy while retaining my commitment to, and struggles with, classroom practice. According to Lusted (1986), pedagogy, as a concept,

> draws attention to the *process* through which knowledge is produced. Pedagogy addresses the "how" questions involved not only in the transmission or reproduction of knowledge but also in its production. Indeed, it enables us to question the validity of separating these activities so easily by asking under what conditions and through what means we "come to know". How one teaches . . . becomes inseparable from what is being taught and, crucially, how one learns. (pp. 2–3)

This focus on the process of knowledge production—on "how" (as how connects to what and why, etc.)—is the meaning I wish to ascribe to "pedagogy" for the purposes of this book. This meaning is not the same "how" of pedagogy that is often associated with "methods" courses in teacher education programs. Rather, following Lusted, it is a kind of focus on the processes of teaching that demands that attention be drawn to the politics of those processes and to the broader political contexts within which they are situated. Therefore, instruction and social vision are analytical components of pedagogy; insofar as the concept implies both, each requires attention.

The meaning I ascribe to "pedagogy" is consistent with the political underpinnings of much radical educational discourse; that is, this particular notion of pedagogy, with its concern for how and in whose interests knowledge is produced and reproduced, shares the concerns of radical educational discourse. Thus, my analysis of radical pedagogies is intended as a critique that allies with the critical and feminist discourses, and offers itself in a general spirit of support. I am committed to the kinds of projects these discourses support, which oppose oppressive gender, race, class, and other social formations, and attempt to facilitate more "democratic" and "emancipatory" schooling for all. Hence, the immediate practical problem undergirding this study is how to use radical pedagogies, whose projects I support, in my own practice as a teacher educator, when these discourses seem to offer minimal assistance in responding to criticisms like Scott's. That is, as Scott identified, some of my difficulties as a teacher educator were located in the instructional act. I struggled to actualize the rhetoric of "radical" teacher education in the details of classroom practice, both in terms of specific content and in terms of instructional strategies.

It is helpful here to elaborate the meaning of pedagogy. If pedagogy is understood as the process of knowledge production, it follows that discourses of radical pedagogy can be seen to have at least two pedagogies: (1) the pedagogy argued for (the claims made about the process of knowledge production in radical pedagogy) and (2) the pedagogy of the argument (the process of knowledge production evident in the argument itself). Scott identified inconsistencies between the pedagogy I was arguing for and the pedagogy of my argument. One theme of this book is to explore possible inconsistencies in the pedagogies of critical and feminist pedagogy discourses. As an example, consider a discourse of radical pedagogy which makes schools its object. To construct such a discourse in a way that would place the burden for change on teachers, but would not offer concrete guidance for what teachers could actually do to facilitate such change, the discourse would seem both partial and hollow. While naming a discourse (that addresses a social vision, but neglects instructional aspects) "pedagogical", might have strong rhetorical value among teachers (in legitimating the academic and her/his discourse to other teachers) this approach could both deny and mystify the experiences of teachers, rather than affirm or interpret them. Attention to politics *and* pedagogy does not necessarily arrive at the politics *of* pedagogy. The distinction I have drawn here, between the pedagogy of the argument and the pedagogy argued for, provides a central lens for this study whereby, as I shall elaborate in Chapter 3, the pedagogy of the argument becomes a major point of my critique.

FRAGMENTED DISCOURSES

At this point, I want to clarify the objects of my study that I have referred to as "discourses of radical pedagogy" or "critical and feminist pedagogy discourses." First, I have deliberately limited the focus of this study to an analysis of those discourses which claim to focus centrally on *pedagogy*, and which also claim to be constructing pedagogies; that is, those discourses that guided my practice as a teacher educator, discourses which are rooted in particular political and theoretical traditions that resonate with my own dissatisfactions regarding "mainstream" educational approaches. This delimitation also emerges from my concern that insufficient attention has been paid to pedagogy, in its broad sense of social vision *and* instruction. Second, while many attempts have been made to develop alternative pedagogies (consider, for example, the work of Dewey and Kohl),[3] my focus is on contemporary discourses of radical pedagogy: discourses which hold academic currency to the extent that they appear in academic journals, are discussed in university departments, and are at stake at professional meetings. Specifically, I address discourses of "critical pedagogy" and discourses of "feminist pedagogy." (I will discuss limitations of these decisions in Chapter 2).

Addressing the range of contemporary academic work that claims the label "critical pedagogy" or "feminist pedagogy" requires an analysis of fragmented discourses. The following chapter explores the various strands of feminist and critical pedagogy which, at the moment, constitute these fragmented discourses. Briefly put, I will outline four strands of radical pedagogy that are distinguished by the various emphases each place on instruction and social vision in the name of pedagogy. (Of course, each has at least some implication both for instruction and for social vision). I identify a strand of feminist pedagogy that emphasizes instructional aspects of pedagogy, emerging primarily from Women's Studies; a strand of feminist pedagogy that emphasizes implications of feminist social visions for education, emerging from Schools of Education; a strand of critical pedagogy that emphasizes a critical social and educational vision, found primarily in the work of Henry Giroux and Peter McLaren in Education; and a strand of critical pedagogy which, in relation to the other strand of critical pedagogy, places more emphasis on instructional practices, found mainly in the work of Paulo Freire and Ira Shor (originally formulated outside the context of Schools of Education).

In Chapter 2, I elaborate the fragmentation and differentiation among discourses of critical and feminist pedagogy. For example, the field of radical pedagogy seems more overtly characterized by a lack of engagement than by disagreement between discourses. That is, rather than addressing the different discourses within radical pedagogy itself, each strand of radical pedagogy tends to situate itself in opposition to dominant/traditional educational theories and practices, each asserting itself as a new alternative. I will argue in Chapter 2 that there is little conversation (in terms of published dialogue) between the feminist pedagogy that emerges out of Women's Studies and the feminist pedagogy that emerges out of Education; there is little dialogue between Freire and Shor, and Giroux and McLaren; and there is virtually no communication between those who practice and/or write about critical pedagogy and those who practice and/or write about feminist pedagogy.

Despite the differences within and between discourses of critical and feminist pedagogy, an examination of their central claims, in terms of the pedagogy argued for, reveals a great number of commonalities. Both critical and feminist pedagogical discourses emphasize student experience and voice (e.g., Berry and Black, 1987; Freire, 1968; Giroux, 1988a; Lewis, 1988, 1990a; McLaren, 1989; Shor, 1980), assert the objectives of self and social empowerment toward broader social transformation (e.g., Culley, 1985; Giroux, 1988a; McLaren, 1988a; Shor and Freire, 1987; Shrewsbury, 1987a), speak about teachers' authority and struggle with the contradictions inherent in the notion of authority for emancipation (e.g., Bright, 1987; Friedman, 1985; Giroux, 1988a; Morgan, 1987; Shor and Freire, 1987; Spelman, 1985), are linked to political and social movements that seek to erase multiple forms of oppression (e.g., Maher, 1985b; McLaren, 1988b) and (when addressed at all) suggest similar classroom practices (e.g., Bell, 1987; Freire, 1968, 1973; Maher, 1985a, 1985b; Mumford, 1985; Schniedewind, 1985; Shor, 1980). If so many commonalities can be named, why is there fragmentation?

The fragmentation of the discourses might be a function of academic work, whereby one can go through an entire academic career without having to read, hear, or see "alternative" discourses. The separation of the discourses might also be the result of strategic moves among intellectuals where, like Bové's (1986) description of the "status quo of intellectual life," "imagining alternatives means competing against other intellectuals and their work" (p. 223). Although such competition might not be manifested in direct confrontations (until recently[4]), competition is nevertheless apparent in separate struggles for ascendancy relative to "dominant" discourses and among "oppositional" discourses. For example, to name these discourses "pedagogies" might be to assert difference vis-à-vis those educational theories that neglect classroom practice, focusing instead on "macro" level critiques of schooling and society; as well, naming certain pedagogies "feminist" is no doubt a strategic move away from those discourses that largely neglect gender oppression in favor of abstractly focusing on issues of class oppression ("patriarchal" discourses). While I support the assertion of these (and other) differentiations, I would argue that they should be made reflexively, and with awareness of how the competitive impulses of academic culture can take precedence over espoused political commitments.

The fragmentation and separation of these discourses, the assertion of difference rather than common interest, the lack of any clear alliances or even substantial engagement with each other's work, and the impulse to dismiss those who do not share the same language, assumptions, commitments, or claim the same label, raises other questions about competition (between intellectuals or discourses) within intellectual fields. Strategies of differentiation and fragmentation might also be explained as political moves to avoid undercutting other oppositional discourses. While those of us who affiliate with "radical" or "oppositional" discourses may need to be careful critiquing each other in ways which would provide "conservative" discourses with more material to use against us, I argue that acknowledging our engagement in complementary enterprises, be they specific projects or particular ideas, has the potential to strengthen our work, and, most certainly, to promote greater self-reflection and self-criticism. Without acknowledging mutual engagement, we risk an insularity that not only reduces the impact of radical work in the field of education generally, but also reduces possibilities for the development of our own work within radical communities locally.

Another, perhaps central reason for strategies of differentiation and fragmentation is that each discourse carries the markings of its own historical struggles for positioning. For instance, feminists have consciously separated themselves from critical pedagogy because they were unable to locate themselves in such discourse. Elizabeth Ellsworth's (1990) summation of the experiences of women of color in "Second

Wave" feminism is similar to the experience of feminists in critical pedagogy (which, until recently, has not attempted to address feminist concerns): "they/we have been included, without making a difference, . . .
have been listened to, without being heard, . . . have been present without being seen" (p. 3). By articulating these kinds of tensions I hope to
offer a clearer sense of the potential for understanding the current fragmentation of the field of radical pedagogy.

In addition to issues of power relations among intellectuals and among
discourses, I consider power relations in the U.S. in comparison with
those of certain other countries as these relations relate to the production
of radical pedagogy discourse; power relations between men and women
as evidenced by the separation of critical and feminist pedagogical discourses along gender lines; power relations at work in the particular
political and theoretical traditions of the discourses; and power relations
that marginalize critical and feminist pedagogy discourses relative to
"mainstream" discourses. Examining discourses of critical and feminist
pedagogy through a lens in which pedagogy is the process of knowledge
production, and in which such production is seen to be connected with
relations of power, helps explicate the fragmentation and inconsistencies
within critical and feminist pedagogies. That is, defining pedagogy as the
"process of knowledge production" draws attention to the fact that the
discourses themselves consist of multiple pedagogies, not just the pedagogies argued for; and, focusing on levels of discursive formation and
practice—where "truth" is constructed—draws attention to the divisive
potentiality of power. I want to focus more closely on the institutional
conditions of critical and feminist discourse construction.

INSTITUTIONAL LOCATION

Broadly defined, the discourses of critical and feminist pedagogy
which are the object of my study are located in the academy. Chapter 2
addresses the particular locations (within the academy) of the various
strands of critical and feminist pedagogy. There are two general issues
that emerge from an analysis of the location and construction of discourses of radical pedagogy in the academy. First, the academic study
of pedagogy has been situated by the rise of schooling within discourses
of social regulation. The notion of pedagogy, historically derived from
the Greek *paidagogia* (where *paidos* is boy and *agogos* is guide), suggests
a kind of guidance of the young. The "birth" of the school, the institutionalization of pedagogy, "arose out of practical needs to cure (ignorance and moral depravity), to reform, to discipline, and to educate

the social body. . . . The school . . . became the site of discursive practice, the practical expression of a discourse of both repression and formation" (Luke, 1989a, pp. 145–146). Despite shifts and movement over time with dynamic social, economic, and political forces shaping the development of "new" pedagogies, pedagogy emerged from and remains enmeshed in discourses of social regulation (Hamilton, 1989).[5] This discursive location of pedagogy introduces another theme of the book; namely, that the regulative aspects of pedagogy are overwhelmingly difficult to throw off, and so the possibilities for "emancipation" and "liberation" in the name of pedagogy (assuming we even know what these terms mean and whom is to be liberated or emancipated from what), are restricted partly by their very location within pedagogy. A specific return to these issues is found in Chapters 4 and 5, where I consider the ways in which the various strands of critical and feminist pedagogy discourse address "authority" and "empowerment," and in Chapter 6, where I elaborate the historical construction of pedagogy.

Second, as academic discourses, critical and feminist pedagogies are historically embedded in institutionally discursive formations of intellectual production. I argue, especially when considering the pedagogy of the argument, that a "will to truth" and a lack of reflexivity are related to these discourses' institutional location. These issues also become major themes of the book as I call for greater reflexivity and humility in the construction of discourses of radical pedagogy.

As a point of introduction to these themes, it is helpful to consider Michel Foucault's references (in translation) at various times to a "will to truth" and a "will to knowledge."[6] What difference (if any) is there between these two expressions? The English "knowledge" apparently combines translations of two French words: *"connaissance"* and *"savoir."* *Connaissance* refers to a particular corpus of knowledge, a particular discipline. *Savoir* is usually defined as knowledge in general, the totality of *connaissances*. Foucault uses *savoir* "in an underlying rather than overall way" (A. M. Sheridan Smith, trans., Foucault, 1972, p. 15).[7] The general distinction appears to be between the will to knowledge as the general desire to know, and the will to truth as the desire to know the difference between truth and falsity in particular disciplines or discourses. This will to truth also requires some knowledge and acceptance of the rules necessary for the acquisition of knowledge in a particular disciplinary field. Because I will be focussing on the desire to construct "truth" within the discourses of critical and feminist pedagogy, I shall use "will to truth" except if referring to a more general desire to know.

The "will to truth" which characterizes much intellectual work is such that the need, desire, or willingness to question one's own work is often lost in the desire to believe that one has found "truth," that one is "right." Although I refer to "one," Foucault did not consider the will to knowledge to be a matter of constitutive agency or individual will, but rather many people acting and struggling with each other within the politics of truth (Rajchman, 1985). Therefore, I also argue that we need to think of an "anonymous, polymorphous" (Foucault, 1977a, pp. 200–201) will to knowledge. My concern is that when discourses of critical or feminist pedagogy present themselves in a fixed, final, "founded" form, that form soon "protects *them* from rethinking and change. It turns what was once 'critical' in their work into a kind of norm or law—a final truth, a final emancipation. For Foucault that is just what critical 'truth' *cannot* be" (Rajchman, 1985, p. 93). As a teacher educator practicing critical and feminist pedagogy, I have wanted to believe that what I am doing is right—it is certainly more difficult to live with uncertainty. But now I am inclined to agree with the function and ethic for the intellectual Foucault proposes: that is, the attempt to constantly question the "truth" of one's thought and oneself.

SUMMARY

The object of my study has been introduced as the discourses of radical pedagogy, within which are located the contemporary discourses of critical and feminist pedagogy. The operative lens views "pedagogy" as the process of knowledge production. This conception of pedagogy draws attention to both the pedagogy argued for and the pedagogy of the argument itself. Pedagogy as the process of knowledge production also begins to draw attention to a power-knowledge connection, particularly as discursive formations and practices are examined. Major themes of the book, emerging from my concerns about the discourses of critical and feminist pedagogy, have also been introduced: (1) the fragmentation of discourses of radical pedagogy; (2) pedagogical constraints that arise from its historical formation as, and institutional location in, discourses of social regulation; and (3) the need for reflexivity to counter dangers of the "will to truth." These themes will be brought together in Chapter 3, and in the subsequent chapters, using Foucault's notion of "regime of truth."

Interest in discourses of critical and feminist pedagogy seems to be growing among certain groups of educators and academics. Consider the increasing number of publications and presentations at professional meetings that address critical or feminist pedagogy. Clearly I have not been alone in my struggle to practice radical pedagogies. However, as I have noted, it seems that radical pedagogies remain marginalized within the broader educational community. This study attempts to understand reasons for the continuing marginalization of critical and feminist pedagogy discourses that might be considered internal to the discourses themselves. I want to re-emphasize that I do so, not in an attempt to destroy or immobilize radical pedagogical work, but rather in an attempt to strengthen that work/my work.

I am well aware of the possibility of negative reactions to this study, particularly from any who should feel threatened by the critique inherent to my pragmatic goal. The continuing marginalization of radical work is likely to set up particularly defensive attitudes, especially toward a critique that claims to emerge from within. In this regard, I share some of the risks articulated by Pierre Bourdieu (1988) in his study of French social theorists around the events of 1968 in France:

> It is well known that no groups love an "informer", especially perhaps when the transgressor or traitor can claim to share in their own highest values. The same people who would not hesitate to acclaim the work of objectification as "courageous" or "lucid" if it is applied to alien, hostile groups will be likely to question the credentials of the special lucidity claimed by anyone who seeks to analyse his [sic] own group. The sorcerer's apprentice who takes the risk of looking into native sorcery and its fetishes, instead of departing to seek in tropical climes the comforting charms of exotic magic, must expect to see turned against him the violence he has unleashed. Karl Kraus . . . says that anyone who rejects the pleasure and easy profits of long-distance criticism, in order to investigate his immediate neighbourhood, which everything bids him hold sacred, must expect the torments of "subjective persecution". (p. 5)

While a study of "foreign" discourses such as, for example, the recently ascendant discourse of cognitive psychology might have been safer and certainly less painful, it seems to me it is time to systematically examine, to take the proverbial "good hard look" at, both critical and feminist pedagogy discourses.

In addition to perhaps stirring the wrath of my "immediate neighborhood," to distance myself from the field of radical pedagogy enough to be able to objectify it is to risk losing the ground I may have gained as an insider—to risk being distanced by others in the field, at the same time as I distance myself in order to complete this study. In so doing, I risk losing touch with the special knowledge to which I might have access as a member of the group. But in order to talk about the group(s) in any objective way I can no longer belong in the same way (Bourdieu, 1988). I make these points to clarify that many aspects of this endeavor have been neither easy nor fun. A celebratory study would have been much more pleasurable, but it was not the study that emerged from my experiences as teacher, student, or scholar of contemporary discourses of radical pedagogy.

Rather, in my re-examinations of the discourses of critical and feminist pedagogy (as well as of myself in relation to the discourses), I have arrived at a skeptical view of both critical and feminist pedagogies. Rather than being paralyzed by this skepticism, or rejecting discourses of radical pedagogy, I have found the work of Foucault helpful in attempting to understand the struggles and contradictions of radical pedagogy and in motivating me to continue to think about (and practice) critical and feminist pedagogies. Foucault says: "Thought is freedom in relation to what one does, the motion by which one detaches oneself from it, establishes it as an object and reflects on it as a problem" (Rabinow, 1984, p. 388). I have certainly found some freedom in problematizing radical pedagogy; freedom which has helped me return to my practical endeavors in teacher education. In publishing this book, it is my hope that others who support radical pedagogies will also find freedom in the analysis I offer.

As already outlined, Chapter 2 provides an elaboration of the differentiation and fragmentation of discourses of critical and feminist pedagogy. Chapter 3 provides an introduction to Foucault's analyses of power-knowledge, particularly to my use of his notion of "regime of truth." Chapters 4 and 5 mark the beginning of a return to specific questions of pedagogy for the radical educator. Taking to task the issues of "authority" and "empowerment" (issues I have found especially troubling in my own practice and which seem to cause internal problems for discourses of radical pedagogy), I demonstrate the analytical power "regime of truth" lends to assist in understanding the difficulties radical pedagogues encounter. The constructions of "authority" and "empowerment" in various strands of critical and feminist pedagogy are analyzed through the perspective afforded by the notion of regime of truth. Chapter 6 provides a discussion of the preceding analysis, examining major findings, comparing the critical and feminist discourses, and revisiting a question introduced in Chapter 3: "Where *does* 'regime of truth' leave us vis-à-vis understanding and practicing radical pedagogy?" Chapter 7 comes full circle to questions of practice in radical teacher education. I consider implications of analyzing discourses of critical and feminist pedagogy as regimes of truth in terms of my own pedagogical practice. Through the process of re-assembling the discourses that have guided my practices as a teacher educator, I also suggest practical and strategic directions toward which this kind of analysis could lead.

While this study focuses on the discourses of radical pedagogy that shape my own work in teacher education, I believe that this analysis engages other educational discourses, indeed, studies outside of education. I deliberately locate this work in the practical site of teacher education in an attempt to avoid getting bogged down in "metatheoretical reflection" (Miedema, 1987, p. 227). I would contradict my own argument if this study were not contextualized. Moreover, given that teacher education is the site of my own practice, I would contradict my own argument to locate the study elsewhere. If this book proves to be of use to academics or teachers in any field, who are concerned with trying to retain a critical openness about scholarship and teaching, it will have served its purpose.

Critical Pedagogies and Feminist Pedagogies: Adversaries, Allies, Other?

Systems of thought are not necessarily opposed in the same way as their authors are: it is always possible to have chosen the wrong adversary. To be sure, differences, sometimes radical ones, do exist: but these differences, being asymmetrical, often elude the simple structure of opposition. (Shoshana Felman, 1985, p. 21)

The primary objects of my analysis are contemporary discourses that claim to be constructing "critical pedagogy" or "feminist pedagogy." Broadly speaking, these discourses outline theories and strategies for the enactment of democratic and emancipatory schooling. One does not have to look far into this literature to notice differences and separations both between and within the two discourses. That is, not only are critical and feminist discourses separated from one another, but there are apparent fragmentations within each discourse, even if the particular distinctions within the discourses are not always clear or articulated in a form of direct opposition or disagreement. The purpose of this chapter is to explore the fragmentation and ambiguity that characterize the critical and feminist pedagogy discourses by identifying various strands within each kind of discourse.[1] I do so by employing the frames established in Chapter 1: first, that pedagogy implies both instructional practices and social visions and second, that the pedagogical presentation of the argument must be considered along with the pedagogy that is being advocated. I emphasize that these frames emerged from my preliminary analysis of differences within critical pedagogy discourse.

I reiterate that this investigation is limited to radical or oppositional discourses that (1) are in invested in constructing a pedagogy and (2) hold academic currency as we move into the 1990s. The first delimitation facilitates a particularly close examination of the instructional side of pedagogy; an examination that has been missing from much radical educational work. As such, it moves toward reconceptualizing radical educational work that does not easily separate broader social visions from questions of what is to be taught and how. A limitation of this move is to neglect other radical educational work with relevance to pedagogy, such as literature from feminist philosophy of education (e.g., Greene, 1978, 1988; Martin, 1981, 1984; Noddings, 1984), literature on gender and schooling (e.g., Clark, 1989; Valli, 1983; Weiner, 1988: also see Kenway and Modra, 1992), and literature on critical educational theory (e.g., Apple, 1979, 1986; Connell, 1985; Pinar, 1981; Popkewitz, 1988, 1991). However, I am primarily concerned with those discourses which, in the very words they use to name themselves, claim to be constructing pedagogies—discourses which I hoped would guide my practice in teacher education.

The second delimitation—focusing on discourses carrying *academic* currency—neglects literature that similarly attempts to articulate and practice radical pedagogy *outside of* the academy (e.g., the publications of radical teachers such as *Rethinking Schools* and *Democratic Education*). I justify this move by calling attention to the power that academic discourses have in legitimating reform attempts of radical teachers, by locating my own teacher education practice in the academy, and by pursuing a desire to avoid the all-too-common unreflexive lapses into which much academic discourse falls by failing to examine itself and the conditions of its own existence.

To identify what I call the strands within critical and feminist pedagogy discourses, I reviewed books and journal articles published between the late 1970s and the time of this writing[2] (with the exception of Paulo Freire's *Pedagogy of the Oppressed*, published in 1968). In the attempt to name strands of these discourses, I run the risk of reducing their complexity and multiplicity and thus of misrepresenting them. The act of categorization is act of simplification. And to simplify is to risk refutations of my arguments by the writers whose work is addressed in my analysis. Hence, I want to acknowledge from the start that my accounts of each discourse will necessarily be partial (in both senses): (1) my own perspectives in terms of intellectual interests, practical and political concerns, will be brought to bear on this analysis of radical pedagogy; (2) I will not be attempting a complete representation of all texts pertaining to each discourse. Furthermore, in relying primarily on textual articulations, I run the risk of all textual analysis, that is, I risk neglecting historical and material practices. The published text represents only a fraction of the struggle for meaning which accompanies its production. Nevertheless, most teachers and academics encounter new ideas in education through the written text, and the written text is a major source of academic capital (Bourdieu, 1988).

Within the discourse of critical pedagogy two main strands can be identified. The central distinction between the two strands lies in their different approaches to the question of pedagogy: one strand emphasizes the articulation of a broad social and educational vision, while the other shows greater concern for developing explicit instructional practices to suit specific contexts. In making this distinction between "systems of thought" in critical pedagogy, the prominence of its "authors"—its key proponents—is striking, with Henry Giroux and Peter McLaren the key advocates and representatives of the first strand and Paulo Freire and Ira Shor the key advocates and representatives of the second. While other "authors," such as Roger Simon, John Smyth, Dan Liston, and Ken Zeichner, have used the language of critical pedagogy, they do not neatly align themselves with a particular strand; nor is critical pedagogy the primary focus of their work.[3]

In the discourse of feminist pedagogy, two strands can also be identified. The central distinction between these strands is that one strand emphasizes instructional aspects of pedagogy, and the other strand emphasizes feminism(s). While "authors" can be affiliated (such as Culley, Schniedewind, Shrewsbury, Morgan with the former strand and Maher, Grumet, Greenberg with the latter), these "systems of thought," represented by diffuse groups of authors, are most closely linked to different institutional locations within the academy. That is, proponents of the first strand of feminist pedagogy tend to be located in Women's Studies departments while proponents of the second strand tend to be located in Schools of Education.[4] Both strands contribute to the construction of the discourse of feminist pedagogy that is available to teacher educators like myself.

The remainder of this chapter will elaborate each of the four strands of radical pedagogy discourse. While I have differentiated the various strands of radical pedagogy relative to their emphases on instruction and social vision, in the interests of less cumbersome labeling, I will refer to them in terms of their institutional or authorial affiliations: that is, the feminist pedagogy constructed in Women's Studies, the feminist pedagogy constructed in Education, the construction of critical pedagogy articulated by Giroux and McLaren, and the construction of critical pedagogy articulated by Freire and Shor.[5] Moreover, naming the objects of my analysis in this way shifts the focus from the method of my inscription to the social groups that can be located within and by such inscription. I briefly describe each strand, attempting to fairly represent its approach to pedagogy and to highlight the features that distinguish it from the other strands in terms of both the pedagogy argued for and the pedagogy of the argument. The conditions for the formation of each strand of radical pedagogy discourse are also elaborated in terms of institutional location and links to particular political and social movements and intellectual traditions. This analysis identifies similarities (often unacknowledged) as well as differences between and among the strands of radical pedagogy and, in so doing, it takes up the task of engaging discourses beyond simply "choosing an adversary". I argue that, beyond oppositional positioning, the discourses have failed to recognize and nurture alliances which could prove fruitful for specific projects, such as improving practices of teacher education.

FEMINIST PEDAGOGY AND FEMINIST *PEDAGOGY*

The question, "What is feminist pedagogy?" is approached differently by two separate groups. One group writes about feminist pedagogy from the context of Women's Studies. Here, the emphasis is on pedagogy; that is, "What is feminist *pedagogy*?" as opposed to feminist theory or feminist research methodology. While there is also attention paid to distinctions between patriarchal and feminist pedagogies, the emphasis remains to come to terms with pedagogy. The other group writes from the context of Education[6] and restates the question, "What makes pedagogy *feminist*?" There is an irony in the emphases of these two groups: in writing about feminist pedagogy, the Women's Studies people seem more concerned about pedagogy/ education while the Education people seem more concerned about feminism. My aim here is to explore possible reasons for this ironic situation, but first I want to explain why I will focus on this distinction rather than on the typical differentiations of feminist thought according to ideologies.

Unlike the discourse of critical pedagogy, the discourse of feminist pedagogy is not so much represented by the books of key proponents as it is by anthologies comprised of many contributors, as well as by journal articles. The distinction might crudely be phrased as feminist community versus critical notoriety. Whether such community results from a kind of positive, non-competitive attitude among feminists concerned with pedagogy, or from a general determination not to create new canons of feminist thought,[7] or from a powerlessness of women in the academic field to "make their mark," or some other reason(s), the diversity and fragmentation found in such collections makes very clear that what is under discussion is not feminist pedagogy but feminist pe-

dagog*ies*. For example, one recent collection of articles on feminist pedagogy (Schniedewind and Maher, 1987) includes pieces on "black feminist pedagogy," feminist pedagogy for "returning women," feminist
pedagogy in a "college for neighborhood women," undergraduate feminist pedagogy, and high school feminist pedagogy. Although such a
volume demonstrates that feminist pedagogy is on some level responsive
to, and differentiated by, the specific contexts in which it is practiced,
there do not appear to be discrete strands of feminist pedagogy discourse, with their own regularities, developing around these contexts.
Rather, differentiation between sites of practice is representative of a
general move to "contextualize" feminist pedagogy, and feminist work
generally, particularly in Women's Studies where the perception is that
there are more possible sites than in the "natural site" of Education, i.e.
schools (although it should be pointed out that feminist pedagogy in
Education also addresses a range of specific classrooms). These are applications of feminist pedagogy discourse. The pedagogy argued for in
the cited different contexts draws upon the same ideas and theorists and
suggests similar practices. The pedagogy of the argument also is constructed in similar ways across contexts. Hence, feminist pedagogy discourse does not construct separate pedagogies according to contexts.

The most common way to distinguish feminist work is to consider its
relation to the main theoretical frameworks of Anglo feminism—liberal,
radical and socialist feminist thought.[8] While writers of feminist pedagogy
do not often locate their pedagogical work or writing within specific
forms of feminist thought, it is clear that liberal, radical, socialist and,
more recently, poststructuralist feminist thought is represented. To date
most of the literature on feminist pedagogy, whether from Women's
Studies or Education, reflects liberal and radical feminisms. Very recently, pedagogy has received attention from poststructuralist feminists
in Education (e.g., Britzman, 1990; Ellsworth, 1989; Lather, 1990, 1991;
Lewis, 1990a, 1990b; Luke and Gore, 1992; Orner, 1989, 1990). The
lack of representation of socialist feminist thought in the discourse of
feminist pedagogy is interesting. Speculatively, I would suggest that this
lack of attention is linked to socialist feminism's emphasis on the
"broader," more abstract, macro questions of ideologies and institutions
rather than on micro questions of classroom pedagogy and/or linked to
socialist feminism's closer alliance with critical pedagogies which have
posed class-based relations as the primary social relation.

While texts of feminist pedagogy could be differentiated by their underlying philosophical and political assumptions and then categorized
according to these strands of feminist thought, to do so would be to

impose distinctions rather than to allow distinctions to emerge from the discourse of feminist pedagogy. That is, the writers who construct feminist pedagogy are not naming certain strands "liberal feminist pedagogy" and certain other strands "radical feminist pedagogy." Nor is it really *possible* to impose such categories on the literature without overlooking the frequent coexistence of different traditions of feminist thought in one text on feminist pedagogy.[9] Given that distinctions around context of practice and feminist thought do not appear salient in the construction of separate strands of feminist pedagogy, I return now to a closer examination of the central distinction between the "feminist *Pedagogy*" of Women's Studies and the "*Feminist* pedagogy" of Education.

Feminist Pedagogy as Constructed in Women's Studies

Women's Studies courses and departments on university campuses emerged out of the women's liberation movement, a social and political movement that has a long history of struggle. Writers of feminist pedagogy who are located in these departments, tend to emphasize the instructional processes of teaching, focusing on pedagogy in terms of *how* to teach and *what* to teach. As I will elaborate in Chapter 4, there are frequent references in this literature to "new" texts, "new" readings, personal experiences, and to cooperative and non-didactic classroom processes (e.g., Boxer, 1988; Maher, 1985a; Mumford, 1985). This emphasis that privileges particular modes of instruction over a particular feminist social vision helps explain why we have not seen the emergence of "liberal feminist pedagogy" or "radical feminist pedagogy." Instead, a general feminist vision is assumed. The how, what and why of pedagogy are separated from each other as well as from the "feminist" of feminist pedagogy, or at least they are viewed as separable. Thus the pedagogy argued for centers on discussions of classroom processes and principles.

Despite the central place given to instructional processes of teaching in this strand of feminist pedagogy, the (re)presentation of pedagogy in this work is rather ahistorical with respect to educational practice. Occasional reference is made to the work of Paulo Freire and his criticisms of "banking education." Otherwise referring to educators is rare.[10] Even in an extensive bibliography on feminist pedagogy in *Women's Studies Quarterly* (Shrewsbury, 1987b), the vast majority of citations are taken from works published outside of the educational field, thus much of the work on feminist pedagogy in Education is overlooked. An exception is the work of Frances Maher whose academic appointment is in Education and who has published in both Education and Women's Studies forums and whose work is cited frequently by both groups. Perhaps a reason for her affiliation with both strands of feminist pedagogy lies in the fact that she composed most of her academic work at Wheaton College, which, until 1988, was an all women's college. Here, the same kind of premises that undergird Women's Studies programs can be found: namely, the need for women to have their own space and their own educational culture, in order to "find their voices" and grow without the threat of male (physical and/or symbolic) violence. These premises are frequently posited as characteristic of the feminist struggle for "self-determination" (e.g., Boxer, 1988). Also raised by this observation is the general issue of student populations as they figure in the different strands of radical pedagogy. I will return to this issue later in this chapter.

The lack of attention to the field of Education might partially be explained by the way in which work in the academy, particularly for fields and individuals still trying to gain legitimacy, offers little time for thorough and systematic reading outside of one's field. It is even possible that the occasional mention of Freire by Women's Studies writers has become part of the "folklore" of feminist pedagogy, passed perhaps uncritically from one writer to another, rather than a reference that indicates each writer's close reading of *Pedagogy of the Oppressed* (1968), let alone any of Freire's later works. That there is any mention of "education folks" at all could be interpreted as part of the game of seeking power to define feminist pedagogy within the academy generally; that is, a game wherein one demonstrates a (cursory) knowledge of general educational discourse in the process of rejecting it and replacing it with feminist pedagogy. The general claim is that Women's Studies does what Education has not done:

> If the path Women's Studies travels is often smoother today than it was two decades ago, it is at least in part because almost everyone can see that Women's Studies excels at just what higher education is supposed to do: educate the young and not so young to lead more rewarding lives in ways that contribute to more democratic societies. (Harding, 1990, p. 17)

Feminist pedagogy discourse is often posed as a challenge to the nature of academic institutions (Schniedewind, 1987).

The lack of attention to Education, including some feminist work in Education, is also related to a more general rejection of Education that is grounded in a critique of the ways in which Education is patriarchal. In this view, "patriarchy is the educational paradigm" (Spender, 1981,

p. 157) and "the worthy content of education is defined by the interests of men, the suitably worthy recipients of educational effort are boys and men, and the primary exemplars and transmitters of advanced knowledge are expected to be men" (Morgan, n.d., p. 16). Given this view, feminist pedagogy informed by radical feminist thought may be particularly reluctant to cite male educators or educational researchers as authorities on pedagogy.

It is interesting to consider why Freire has become something of an exception. Despite Freire's location in a particularly patriarchal culture and his general neglect of gender issues, his work has been embraced within much feminist pedagogy discourse. Freire's connection to and embodiment of "Third World" identities and politics fits with the general social vision of feminist pedagogy: the liberation of "women and minorities" (e.g., Maher, 1985b) from the oppression of the white male patriarchy.

Kenway and Modra (1989) urge feminist educators to consider the broad range of viewpoints on Freire's work rather than uncritically accepting it. "At the moment it looks very much as if Freirean idolatry is taking the place of the development of critical consciousness *in the very project of liberatory education itself*" (p. 12). Moreover, Maglin (1987) points out that it is rather contradictory to name Freire as a "father" of feminist pedagogy; she recommends looking at some of "our mothers of pedagogy" (p. 15). Apparently, among the Women's Studies writers, such "mothers" are not to be found in schools or in Education. Indeed, there is little attention drawn to what women teachers have accomplished within mass public education in much of the Western world since the latter half of the nineteenth century (Apple, 1987), or to the recently burgeoning literature on feminist pedagogy which has emerged within Education.

A related, more general, reason that there has been little attention directed to the development of pedagogical discourse more generally might be that many of the writers in this group view schools and colleges as having alienated them/denied their experience/silenced them; that is, perhaps they personally experienced schooling as patriarchal and thus now reject Educational thought, considering it irrelevant to, and contradictory for, feminist practice. Even when they think back to some teachers with particularly fond memories, the commitment to feminist pedagogy of these women writers emerges from their memory not of pedagogy but of school, not of those wonderful (or horrible) women (and men) but of the institution. "When we went to college, most of us were presented with a male authority structure that sought to intimidate us and impress us with its academic credentials" (Jhirad, 1990, p. 30).

Thus, the pedagogy espoused by the writers I have cited in this group (e.g., Culley, 1985; Morgan, 1987, n.d.; Schniedewind, 1987; Spender, 1981) emerged more directly out of the women's liberation movement and "consciousness raising" activities (Fisher, 1987, p. 47) than out of formal academic study in Education. Spender (1981) claims: "Equality and cooperation were almost the inevitable outcome of the circumstances in which feminists found themselves" (p. 169). She makes this statement in the context of cautioning against the weakening of the feminist movement that could result with the institutionalization of feminism via Women's Studies. With the growth of a body of feminist knowledge and the possibility for "transmission" of that knowledge, Spender points out that Women's Studies risks taking on the same hierarchical and competitive characteristics as the rest of the patriarchal academy. While this caution seems appropriate given that the academy is undeniably patriarchal (Luke and Gore, 1992), the alternative suggested by citing early (Anglo) feminist consciousness-raising efforts outside the academy, risks uncritically valorizing consciousness-raising as an end in itself. As Kenway and Modra (1989) point out, praxis is not a necessary outcome of raised consciousness.

Rather than having had formal, academic study in Education, many of the professors in Women's Studies departments had backgrounds in the humanities and social sciences. Thus, another reason for paying little attention to Education might stem from an elitism among some Women's Studies scholars who valorize their disciplinary backgrounds over professional training in education.[11] Susan Laird (1988) provides a related explanation of the lack of attention to schools, colleges and departments of education, as she considers it part of "the female struggle for intellectual dignity" (p. 462). From this perspective, the woman teacher is portrayed "as a hopeless victim of unreasonable demands and deprivations, who had better find other work than teaching if she wants to be a self-respecting person" (p. 461). Laird argues that this attitude is reflected in the following "feminist disincentives" for women to enter school teaching:

> women's colleges that discourage bright students' interests in childhood or adolescent education, women's research centers that conceive their projects of curriculum transformation in a top-down relationship between colleges and schools, the tendency to locate Women's Studies in liberal arts colleges and apart from those more "practical" colleges where women traditionally have predominated within the university,

general feminist silence and inaction in response to the recent teaching
reform movement in which corporate and state efforts flourish, and
the "feminist pedagogy" movement itself with its almost exclusive focus
upon women teachers as professors or as community educators of
adults. (p. 457)

Here, the issue of different student populations ought to be addressed. The clients and primary target of this strand of feminist pedagogy are undergraduate women in Women's Studies courses. The primary population assumed for work in Education, namely elementary and
secondary school boys and girls, is perceived to be markedly different
and apparently unrelated. For example, Smithson (1990) claims that
"Women's Studies investigators are far from understanding the differences in the ways women and men learn" (p. 8) and yet he turns, almost
exclusively, to the field of Literature as the source of knowledge on
learning. It seems he does not value, or at least has overlooked, the vast
body of literature produced in Education on the differential learning
strategies of males and females (e.g., Kelly and Nihlen, 1982; Walkerdine,
1988). Such a lack of acknowledgment of the contributions made by male
and female education theorists, researchers, and teachers toward the
understanding of feminist pedagogical practice is to be expected in the
context of struggles within a field or discourse. The "will to truth," as
introduced in Chapter 1, helps explain such differentiations or oversights
(depending on one's perspective).

An effect (probably unintended) of this approach to feminist pedagogy
is to erase the experiences of teachers who have practiced "democratic"
forms of pedagogy. The following statement, made by two high school
teachers, is illustrative. They believe that feminist pedagogy,

> builds on existing traditions in education . . . [which include] group
> learning, peer tutoring and evaluation, differentiated standards, eval-
> uation modes, dialectic between cognitive and affective domains, writ-
> ing process, learning theory, critical and creative thinking, case study
> methods and educational reform movements. Without particular con-
> cern for gender issues, then, many teachers are already practicing
> pedagogy that parallels the efforts of feminists. (Roy and Schen, 1987,
> pp. 110–111)

There is a sense in which I hear these teachers saying that some of the
writing on feminist pedagogy has denied their knowledge and experience.
It's almost a "Hey, hang on, you're not the first to think of, talk about,
or do this stuff! We've been doing it, and doing it well, for years!" Because
the pedagogical practices to which Roy and Schen (1987) refer are not

directly or necessarily linked to an awareness of women's oppression and a commitment to ending it, the existing practices in Education have been ignored.

Hence, a contradiction is evident within this strand of feminist pedagogy: despite the claim that "feminist pedagogy encourages us to validate women's sensitivity to and perceptions about the world and to understand and explore our commonalities and difference" (Bell, 1987, p. 77),[12] this strand of feminist pedagogy has denied the experience of these women teachers. In their (often strategic) separation from schools and from educational discourses, feminist pedagogy writers from Women's Studies demonstrate "little sense of either the humanist, progressive [or] critical challenges to the mainstream by educators, male, female and feminist" (Kenway and Modra, 1989, p. 14), which not only leads them "to make inappropriate claims about the inventiveness of Women's Studies pedagogy but it robs them of powerful support for their own work" (Kenway and Modra, 1989, p. 13). To be sure, as Grumet (1988a) has said, there are senses in which teachers have joined Virginia Woolf's "procession of the sons of educated men" (p. 57), but this view denies the moments of resistance (and not just "defensive, passive resistance" [p. 57]) and the moments of contradiction—the moments when women have successfully and powerfully emerged in classrooms. It is a rather unitary view of teachers' work; one which foregrounds the operation of gender oppression to the marginalization of personal and private interventions made in the classrooms of individual teachers and schools.

Feminist Pedagogy as Constructed in Education

I want to turn now to the other strand of feminist pedagogy which is located within Education Departments (and occasionally in pre-tertiary schools; see Roy and Schen, 1987). As already indicated, this group brings a long history of educational thought and practice to questions of feminist pedagogy, a history that has been dominated by scientism, professionalism, technical rationality, patriarchy. Feminist pedagogy emerged in Education from a growing discontent with the patriarchy of schooling and with mainstream and radical masculinist educational discourses, the analyses of which were clearly connected to and resonant with the feminist movement(s).

This strand of feminist pedagogy largely rejects the more technical, instructional meaning of pedagogy: pedagogy as a method of teaching within a context of awareness of women's oppression and a commitment to ending it (the meaning which seems prominent within the Women's

Studies strand). Pedagogy is instead approached more broadly, emphasizing how gendered knowledge and experience are produced. In the following statement, Maher and Rathbone (1986) demonstrate a more comprehensive sense of the history of pedagogical practice, and focus more specifically on gender issues insofar as they characterize feminist pedagogy:

> While collaborative, interactive pedagogical techniques have a long history in education outside of women's studies scholarship (e.g., in the works of John Dewey and Paulo Freire), they receive supplementary justification, and a new context, when viewed from the perspective of women's studies. (p. 217)

Here, gender issues are the focus of feminist pedagogy; this focus makes pedagogy feminist.

In another article, Maher (1987) contrasts feminist pedagogy with conventional approaches to inquiry teaching claiming that "what is most important [about feminist pedagogy] is that it draws both male and female students into a process of learning that gives both them and the subjects of their study actual lives, lived as men and women in both the public and private spheres. In this way, students are involved in the classroom as whole people" (p. 192). Feminist pedagogy is "to help students and ourselves listen to and come to terms with our differences and the multiple capacities and social responsibilities within ourselves" (p. 192).

One might still ask, as does Peter Taubman (1986), how this view of feminist pedagogy differs from "good teaching". Taubman describes feminist pedagogy as "a pedagogical method based to a great extent on progressive educational theory and the radical critique of education which emerged in the late 1960s and early 1970s" (p. 89). In his view, "what makes the overall critique of education and schooling and the pedagogical method . . . different from the radical critiques to which they tip their hat is that they infuse or imbue that radical critique with feminist theory. In many respects feminist pedagogy is a reformulated and represented version of radical pedagogy" (p. 89). While many feminists would reject and resent Taubman's characterization of feminist pedagogy in relation to the "center" of white, male discourse (even if radical), there are clearly commonalities between the feminist and critical pedagogy discourses in Education. Maher, for example, characterizes her own work as bringing the "new scholarship on women" into education and teacher education (Maher, 1985b, 1987; Maher and Rathbone, 1986). Even if this strand of feminist pedagogy is said to be a reformulated version of radical pedagogy, it resonates with feminist educators' dissatisfaction vis-à-vis critical pedagogy's "gentle genuflections" of gender-sensitivity, but lack of serious engagement with feminist literature (Kenway and Modra, 1989).

At the same time, however, feminist pedagogy literature in Education engages minimally with critical pedagogy literature. Critical pedagogy discourse is often dismissed as patriarchal and masculinist with little demonstration that this is so. Reasons not to engage these criticisms might include reluctance to spend intellectual time and energy on this material, a belief/"knowledge" that critical pedagogy *is*, by definition, patriarchal and masculinist, and the attitude (common among oppressed peoples) "besides, why should feminists constantly offer men this service?" (Kenway and Modra, 1989, p. 1).[13]

Thus, while the history of schools and teaching is more central in this strand of feminist pedagogy than in the Women's Studies strand, as captured eloquently in the following statement by Madeleine Grumet (1988a), their central engagement, as I shall elaborate shortly, is with feminist discourses rather than with educational discourses:

> We have burdened the teaching profession with contradictions and betrayals that have alienated teachers from our own experience, from our bodies, our memories, our dreams, from each other, from children, and from our sisters who are the mothers of those children. Perhaps it is time for women who call ourselves educators to question our participation and practice in the schools. (p. 57)

Just as Women's Studies writers appeal to Freire, perhaps in search of some legitimacy in Education, the Education writers more generally draw on Women's Studies and feminist theory in ways that are very supportive of Women's Studies and the whole concept of feminist pedagogy. Hence, there appears to be very little challenge to the concept of feminist pedagogy; it is accepted rather uncritically, may contain frequent citations to certain major anthologies, but offers little in terms of close engaging discussion, critique, or detailed analysis. Perhaps it is a case of "not biting the hand that feeds you." Perhaps it is the discomfort of challenging the notion of feminist pedagogy from a feminist perspective: to do so would be to risk accusations of betrayal and consequences of exclusion. Perhaps there is a level of discomfort reached which then inhibits reflexivity. It is certainly interesting that (until recently[14]) one of the strongest critiques of feminist pedagogy comes from a male teacher, Peter Taubman.

Despite the consistent citations of *Gendered Subjects* (Culley and Portuges, 1985), *Learning Our Way* (Bunch and Pollack, 1983) and the *Wom-*

en's Studies Quarterly (Schniedewind and Maher, 1987) special issue on feminist pedagogy, the writers in this group tend to draw directly from feminist theory and women's studies more generally. This limited and uncritical engagement with the Women's Studies strand of feminist pedagogy might arise from a certain elitism that considers it insufficient in legitimately addressing pedagogical issues—perhaps with good reason in light of my analysis of the construction of feminist pedagogy in Women's Studies. And yet, it could be argued, in their haste to articulate feminist positions in Education, these writers have been uncritical of the feminist literature.

My concern is one that urges feminists in Education to be reflexive and critical of ourselves and our discourse(s) of feminist pedagogy. As an example, I want to consider, in some detail, an article by Selma Greenberg (1982) published in the *Journal of Curriculum Theorizing* which illustrates some of the dangers in uncritically accepting "all things feminist" in the name of promoting feminist pedagogy. Greenberg (1982) claims "feminists have, with incredible effectiveness, made operational the ideas, insights and practices educational philosophers and theorists have engendered and promulgated" (p. 194). While this statement implies that "feminists" have drawn on the work of educational philosophers and theorists, as I have already discussed, the practices of "teachers" in women's studies do not appear to have emerged from the study of education but, rather, from within the pragmatic context and conditions in which feminists found themselves. Greenberg also claims that in the women's movement, "feminists have practiced the theories the educators only preach, they have developed educational strategies at once powerful, non-hierarchical, loose, and voluntary" (p. 193). Here, Greenberg attempts to define, in a universalizing way, what is "good pedagogy." As just one criticism of this attempt, Greenberg's "voluntary" criterion, which refers to the voluntary participation of women in consciousness-raising groups, ignores the institutional constraints of much educational practice. Schools are rarely (if ever) the "mutually supportive, accepting, non-hierarchical, and free" (p. 196) environments of Greenberg's consciousness raising groups. Greenberg's characterization of women's studies also sounds rather celebratory, optimistic and simplistic to me. It fits with what Schilb (1985) has called "the cherished stereotype of the feminist classroom as a scene of perpetual collaborative bliss" (p. 256). Lewis (1988) points out that this myth denies "the difficult undertaking of uncovering social realities the pain of which sometimes makes us wish we didn't know what we know, [and] undermines the political aspects of feminist analysis and the women's movement" (pp. 154–5). Hence, without critically engaging the feminist literature we risk making unsupported claims, denying the experiences and knowledge of others, and shattering the potential for wider legitimacy.

Greenberg (1982), however, raises some advantages of women's studies over "establishment" education which are, perhaps, more reasonable. She claims that feminism has developed the ability to be comfortable with one's own ignorance: "For one of the basic tenets of feminism is that sexism robs both women and men of half the world of knowledge, skills, ability" (p. 195). This might be a strength of feminist, over critical, approaches to education. Instead of the "critical" assumption that false consciousness can be transformed by someone who "knows," feminism purports to acknowledge that women have simply been denied the opportunities to develop and realize their own knowledge, have been denied multiple interpretations of their experiences. However, as I shall demonstrate in Chapter 4, there is still a strong reliance on feminists who "know" to be the agents who empower through feminist pedagogy.

Another claim Greenberg makes is that many "establishment reformers" have been almost "eerily ahistorical" (p. 196). She says, "it is particularly ironic that it is the professional educators who often turn out to be the group with unrealistic educational expectations" (p. 195). On the other hand, Greenberg explains that "feminists have always appreciated that their reeducation efforts would be long drawn-out efforts. Believing women and men to exhibit different intellectual, social and emotional patterns as a result of behavioral shaping begun before the dawn of consciousness, they have had little trouble appreciating the enormity of their task" (p. 196). There is certainly a tendency among educational reformers to deny the history of failed reforms (Cuban, 1984; DeLone, 1979; Sarason, 1982; Popkewitz, 1991). That educational reformers are primarily located in ideologies of technical rationality, scientism, and professionalism, all of which are avowedly apolitical, helps explain this tendency. On the other hand, that feminists are located in a social and political movement with a long history of struggle, helps explain Greenberg's claim that feminists have set themselves more manageable educational aspirations.

Greenberg's paper is typical of the earlier work on feminist pedagogy in Education. Rather than comparing itself with its "sister" in Women's Studies, this strand of feminist pedagogy compared and celebrated itself, and Women's Studies, as working against efforts in mainstream education. While the Women's Studies strand makes such comparisons in generalized, totalizing ways, dismissing the patriarchal institution, the Education strand makes more specific comparisons with particular educational theories and practices (although, these comparisons rarely form "explicitly deconstructive work on educational theoretical metan-arratives" [Luke, 1989b, p. 1]).

A final point made by Greenberg is that the professional educator can be most helpful by warning feminists "to be wary of the temptation to make raised consciousness a requirement" (p. 198). Perhaps Green-berg's warning is timely as Women's Studies moves into a stronger place, at least within some universities, as courses proliferate, and as courses in women's studies increasingly become requirements for all undergrad-uate students on some campuses. This increasing institutionalization of feminism, and simultaneous movement away from the "free and vol-untary" contexts of consciousness-raising may account for increasing attention, within the discourse of feminist pedagogy, directed to ques-tions of power and authority, and increasing accounts of the difficulties in classrooms of difference: mixed gender classrooms (Lewis, 1990a); classrooms in which differences in knowledge, class, sexuality (race, age, religion, and so on) become visible/cannot be ignored (Gardner, Dean and McKaig, 1989); classrooms which end up, despite their feminist intentions, following "the conventional academic model" (Mahony, 1988). Such accounts highlight one theme of this book—the institutional exigencies of pedagogical practice and the nature of pedagogy itself. The trend toward *teaching* feminism is different from *doing* feminism outside of the academy.

Despite my concerns about Greenberg's claims, her article is illustra-tive of the fundamental difference I find between the construction of feminist pedagogy discourse within Education and its construction in Women's Studies. The approach in Education is to place feminism in central place; discussions of feminist pedagogy are thus less concerned with details of classroom practice than with bringing feminism into ed-ucation, making the theoretical links. Indeed, in this articulation of a feminist vision of schooling, the instructional aspect of pedagogy has often been neglected. Although (or perhaps because), as a field, Edu-cation has more legitimacy, and certainly has a longer history in the academy, compared to Women's Studies, feminist educators have not yet acquired a "home" in Education in the way that feminists have in Women's Studies. As evidence, consider that women/feminists/gender issues have not yet (1992) achieved Divisional status within the American Educational Research Association; they only hold spaces under "Special Interest Groups": namely "Research on Women and Education," and "Critical Examination of Race, Ethnicity, Class and Gender in Educa-tion." This is not to advocate or celebrate such separation/separatism/

ghettoization, but simply to signal another of the material conditions that differentiates the two strands of feminist pedagogy, a difference that helps to explain the emphasis on feminism and neglect of instructional aspects which characterize this strand of feminist pedagogy.

The Women's Studies approach, in which feminism is already central, is more inclined to address feminist pedagogy as strategy, technique, methodology. This approach emphasizes classroom practices probably because theories of the gendering of knowledge itself are being addressed throughout the field of Women's Studies. However, its ahistorical approach to pedagogy results in accounts of feminist pedagogy that tend to be very descriptive: a rather uncritical and often celebratory sharing of stories about activities and strategies used in feminist classrooms (see, for example, the *Women's Review of Books*, February, 1990).

It is interesting, however, that despite their different institutional locations, carrying their different theoretical histories and traditions, the two strands of feminist pedagogy seem to similarly address classrooms. This similarity may have something to do with the fact that, in both contexts, women have been the central agents, the key actors, of the classroom; women's shared experiences of oppression have led to a general commitment *not* to reproduce patriarchal relations in the classroom. And even though women have at times functioned as the agents of patriarchy (Grumet, 1988a), their rejection of patriarchy may account for the emphasis on nurturing, experiential learning, and an ethic of caring that characterize the pedagogical commitments espoused from both contexts. Their common roots in the consciousness-raising of the women's movement also account for a number of shared claims made about feminist pedagogy, such as their emphasis on experience, voice, and empowerment (to be elaborated later in this book). As I will argue (especially in Chapter 6), these similarities might result from the limited options within progressive pedagogy as it is currently institutionalized and practiced.

Before turning my attention to discourses of critical pedagogy, I want to briefly address the recent articulation of poststructuralist feminist pedagogical practice among some of the Education writers. This work currently provides what is perhaps the most significant challenge to extant radical pedagogy discourses. However, I am not posing this work as a third strand of feminist pedagogy discourse because, at this stage, it does not purport to be centrally concerned with constructing a "feminist pedagogy."

Poststructuralist Influences on Discourses of Feminist Pedagogy

The recent move to poststructuralist feminist analysis of pedagogy among feminist educators can be viewed as part of a broader shift in the women's movement(s) from emphasizing commonalities among women, which led to the erasure of differences and the exclusion of some women, to a perspective which attends to the differences among women.[15] This move was in some ways foreshadowed by feminism's attention to the specificities of context, especially apparent in the Women's Studies strand of feminist pedagogy, and by socialist feminism's analyses of class and gender "double oppressions," the particularities of which challenged essentialisms of liberal and radical feminisms. The shift to poststructuralist feminist work on pedagogy (occurring primarily in Education rather than in Women's Studies) is also evidence of the theoretical emphasis of feminist work in Education, and of its familiarity with the current shifts in social theory, particularly, in this case, feminist theory.

While poststructuralist feminist work in Education makes pedagogical practice a central concern, claims to develop an alternative or post-structuralist "feminist pedagogy" are rare among these writers (see Luke and Gore, 1992). Rather, they emphasize the inappropriateness of pe-dagogical prescriptions, arguing for pedagogies that remain specific to the multiplicities of particular contexts. To date, such work has been concerned, reflexively, with the pedagogical practices of its proponents in undergraduate and graduate education (e.g., Britzman, 1990; Ell-sworth, 1989, 1990; Lather, 1990, 1991; Lewis, 1990a, 1990b; Orner, 1989, 1990) rather than with issues of elementary or secondary school-ing. As such, it is similar to the Women's Studies strand of feminist pedagogy, the potential weakness being limited theoretical use for prac-titioners who work within the particular conditions of schools. (I frame this concern in terms of my own practice in teacher education).

While the recent poststructuralist feminist move in Education seems to be gaining momentum, it certainly has not subsumed "earlier" analyses of pedagogy from feminist perspectives. That is, the strands of feminist pedagogy discourse which have been the focus of this chapter thus far continue to flourish. For example, the recent publication of a volume titled *Gender in the Classroom: Power and Pedagogy* (Gabriel and Smithson, 1990) makes limited use of poststructural scholarship in the direct at-tention it gives to pedagogy as practice.

CRITICAL PEDAGOGY AND CRITICAL *PEDAGOGY*

The literature of critical pedagogy, like the literature of feminist ped-agogy reveals considerable diversity. Again, the object of my analysis is pedago*gies* rather than a unitary discourse. Unlike the feminist literature, however, in which different strands are identified in relation to communities of writers, the strands of critical pedagogy are distinguished by individual figures. Given that, as Bourdieu (1988) puts it, "there are surely few social worlds where power depends so strongly on belief, where it is so true that, in the words of Hobbes, 'Reputation of power is power' " (p. 91), I will limit this analysis to the following central figures: namely, Henry Giroux, Peter McLaren, Paulo Freire, and Ira Shor. The centralization of authors/authorities in the discourse of critical pedagogy risks overemphasizing individuals in comparison to the diffusion of referents employed in my discussion of feminist pedagogy. I want to emphasize that my object is the *discourse* of critical pedagogy; for better or worse, however, this discourse is represented by these authors. Furthermore, in focusing on the construction of different strands, and on commonalities within each strand, there will be a tendency to obscure differences among the individual authors. Like the feminist pedagogy discourse, distinctions can be drawn within critical pedagogy according to the location of authors in different disciplines within the academy. Giroux and McLaren, until recently, were both professors of Education (at Miami University, Ohio). Giroux recently accepted an endowed Chair position at Pennsylvania State University. Shor is an English professor (at Staten Island College, the City University of New York). Freire's position is somewhat anomalous, due to his location outside of the U.S.: Freire is currently Minister of Education, directing the state schools in Sao Paulo, Brazil. Considering for a moment, the strands of critical pedagogy which have been constructed within the U.S. (all of which make reference to Freire), one finds a rather interesting parallel to the feminist pedagogy discourse. The writers who can be located outside of Education (namely, Shor and the Women's Studies people) focus more directly on pedagogy in specific contexts, while the writers located in Education (Giroux and McLaren, and those who write about feminist pedagogy in Education) seem more concerned with articulating critical (or feminist) theories of education. As with the previous section on feminist pedagogies, my aim here is to further elaborate the tendency for one strand of critical pedagogy to emphasize the social vision, and the other strand to emphasize context-specific instruction.

Critical Pedagogy as Constructed by Giroux and McLaren

While Giroux and McLaren share school teaching experiences that preceded their work as professors, their writing on critical pedagogy is more directly related to their academic study of Education and social theory than to those early, or even later, teaching experiences.[16] Rather than attending to instructional practices, what is most evident in this particular construction of critical pedagogy is Giroux's and McLaren's commitment to a particular political vision. Theirs is a discourse with theoretical and political roots in Neo-Marxism and the Critical Theory of the Frankfurt School, and so it emphasizes a critique (embedded within a language of possibility) of social injustices and inequities, particularly those constructed around class differences, but also (recently—and some would argue, superficially[17]) gender and racial differences, which are perpetuated through schooling.

Some critics have considered the resultant discourse to be contradictory in its attention to "oppressed groups." For instance, Wexler (1987) states: "This discourse included 'gender', but in a male language. It included 'the working class' but in the language of critical theory that suppressed the articulated speech of working people" (p. 94). In a statement of potential self-criticism, Giroux (1988a) recently declared that radical educational theory has "been unable to move from criticism to substantive vision" (p. 37). "Bereft of a language of moral purpose, radical educational theory has been unable to posit a theoretical discourse and set of categories for constructing forms of knowledge, classroom social relationships, and visions of the future that give substance to the meaning of critical pedagogy" (Giroux, 1988a, pp. 37–38).

Perhaps in response to these criticisms, recent years have seen Giroux and McLaren make links with the works of Foucault, poststructuralists, literary theorists, feminist theorists and liberation theologians (see for example, Giroux, 1988a, 1991; McLaren, 1988b). Despite this theoretical broadening, it is my contention, drawing on the lens established in Chapter 1, that their general approach to the question of pedagogy has changed little.[18]

To elaborate, their approach is centered on articulating a "pedagogical project," rather than "pedagogical practice"; that is, a social vision for teachers' work rather than guidelines for instructional practice—it is a vision of teachers who work to create "a politicized citizenry capable of fighting for various forms of public life and informed by a concern for equality and social justice" (McLaren, 1989, p. 158). Like their feminist colleagues/counterparts in Education, Giroux's and McLaren's neglect of classroom practice may stem from the explicit opposition of critical pedagogy to "dominant discourses" which prescribe practices in rather rigid and technical ways (e.g., Gentile, 1988, on "essential elements of instruction"). Instead, Giroux (1988a) argues that his work represents

> a particular way of seeing, a view of theory as a form of practice, one that rejects the fetish of defining the practical as the flight from theoretical concerns. . . . Theory as a form of practice points to the need for constructing a critical discourse to both constitute and reorder the nature of our experiences and the objects of our concerns so as to both enhance and further empower the ideological conditions for a radical democracy. (p. 36)

His aim is to "help illuminate the specifics of oppression and the possibilities for democratic struggle and renewal for those educators who believe that schools and society can be changed and that their individual and collective actions can make a difference" (p. 36). However, the emphasis is on the critique of oppressions and the abstract outline of possibilities rather than on the specific actions or strategies of educators or others.

Ellsworth (1989) has situated her critique of critical pedagogy in what she calls the "repressive myths" which accompany the emancipatory rhetoric. She states that "when participants in our class attempted to put into practice prescriptions offered in the literature concerning empowerment, student voice, and dialogue, we produced results that were not only unhelpful, but actually exacerbated the very conditions we were trying to work against" (p. 298). I would argue that the critical pedagogy of Giroux and McLaren does not prescribe specific practices for use in classrooms. Questions of process, of how, are not addressed even though such questions are central to the everyday practice of teachers.[19] Giroux (1981) is quite aware of this kind of criticism and responds in the following way: "The real issue at stake here is whether theoretical work itself is a form of practice and whether it can be used to create the terrain and necessary preconditions for a radical pedagogy. For me, the answer is a resounding yes" (p. 219).

The question becomes then, what is meant by the term "pedagogy" in this strand of critical pedagogy? Specific statements about the instructional part of critical pedagogy are difficult to locate in the writings of Giroux and McLaren. Giroux (1988b) and Giroux and Simon (1988) refer to pedagogy as: "a deliberate attempt to influence how and what knowledge and identities are produced within and among particular sets of social relations" (p. 120; p. 3). McLaren (1989) cites Roger Simon (1987):[20]

> "Pedagogy" is a more complex and extensive term than "teaching", referring to the integration in practice of particular curriculum content

and design, classroom strategies and techniques, a time and space for the practice of those strategies and techniques, and evaluation purposes and methods. All of these aspects of educational practice come together in the realities of what happens in classrooms. Together they organize a view of how a teacher's work within an institutional context specifies a particular version of what knowledge is of most worth, what it means to know something, and how we might construct representations of ourselves, others, and our physical and social environment. In other words, talk about pedagogy is simultaneously talk about the details of what students and others might do together *and* the cultural politics such practices support. To propose a pedagogy is to propose a political vision. In this perspective, we cannot talk about teaching practice without talking about politics. (Simon, 1987, p. 371)

It is interesting that the two major statements which deal directly with pedagogy, are connected in some way to Roger Simon. While Simon also writes about critical pedagogy, "a pedagogy of possibility" (Simon, 1987; Lewis and Simon, 1986), I have excluded his work from this analysis because he is less centrally linked with this particular strand of critical pedagogy discourse.[21] Nevertheless there is an irony in this reliance on Simon for definitions of pedagogy when Giroux is sometimes referred to as *the* authority on critical pedagogy (see for example McLaren, 1989) and the irony is further indication that Giroux and McLaren do not deal directly with instructional aspects of pedagogical practice themselves.

While these "definitions" reflect clear attention to classroom practice, the statement "to propose a pedagogy is to construct a political vision" (Giroux and Simon, 1988, p. 3) seems to be at the heart of this approach to critical pedagogy. Given that they direct little attention to instructional aspects of pedagogy, Giroux and McLaren seem to assume that the converse is also true: that is, that to construct a political vision is to propose a pedagogy. The assumption is, to focus on a political vision is also to create or support a particular pedagogical form; yet, such an assumption neglects the politics of the pedagogical form itself.

In a review of Giroux's (1983) book, *Theory and Resistance in Education*, Simon (1984) concludes that some readers "will be frustrated with Giroux's vagueness and will fault him for not coming to grips with the question, "What's to be done?" But it must be understood that Giroux's intent is to frustrate such readers. He refuses them answers, for he knows that any answer will always have to be contingently and collectively developed" (p. 387). While I would agree that pedagogical practice needs to be context-specific, I believe that practice can be addressed in the specific contexts of this particular historical conjuncture. There are "partial equivalences" (Bourdieu, 1984), commonalities, objective relations, that exist (in all universities for example), independent of the particular contexts in which we work (University of Wisconsin-Madison or The University of Newcastle, for example).

Giroux does not appear to have escaped the schizophrenia which he claimed, in 1979, characterized radical pedagogy in North America: "Caught between the imperatives of radical content and radical classroom social relationships, radical educators in general have settled for one at the expense of the other" (p. 257). At the micro level, one could say that Giroux has done neither—has neither addressed specific content nor specific practice. This situation must be explained in light of the historical and social conditions of the emergence of radical pedagogical work (Liston and Zeichner, 1991). Wexler (1987) explains it thus:

> Radical professional identity placed a contradictory demand on the new sociologists. They had at once to articulate and rationalize a radical or critical paradigm within the academy . . . and also, especially as radical educators, to act on the social world by developing a radical practice. The experience of contradictory pulls from professional institutional demands and from traditional radical political ideals was further complicated by continuing professional and political uncertainties in a climate of defeat. The solution that developed . . . was equally contradictory and complex: an abstract academic theory of practice . . . with no reference to any real, concrete, social movement. . . . The effect was to create a transformative pedagogy in general. (p. 86)

Despite the explanatory power of Wexler's argument, these historical circumstances cannot fully account for the direction taken, or priorities shown, in this strand of critical pedagogy. Moreover, changes in historical circumstances from the 1980s through the 1990s, have not been reflected in shifts of attention within this strand of critical pedagogy in terms either of specific practices or content.

The pedagogy of the argument also gives shape to this strand of critical pedagogy. Lusted (1986) locates "the fundamental refusal to take the need for pedagogy seriously" (p. 4) within the divisions between academic and teacher. "Theorists theorise, produce; teachers teach, reproduce. Therefore, such a logic would run, if anyone need be concerned about their pedagogy it is only the teacher—with a heavy stress on *only*" (p. 4). While Giroux would argue vehemently that neither his intention nor the meaning of his work is to place the burden of pedagogy on teachers (see for example, Giroux, 1981), his writing, as well as the writing of McLaren, emphasizes, in fairly abstract terms, what teachers should do to change schools, but makes little suggestion of strategies they might use.[22] Furthermore, and not surprisingly, with the exception of limited mention of events that have taken place in his graduate classes, Giroux's writing provides no sense of his own attempts to implement the critical pedagogy he espouses. One reading of the pedagogy of this argument is that it functions to reposition the theorist in his own interest—namely, to achieve influence and an audience (Bové, 1986). Surely social change, especially within that which is articulated within a language of possibility, requires that attention be directed to strategy, to specific practices. I don't want to argue that Giroux and McLaren should return to the schools and "get their hands dirty!" Their roles as theorists are important. My objection is that placing the burden for change on teachers, while simultaneously refusing to offer concrete suggestions, seems inconsistent with their project. My critique is not about Giroux and McLaren refusing prescription; rather, it is concerned with the abstract ways in which their discourse produces prescriptive effects which limit its applicability to the very practitioners at whom it is directed.

Thus, while Giroux and McLaren might argue that their writing constitutes a pedagogy, that theoretical work *is* practice, I argue that their pedagogy might be seen to restrict its audience to those readers who have the time, energy, or inclination to struggle with it (namely, other academics and graduate students; *not* the avowedly targeted teachers or, in many cases, undergraduate students) and, in so limiting its audience, it subsequently limits its political potential. Lusted (1986) puts it more strongly:

> The problem with a great deal of cultural and educational theory alike, shared even by critical/radical theory which should know better, is that it makes ritual nods in the direction of acknowledging a pedagogy of sorts in its production while, in its form, disavowing its importance entirely. This reflex practice has a politics and that politics is deeply reactionary. It is based on two unquestioned assumptions. The first is that to transmit ideas is enough. . . . The second . . . is that the pedagogy of its address follows its production rather than being integral to it. . . . The first assumption is irresponsible, the second is self-deluding. (p. 5)

That the pedagogy of their argument is of widespread concern becomes evident in the number of comments made at conferences that plead for clarity, the various reactions of my students (in teacher education programs)[23] who attempt to read the work of Giroux and McLaren, and the publication of certain academic critiques (see for example Bowers, 1991a, 1991b; Schrag, 1988; Miedema, 1987). Giroux (1988a, p. 163) and

McLaren (1989, p. 227) cite Lusted themselves, on the process of knowledge production:

> Knowledge is not produced in the intentions of those who believe they hold it, whether in the pen or in the voice. It is produced in the process of interaction, between writer and reader at the moment of reading, and between teacher and learner at the moment of classroom engagement. Knowledge is not the matter that is offered so much as the matter that is understood. (Lusted, 1986, p. 4)

Yet, the pedagogy of their argument seems to have overlooked this/their own insight.

Before turning to the other strand of critical pedagogy, I want to comment briefly on Giroux and McLaren's recent poststructural/postmodern turn. In recent essays (e.g., Giroux, 1988d, 1988e, 1991; McLaren, 1988b), Giroux and McLaren have considered postmodernist and poststructuralist thought and its implications for educational criticism and practice. While they seem willing to accept, in principle, the questioning of grand narratives, the regulation of social and moral experience, the need to redraw the borders of meaning, desire, and difference, the importance of the contingent, the specific, and the historical, they also call for the maintenance of "those strategic modernist elements that contribute to a politics of radical democracy" (Giroux, 1988d, p. 26).

Hence, when directing attention to questions of pedagogy in light of postmodernist thought, their focus shifts little. This strand of critical pedagogy is centrally concerned with the articulation of a particular, however shifting, social vision—one that is perhaps more fragmented, but nonetheless abstract. In his list of principles "towards a postmodern pedagogy," Giroux (1991) calls for "a critical pedagogy defined, in part, by the attempt to create the lived experience of empowerment for the vast majority" (p. 47), a critical pedagogy which involves "providing students with the opportunity to develop the critical capacity to challenge and transform existing social and political forms" (p. 47). "At stake here is a pedagogy that provides the knowledge, skills, and habits for students and others to read history in ways that enable them to reclaim their identities in the interests of constructing forms of life that are more democratic and more just" (p. 50). The pedagogy of the argument remains a directive one. The goal remains a universal, rather than partial and contradictory, one of empowerment. Critical pedagogy remains a source of great hope for the transformation of social and political forms. In short, despite their presentation of poststructural challenges to grand narratives, this strand of critical pedagogy presents little revision in its address of classroom practice.

Critical Pedagogy as Constructed by Freire and Shor

Turning to the other strand of critical pedagogy, Freire's approach in relation to the pedagogy of the argument is quite different. He says:

> We intellectuals should examine the nature of our own idiom. The challenge to liberating educators is to transform the abstract speech we inherit from our training in the bourgeois academy. This takes some courage to re-invent our idiom while we are still being rigorous and critical . . . Finding that idiom requires intellectuals to break with the elitism of their training and with the discourse that currently guarantees them prestige of rewards in the academy. (Shor and Freire, 1987, pp. 181–182)

(I should note that Freire has not always been so reflective about his language). Freire (in particular) and Shor are theoretically sophisticated, like Giroux and McLaren; yet Freire and Shor have been able to construct a strand of critical pedagogy which offers concrete suggestions and examples taken from their own pedagogical practice, and which is intended to help other educators.

Even the titles of some of their publications reveal this distinguishing difference between the two strands of critical pedagogy. Compare, for example, the following books:

Giroux (1988a) *Schooling and the Struggle for Public Life*
Giroux (1988b) *Teachers as Intellectuals*
McLaren (1989) *Life in Schools: An Introduction to Critical Pedagogy in the Foundations of Education*
Freire (1978) *Pedagogy in Process: Letters to Guinea-Bissau*
Shor (1980) *Critical Teaching and Everyday Life*
Shor (1988) *Freire for the Classroom*
Shor and Freire (1987) *A Pedagogy for Liberation: Dialogues on Transforming Education*

The titles of Freire and Shor's texts certainly suggest greater focus on classroom practice. The following reflective statements further support the difference through which I delineate the strands: From Freire, "Without exception, every book that I have written has been a report of some phase of the political pedagogical activity I have been engaged with ever since my youth" (Freire, 1978, p. 176) and, from Shor, "The problem of pedagogy forced itself on me . . . In the past, only a scholastic fraction of worker-students like me had been admitted to the academy. Now, millions were in. What kind of teaching could make critical learning happen?" (Shor and Freire, 1987, p. 19). For both writers, the question of pedagogy is approached as a search for ways of teaching that would remain consistent with their politics. As I will elaborate in Chapter 5, specific practices include the use of "generative themes" (Freire, 1973), and "re-experiencing the ordinary" (Shor, 1980) through such "progressive" pedagogical techniques as collective and cooperative work styles, and peer and group instruction and evaluation.[24]

Shor, like Giroux and McLaren, is most easily identified with Leftist politics. His writing is concerned with issues of class, race, and gender oppression, concerns which have moved his work into an anthology titled *Studies in Socialist Pedagogy* (Norton and Ollman, 1978). Although, in that same anthology, Freire's work appears in the section entitled "Classics of Socialist Pedagogy," he is more difficult to place. He has been called a Christian, a Marxist, a humanist, a radical, a revolutionary, an existentialist, a phenomenologist (Stanage, n.d.), all of which are supportable with passages from his writing. However difficult to place theoretically, he is clearly identified with what is typically referred to as the politics of the Left.

Like Giroux and McLaren, this strand of critical pedagogy is grounded in a critique of dominant approaches to education. Freire's (1968) nomination and description of "banking education" captures, most clearly and simply, the details of this critique:

a. the teacher teaches and the students are taught;
b. the teacher knows everything and the students know nothing;
c. the teacher thinks and the students are thought about;
d. the teacher talks and the students listen—meekly;
e. the teacher disciplines and the students are disciplined;
f. the teacher chooses and enforces his [*sic*] choice, and the students comply;
g. the teacher acts and the students have the illusion of acting through the action of the teacher;
h. the teacher chooses the program content, and the students (who were not consulted) adapt to it;
i. the teacher confuses the authority of knowledge with his own professional authority, which he sets in opposition to the freedom of the students;
j. the teacher is the Subject of the learning process, while the pupils are mere objects. (p. 59)

The major difference between the two strands of critical pedagogy is that, whereas Freire and Shor attempt to respond to the critique through articulating and practicing alternative pedagogical strategies, Giroux and McLaren respond by articulating an abstract political vision. Part of the difference might be attributable to the content-specific concerns of Freire, i.e., literacy, and Shor, i.e., English, which somewhat contrast with the more general, yet substantive concerns of Giroux and McLaren.

In summary, from the perspective on pedagogy which frames this book, Giroux and McLaren's self-proclaimed discourse of critical pedagogy is a misnomer. Theirs is not critical *pedagogy*, but critical *educational theory*, which is aimed at enabling "teachers as intellectuals" (see Aronowitz and Giroux, 1985; Giroux, 1988b) to develop their own critical pedagogy. Certainly, pedagogy encompasses more than classroom practice/instruction, but I want to draw attention to the slippage away from instructional aspects precisely because they seem so often to get lost in the "grand theories" of critical pedagogy. Giroux and McLaren provide an exciting vision of more democratic schooling and society, one that captured my imagination and energy many years ago. But that vision has not been actualized, and it is my contention that the "failure" to live out its own politics is resultant, *in part*, from insufficiently attending to pedagogy; that is, pedagogy as the politics *of* classroom practice, not pedagogy as politics (articulated by the theorist) *and* classroom practice (left for the teacher to create). Mazza (1981) concludes that the radical, and not just practical, potential of such theories is in question: "While the two factors are related, the former connotes an emphasis on transforming extant situations, including but transcending the narrower concern for implementing theory in practical situations" (p. 83). For this strand of critical pedagogy "to be able to serve as an emancipatory theory that will lead to radical praxis, it must be capable of providing alternative theories *and practices* that can contribute to the transformation of both the curriculum field and schooling" (Mazza, 1981, p. 83, emphasis added).

Shor and Freire's construction of critical pedagogy makes pedagogy the central concern; that is, pedagogy as classroom practice consistent with liberatory politics. In fact, of all the strands of radical pedagogy discussed in this chapter, theirs most clearly exemplifies the definition of pedagogy established in Chapter 1, in that it attends more explicitly both to social vision and to instruction. Perhaps this is one reason why Freire is not only cited, but often revered in most other discourses of radical pedagogy. Of course, just because a pedagogical discourse explicitly attends both to social vision and to instruction, it is not necessarily better than other discourses. For instance, the social vision and/or instructional strategies might run counter to democratic principles or to a particular stance on democracy. More specifically, from a radical feminist stance, Freire's radical pedagogy might be unacceptable in its masculinism, in its having emerged from a strongly patriarchal culture, and in its failure to theorize gender. As another example, Jim Walker (1980) has challenged Freire on the potentially manipulative dangers of his pedagogy. Nevertheless, the label "critical pedagogy" seems appropriate for this strand. It is interesting that Freire and Shor do not usually claim this label, referring to their work, instead, as "dialogical pedagogy" or "liberatory learning." Quite possibly, they do so in order to maintain some distance from the related-but-different area of work found in the writings of Giroux and McLaren.

From an examination of the literature, it is difficult to clarify the relationships between these two strands of critical pedagogy. On the one hand, Freire's work is highly regarded and respected, and is frequently cited by the other writers. On the other hand, I only located two references to Shor by either Giroux or McLaren, one in relation to problems of public schools (Giroux, 1988a, pp. 45–46), and the other in relation to a critique of Shor's critical pedagogy, "overly shaped by the discourse of modernism" (Giroux, 1988e, p. 164). Shor and Freire do not appear to make reference to McLaren's work at all. Furthermore, I located only fleeting references to Giroux's work in Freire's writing (e.g., Freire, 1985), none of which were found in the body of the text, but in a dialogue with Donaldo Macedo located at the end of a book. It would appear that the two discourses are keeping rather separate.[25] Similar to strands of feminist pedagogy, the strands of critical pedagogy seem to be struggling with meanings; struggles which are taking place between writers in positions to compete for ascendancy in a field fueled by a pervasive academic ideology of individualism. Then again, maintaining distance from each other, in separate discursive spheres, may also enable the pedagogues to avoid competition and continue their work with minimal immanent critique.

SUMMARY

I have constructed the following diagram to help clarify the discursive formations of the various strands of critical and feminist pedagogy. The utility of this diagram is to draw clear distinctions. Its limits lie in making static that which is relational.[26] The strands of radical pedagogy discussed in this chapter are shown in their differentiation along the vertical axis; that is, the critical and feminist discourses are represented by their different political projects—a differentiation that has as one of its effects

		Aspects of pedagogy	
		Social Vision	Instruction
Discourses of radical pedagogy	*Feminist Pedagogy*	Education	Women's Studies
	Critical Pedagogy	Giroux/McLaren	Freire/Shor

Figure 2.1. Discursive and institutional differentiations: Strands of radical pedagogy.

the perpetuation of a split along gender lines (I shall elaborate this shortly).

At the same time, employing the lens of pedagogy constituted by both social vision and instruction makes differentiation possible between various approaches to pedagogy—as represented on the horizontal axis. If social vision and instruction are considered differential aspects of pedagogy, then the horizontal axis will bring together the complementary emphases of the different strands, of the two feminist pedagogy strands and of the two critical pedagogy strands. If, although it cannot be assumed, a linking concern of these discourses is indeed pedagogy, then discussions about the horizontal axis may prove as or even more fruitful in efforts to change schooling practices (and to directly address pedagogy) than current discussions which tend to center on the vertical axis of differentiation (and focus on the feminist and the critical rather than on pedagogy).

The diagram also distinguishes between the discursive differentiations and the institutional location differentiations among the various strands represented within the matrix. This points to a commonality between the critical and feminist pedagogies within Education and, perhaps less obviously, between those strands of critical and feminist pedagogy located outside of Education.[27]

OBSERVATIONS OF THE CONTEMPORARY FIELD OF RADICAL PEDAGOGY

From this outline of the contemporary field of radical pedagogy, the lack of close engagement between the various discursive strands becomes striking. The field of radical pedagogy is not constituted by adversaries (opponents, antagonists, enemies)—the various strands do not directly challenge one another (except perhaps for some challenge to critical pedagogy by the Education feminists); nor is the field constituted by allies (combined or united for a special purpose) — except in the general commitment to feminist politics within the strands of feminist pedagogy, and perhaps in the broad, abstract, general commitment to social democracy contained in all strands. Certainly there are no explicitly formed alliances. Rather, the field of radical pedagogy appears to consist of separate strands of radical discourse, each existing and developing relatively autonomously as it tries to create its own spaces within its immediate intellectual and institutional contexts.

There are, however, many similarities between and among the different strands. Of particular relevance to this book, they all avow pragmatic concerns about improving conditions, they all hold positions of marginality relative to the "dominant discourses of our present" and, as pedagogical discourses with social visions and instructional processes (made more or less explicit), they all are, at least in part, discourses of social regulation. In the remainder of this book I will assert, drawing on the work of Foucault, that these strands of radical pedagogy discourse can be seen as caught up in, and operating like, "regimes of truth."

Before moving to the task, I want to highlight and explicate the following observations pertaining to the preceding identification of strands of radical pedagogy: first, the primary geographic location of the cited work is the U.S.; second, there exist different connections between the various pedagogies and political movements; third, men and women are differently inscribed in the strands of radical pedagogy; and finally, in keeping with social theory generally, there is a current trend toward poststructural theories.

US–Centric Discourses?

Consider that the US is the location of much of the critical and feminist pedagogy discourse. Does this reflect an ethnocentrism or US–centrism[28] that ignores important pedagogical work going on elsewhere? Is this also indicative of a focus on "us" rather than others, at the level of discursive production?[29] It is interesting that in Australia, according to Kenway and Modra's (1989) analysis of feminist pedagogy, the Women's Studies strand is similar to what I have outlined here, but in Education there is more of a practical interest in providing non-sexist education than in the theoretical articulation of any "feminist pedagogy." Kenway and Modra refer to this as the "gender and schooling" strand, characterizing it as less informed of most current feminist thought than the Women's Studies strand.

How might differences between Australia and the U.S. (and other countries) be explained? Does radical pedagogical work outside of the U.S. locate itself more clearly in particular, practical, political concerns rather than in the abstract, universalizing concerns of some of the work conducted in the U.S.? Does the U.S. have a greater interest in questions of radical pedagogy, and, if so, why? Is the U.S. a leader in the field of radical pedagogy? Or is radical pedagogy devalued, or considered trivial in other countries? Is there radical pedagogical work available in non-English languages to which the U.S. community has not gained access? Are radical educational discourses more widely accepted outside of the U.S., and are specialized discourses of radical pedagogy therefore unnecessary? Is there something about the structure of the academy in the U.S. that has allowed a space for this work where elsewhere the structures have not? Does the large number of publication outlets (journals) in the U.S. contribute to the formation of specialized discourses of radical pedagogy? While it is not within the scope of this book to explore these questions, they point to the need for more detailed analyses of historical, material, and social conditions that contribute to the construction of radical pedagogies.

Politics and Pedagogy

A comparison of critical and feminist pedagogy discourses reveals a shared concern for democratic schools and societies. For the feminist pedagogy discourse, however, this concern is mediated by a fundamental concern for women as a "class" (Scholes, 1989). Even in those discourses that claim that feminism seeks to redress the oppression of "women and minorities," and in poststructuralist discourses that name "multiple and intersecting oppressive formations," gender is the fundamental category. And by emphasizing feminism, these academic discourses are connected to particular forms of practice and politics. The personal *is* political. What we see, then, is that feminist pedagogy is driven by a more distinct and focused politics than critical pedagogy, the latter which has tended to claim a universalized notion of humanity as its object. As suggested earlier, the strong sense of feminist solidarity and identity (often in opposition to men as patriarchs) that is integral to feminist politics might account for the lack of historical attention to the field of Education from the Women's Studies group.

As Wexler (1987) has so provocatively argued, the critical discourses, particularly those constructed in the U.S., "removed education from practice within social movements into a universal radical pedagogy" (p. 87). This different relation to particular politics also helps explain the lack of attention to instructional practices, especially in the critical pedagogies of Giroux and McLaren. Practices have to be "contingently and collectively developed" within such a universalized radical pedagogy, perhaps so much so that no guidelines can be given even for our current historical conjuncture. While feminist poststructuralists also argue for context-specific pedagogies, their feminist politics seem to give more direction to the practical project.

Finally, as has become characteristic of leftist politics in general, the failure to clarify and unify can be seen to weaken their political potential, creating spaces for "the Right" to move in. Richard Sennett (1980) points to a way in which fruitful alliances might be formed: "Powerlessness comes from the very attempt to define a collective identity instead of defining the common interests of a diverse group of people" (p. 312). While this is a typical response to overcoming fragmentation, it presumes that common interests can be found. Questioning that perspective, Ellsworth (1990) argues that common interests can be identified only in relation to specific projects and specific contexts. In Chapter 7 I will return to this issue and try to identify specific projects in "radical" teacher education around which similar interests might be identified.

Men and Women in Radical Pedagogy

The strong correlation between critical pedagogy and men, feminist pedagogy and women, seems in part to be connected to the neglect of gender oppression analysis in the early (and, some would argue, current) critical pedagogy work in education. Critical pedagogy's "adding-on" of gender is viewed by many women as simply inadequate. As Carmen Luke (1989b) states it: "The general refusal by male academics to engage with feminist theory and to self-reflect on their own work from the perspective of a male reading of feminist critiques, seriously undermines whatever gender(ed) messages they may claim to have for women about women" (p. 23).

Another reason for this strong separation of men and women in radical pedagogy is the broader construction of feminism as women's domain.[30] Feminism, as discourse and as political movement, is grounded in the patriarchal oppression of women. Many men feel, often accurately, unwelcome in feminism. While women do not want men to appropriate feminist discourse, many would like men to intellectually and politically engage with feminist discourse. The historical marginalization of women and of feminist perspectives in the academy can help explain (but not excuse) critical pedagogy's lack of serious engagement with feminist theory. Also finding such marginalization in critical pedagogy, feminists have dismissed much critical work in their construction of feminist pedagogy discourse. In so doing, they might have contributed to the continuing marginalization of their perspectives but, to draw on Ellsworth's (1990) words again, it is not enough to be included without making a difference.

Of course, there are other circumstantial reasons for developing separate discourses of radical pedagogy along gender lines, such as the specificities of the campuses and departments in which one does graduate work.[31]

A danger of this separation between men and women is the deepening of divisions and the possibility that certain strands of radical pedagogy will be unable and unwilling to engage with each other. In itself, this is not so problematic. But if, indeed, these discourses are primarily concerned with the improvement of schools and education for all people, then such separation will likely be counterproductive.

The Poststructural Move

The move to poststructural theory (in both feminist and critical pedagogy discourses) seems to be linked to three phenomena. First, the production of academic discourse is increasingly located in post-industrial, semiotic conditions (Wexler, 1987), and in order to maintain or acquire positions of "power" in the academic field one is required to attend to "new" theoretical discourses.

Second, as "oppositional" discourses, radical discourses tend to counter dominant discourses by providing actual accounts of classroom situations that put into question broader theories (although these seem to be selectively applied—consider the application of poststructuralism to counter masculinist, phallogocentric, patriarchal discourse but the tendency to maintain essentialist notions of "women").[32] "Metatheoretical narratives" such as Marxism, Critical Theory, Feminism (in the singular) have not fully achieved their own political goals specifically because their assumptions of unity and sameness (The Working Class, The Oppressed, Women) disrupt their coming to grips with difference within and among social agents.

Third, and moreover, it seems that the grand, broad theories of Marxism, Critical Theory, and Feminism, in their fundamental acknowledgment of structured inequalities and oppressions, in their pedagogical enterprise, arrive at the need to theorize the contradictory moments— to introduce theories that make spaces for the many exceptions found in the experiences and classrooms of teachers and students. That is, much of the educational production of knowledge takes place at the very private, personal level of teacher and student, and therefore cannot all be explained (away) with structuralism or structuralist politics. It seems to me that there is something about the educational enterprise that leads to the local, partial, and multiple foci of poststructural theories; there is something about the lives of those in classrooms, as well as the lives of (social) "classes," about activities that deal with people as thinking, feeling individuals, that requires the phenomenological, personal accounts of multiplicity and contradiction that are beginning to emerge in the work of feminist poststructuralists in education.[33] (Poststructuralist work in critical pedagogy discourse has not yet applied itself in this way to the micro level of classrooms).

Each issue outlined, if closely attended to, will assist in the project of understanding radical pedagogy. My particular project necessarily has a more limited focus. My concern is with the internal relations of power and knowledge among strands of critical and feminist pedagogy, evident in the separation of the various strands and in the contradictions and inconsistencies between the pedagogies they argue for and the pedagogies of their arguments.

THREE

Regimes of Truth

No discourse is inherently liberating or oppressive. The liberatory status of any theoretical discourse is a matter of historical inquiry, not theoretical pronouncement. (Jana Sawicki, 1988a, p. 166)

Having argued that strands of radical pedagogy discourse are neither adversaries nor allies, I suggested in the preceding chapter that it may be helpful to think of discourses of radical pedagogy as caught up in, and operating as, regimes of truth. In this chapter, I elaborate Foucault's concept of "regime of truth" which entails engaging with the related concepts of "power-knowledge," "governmentality," and "technologies of self." Having taken Foucault (1980a) at his word, that "If one or two of these 'gadgets' of approach or method that I've tried to employ with psychiatry, the penal system or natural history can be of service to you, then I shall be delighted" (p. 65), I focus on regime of truth as a tool for the analysis of radical pedagogy discourses. Despite employing this tool and its related concepts, I do not claim to be a "Foucauldian" or to be consistent "to the letter" with Foucault's ideas. My primary purpose is not to do a Foucauldian analysis of radical pedagogy but rather, to use whatever tools seem propitious or helpful in better understanding and practicing radical pedagogy. Thus, my project has what (to some) might be seen as a more immediate pragmatic intent than did Foucault's analyses.

Next, also responding to Foucault's (1980a) general invitation—"If you find the need to transform my tools or use others then show me what they are, because it may be of benefit to me" (p. 65)—I have modified Foucault's use of regime of truth to be able to apply it to the analysis of strands of radical pedagogy discourse; thus, I will apply the concept at a more microscopic or local level than Foucault did in his own writings. I argue however, that this modification is consistent with Foucault's thought on power-knowledge and discourse. I then turn to consider the special relevance of regime of truth vis-à-vis pedagogy, and, more particularly vis-à-vis this analysis of discourses of radical pedagogy (in terms of both the pedagogy argued for and the pedagogy of the argument). Finally, I move from the general argument to outline a methodology for the identification of regimes of truth in radical pedagogy.

FOUCAULT'S CONSTRUCTION AND USE OF "REGIME OF TRUTH"

In order to understand "regime of truth," I turn to Foucault's use of power and knowledge (*pouvoir* and *savoir*). It is helpful to begin by clarifying what power and knowledge, in Foucault's idiom, are *not*. First, although many readers and critics of Foucault's work use the expression "power/knowledge," it should be clarified that Foucault used "power-knowledge." What is in the stroke or the dash? Tom Keenan (1987) argues that the dash holds the words together *and* apart, showing both their presupposition of each other and their difference from each other. Foucault (1983a) emphatically insisted that power and knowledge are different:

> When I read—and I know it has been attributed to me—the thesis "knowledge is power" or "power is knowledge," I begin to laugh, since studying their relation is precisely my problem. If they were identical, I would not have to study them and I would be spared a lot of fatigue as a result. The very fact that I pose *the question of their relation* proves clearly that I do not identify them. (p. 210)

Where the oblique stroke is sometimes employed to separate terms used to mean much the same thing, or to indicate that one can read either/ or both term(s) joined by the stroke/slash, the dash joins terms that are at some level different. I will therefore retain the dash.

Second, Foucault breaks away from the standard definitions of power and knowledge by reversing the negative articulation in which power (as domination, coercion, constraint, negativity) operates through fraud, illusion, false pretenses—preventing our purposes and desires from reaching fulfillment—and then masks that fact, and in which truth or knowledge can reverse or erase the imposed errors and challenge dominating or repressive power (Dreyfus and Rabinow, 1983; Keenan, 1987). As shall be clarified in the following chapters, this standard definition of the relation of power and knowledge is found in much of the radical pedagogy discourse, whereby, through consciousness-raising and education (generally), dominant powers can be unmasked to reveal "truth," and, in so doing, the potential to overthrow the capitalist and/or patriarchal system increases (Fay, 1987). I recall the "will to knowledge" introduced in Chapter 1. Interestingly the French phrase *vouloir-savoir* means both the will to knowledge and knowledge as revenge. Instead of conceiving of knowledge as revenge, Foucault's notion of power-knowledge "challenges assumptions that ideology can be demystified and, hence, that undistorted truth can be attained" (Diamond and Quinby, 1988, p. xi); it "delimits the intellectuals' dreams of truth's control of power" (Bové, 1988, p. xviii).

Foucault offers an alternative, and, for many, a compelling understanding of power and knowledge in their relation as power-knowledge. As Foucault (1980b) sees it, every relation between forces is a power relation, where force "is never singular but essentially exists in relation with other forces, such that force is already a relation" (Deleuze, 1988, p. 70). Power is not necessarily repressive since it incites, induces, seduces, makes easier or more difficult, enlarges or limits, makes more or less probable and so on (Foucault, 1983b). Power is exercised or practiced, rather than possessed, and so circulates, passing through every related force. Students, as well as teachers, exercise power. In order to understand the operation of power contextually, we need to understand the particular points through which it passes (Foucault, 1980b).

In Foucault's analyses of power, he especially concerned himself with forms of "government," as the sixteenth-century conception of this word "did not refer only to political structures or to the management of states; rather it designated the way in which the conduct of individuals or groups might be directed: the government of children, of souls, of communities, of families, of the sick. . . . To govern, in this sense, is to structure the possible field of action of others" (Foucault, 1983b, p. 221). Foucault (1988a) argued that modern forms of government reveal a shift from sovereign power which is overt, visible and located in a monarchal structure to "disciplinary" power which is exercised through its "invisibility" via normalizing technologies of the self:

Traditionally, power was what was seen, what was shown and what was manifested. . . . Disciplinary power, on the other hand, is exercised through its invisibility; at the same time it imposes on those whom it subjects a principle of compulsory visibility. In discipline it is the subjects who have to be seen. Their visibility assures the hold of power that is exercised over them. It is the fact of being constantly seen, of

being always able to be seen, that maintains the disciplined individual
in his [sic][1] subjection. (Foucault, 1977b, p. 187)

This notion of disciplinary power is vividly illustrated in Foucault's presentation of Bentham's Panopticon, an architectural structure wherein
individual cells located around the periphery of the building surround
a central tower. The backlighting, created by inner and outer windows,
enables observation of each cell from the central tower, while, at the
same time, ensuring that the inmates cannot see if they are being ob-
served. "Hence the major effect of the Panopticon: to induce in the
inmate a conscious and permanent visibility that assures the automatic
functioning of power" (Foucault, 1977b, p. 201).

Disciplinary power thus becomes internalized:

> He [sic] who is subjected to a field of visibility, and who knows it,
> assumes responsibility for the constraints of power; he makes them
> play spontaneously upon himself; he inscribes in himself the power
> relation in which he simultaneously plays both roles; he becomes the
> principle of his own subjection. (Foucault, 1977b, pp. 202–203)

Foucault's notion of "technologies of self" is closely linked with his
(rather idiosyncratic) conception of ethics. For Foucault (1983c), ethics
is separate from and located within the broader realm of morals: "in
what we call morals there is the effective behavior of people, there are
the codes and there is this kind of relationship to oneself" (pp. 239–
240). Foucault distinguishes between the imposed "prescriptions" or
moral codes that determine which acts are permitted or forbidden, which
acts are attributed positive or negative values in a constellation of possible
behaviours, and the ways and means by which individuals constitute themselves as the moral subjects of their own actions. In other words, he
draws a distinction between socially-imposed and internally-constructed
moralities. The technologies or practices of self are, of course, not something that individuals invent in any original sense. Rather, they are patterns found in culture which are proposed, suggested, and imposed on
individuals by their culture, their society, and their social group (Foucault, 1988b).

According to Foucault, the authority for these "technologies of the
self" is located in the human sciences which, in their production, regulation, surveillance, and labeling of human activities, have dominated
Western society from the eighteenth century. Knowledge or "truth," by
which Foucault (1980b) means "the ensemble of rules according to which
the true and the false are separated and specific effects of power attached
to the true" (p. 132),

is centred on the form of scientific discourse and the institutions which produce it; it is subject to constant economic and political incitement (the demand for truth, as much for economic production as for political power); it is the object, under diverse forms, of immense diffusion and consumption (circulating through apparatuses of education and information whose extent is relatively broad in the social body, not withstanding certain strict limitations); it is produced and transmitted under the control, dominant if not exclusive, of a few great political and economic apparatuses (university, army, writing, media); lastly, it is the issue of a whole political debate and social confrontation ("ideological" struggles). (pp. 131–132)

It is clear that Foucault does not address power or knowledge in isolation of, or in opposition to, the other. The two are connected: "power and knowledge directly imply one another . . . There is no power relation without the correlative constitution of a field of knowledge, nor any knowledge that does not presuppose and constitute at the same time power relations" (Foucault, 1977b, p. 27). Explaining the connection of power and knowledge, Foucault (1980a) said, "There is an administration of knowledge, a politics of knowledge, relations of power which pass via knowledge and which, if one tries to transcribe them, lead one to consider forms of domination designated by such notions as field, region and territory" (p. 69).

Consider, for example, the politics of knowledge in the field of radical pedagogy and the observation (Chapter 2) that feminist pedagogies have become by and large the domain of women, while critical pedagogies are solidifying as the domain of men. In part, we can view this differentiation within different discourses as an effect of power-knowledge, and the power relations that undergird the struggles of groups for territory within a certain field. Moreover, within each discursive strand, power relations are constructed in ways that specify which subjects are authorized to speak. In this way, the feminist and critical pedagogical "self" is constructed.

This alternative conception of power and knowledge and its relation to self should be seen not simply as a set of concepts employed by Foucault. Rather, power, knowledge, and self constitute the objects of Foucault's abbreviated lifetime[2] of work. Typically, there are considered to be three domains of analysis in Foucault's work: an archaeological study of knowledge, a genealogical study of power, and an ethical study of the self. The chronological shift in his work from one to the next of these domains was not a move to replace the previous intellectual concern but, instead, a move to widen the analysis (Davidson, 1986). Foucault's work shifted from an analysis of discursive formations to an inclusion of "nondiscursive" practices and regularities, and, later, to a consideration of the "technologies of self" that coincide with the technologies of power. "Regime of truth," although first articulated in the "genealogical" phase of his work, encompasses all three of these concerns.

Foucault (1980b) explains "regime of truth" as follows: " 'Truth' is linked in circular relation with systems of power which produce and sustain it, and to effects of power which it induces and which extend it" (p. 133). Also:

> Each society has its regime of truth, its "general politics" of truth: that is, the types of discourse which it accepts and makes function as true; the mechanisms and instances which enable one to distinguish true and false statements, the means by which each is sanctioned; the techniques and procedures accorded value in the acquisition of truth; the status of those who are charged with saying what counts as true. (p. 131)

As an example, in what Foucault refers to as modern disciplinary society, the regime of truth includes discourses of the human sciences—education, psychology, medicine—which are accepted and made to function as true. Scientific reason is seen as the primary means by which these discourses are sanctioned. Professional, intellectual, or scientific status is accorded to those charged with saying what counts as true (be they the intellectuals involved in the production of knowledge, or the media, politicians, teachers, and others involved in its circulation).

In summary, I understand *regime of truth* to convey the connection between *power* and *knowledge* which is produced by, and produces, a specific *art of government*. For Foucault (1983b), "power is less a confrontation between two adversaries or the linking of one to the other than a question of government" (p. 221). In what Foucault (1988a) calls our "modern political rationality," such government has increasingly produced *self*-disciplining or self-styling. It is an art of government that relies on *technologies of the self* which are actualized and resisted/get acted out through the body. Power exists only in action[3] and is actualized at the site of the body, in our actions and behavior, and thus we can identify *political regimes of the body* (Feher, 1987). Political regimes of the body refers to the actualizing of a regime (or regimes) of truth in, on, through, and around the body.

"REGIME OF TRUTH" AT MICRO LEVELS

While Foucault referred to "regime of truth" in relation to "each society," the focus of his studies suggests that he conceived of "society" in broad temporal and geographic terms. Hence, he focused on early Greek society and the Classical Age, and early Christian society and modernity in his investigations (archaeological, genealogical, ethical) of "What are we today?" (Foucault, 1988a). It is my contention that "society" can be conceived at a more local level whereby discourses and practices can contain a local politics of truth. Thus regime of truth can be applied to discourses and practices that reveal sufficient regularity to enable their immanent naming, such as discourses and practices of radical pedagogy. I intend to demonstrate that such an application of the concept, regime of truth, is not only appropriate but helpful in identifying specific dangers in the functioning of critical and feminist pedagogy discourses.

Foucault (1978) argued that "it is in discourse that power and knowledge are joined together" (p. 100). Because of their articulation in discourse, Foucault (1978) argued:

> we must not imagine a world of discourse divided between the accepted discourse and excluded discourse, or between the dominant discourse and the dominated one; but as a multiplicity of discursive elements that can come into play in various strategies. . . . Discourses are not once and for all subservient to power or raised up against it, any more than silences are. We must make allowances for the complex and unstable process whereby discourse can be both an instrument and an effect of power, but also a hindrance, a stumbling-block, a point of resistance and a starting point for an opposing strategy. Discourse transmits and produces power; it reinforces it, but also undermines and exposes it, renders it fragile and makes it possible to thwart it. . . . There is not, on the one side, a discourse of power, and opposite it, another discourse that runs counter to it. Discourses are tactical elements or blocks operating in the field of force relations; there can exist different and even contradictory discourses within the same strategy; they can, on the contrary, circulate without changing their form from one strategy to another, opposing strategy. (pp. 100–102)

My analysis is consistent with these claims inasmuch as I have named different discursive strands that operate alongside one another in a field of radical pedagogy in which the strands are identified both by their differences and by their partially equivalent tactics and strategies. Thus, when educational theorists draw on Foucault to claim that we can consider *dominant* educational discourses (those produced by the dominant culture) as "regimes of truth",[4] and yet do not examine radical work as regimes, they fail to emphasize Foucault's (1983c) point that "everything is dangerous" (p. 231).

Keenan (1987) argues that *"because* the articulation between power and knowledge *is* discursive, then the link can never be guaranteed. . . . If the vehicle of the coincidence is discourse, the transference between the two cannot be totalized, unified, integrated, or otherwise stabilized. It is unpredictable. . . . The discourse that makes [the link] possible also undermines it, precisely because power and knowledge *are* different" (pp. 17–18). Sawicki (1988b) also asserts the following point in her analysis, framed by Foucault and feminism, concerning identity politics and sexual freedom. Where she refers to "sexuality," I have substituted "pedagogy" in order to demonstrate the relevance of the argument to this discussion of discourses of radical pedagogy.

> Discourse is ambiguous . . . a form of power that circulates in the social field and can attach to strategies of domination as well as to those of resistance. Neither wholly a source of domination nor of resistance, [pedagogy] is also neither outside power nor wholly circumscribed by it. Instead, it is itself an arena of struggle. There are no inherently liberating or repressive [pedagogical] practices, for any practice is co-optable and any capable of becoming a source of resistance. After all, if relations of power are dispersed and fragmented throughout the social field, so must resistance to power be. Thus evaluating the political status of [pedagogical] practices should be a matter of historical and social investigation, not a priori theoretical pronouncement (pp. 185–186).

In this view, radical pedagogies must examine their "sacred" goals and practices for the specific effects they have in particular contexts.

Some examples may be helpful at this point. Consider the circle seating formation so common to progressive pedagogical practice. The circle is frequently employed to shift the classroom interaction away from the direct control of the teacher. The circle counters the traditional classroom in which "Stillness is the achievement of the science of supervision, an arrangement of persons in collective units accessible to constant surveillance. By arranging students in rows, all eyes facing front, directly confronting the back of a fellow's head, meeting the gaze only of the teacher, the discipline of the contemporary classroom deploys the look as a strategy of domination" (Grumet, 1988a, p. 111). The circle opens the possibilities for every student to voice her or his opinion, and to be heard. With students sitting on the floor or on portable chairs they are freed from the restrictive confines of their desks, separated from each other.

Most of us who teach within critical or feminist pedagogies have used a circle seating arrangement at some time, with these kinds of intentions.

Foucault, Sawicki and others (e.g., Walkerdine, 1985, 1986) point out that there is nothing inherently liberating about this practice, even when located within a radical discourse, and nothing inherently oppressive about rows. For instance, the partial privacy allowed by the traditional placement of desks, whereby one is under the surveillance or supervision primarily of the teacher, might be forfeited as students come more directly under the surveillance of their peers as well. The student who prefers not to speak up is less obvious when all desks face the front, as is the student who cannot afford new shoes, who blushes, who is bored and so on. I am not trying to make an argument for a return to rows of desks—I will continue to try to make the circle seating formation work in my own practice. I am arguing that our "liberatory" practices have no guaranteed effects.

As another example, consider the practice (often well-intentioned) in the U.S. of acknowledging the contributions of marginalized people by adding "Women's History Month" and "Black History Month" to the elementary school curriculum. The effects of this practice can be quite conservative in terms of continuing to place the experience of white men at the center and maintaining all other experience in a marginal position. Even curricula which try to more radically transform the perspective from which the social world is viewed, can overlook other marginalized groups. For example, in efforts to deal with race, class and gender, other oppressive formations such as heterosexism and ageism often prevail.

The realizations that there are no inherently liberating practices or discourses and that power-knowledge and "technologies of self" can be seen to operate at the micro level of discrete pedagogical practices (in terms of instruction and curriculum content), are the touchstones that enabled me to see the applicability of the concept, "regime of truth," to my work as a teacher educator. Foucault (1980a) said "the longer I continue, the more it seems to me that the formation of discourses and the genealogy of knowledge need to be analysed, not in terms of consciousness, modes of perception and forms of ideology, but in terms of tactics and strategies of power" (p. 77). In an interview titled "Truth and Power," Foucault (1980b) introduced "regime of truth" immediately following his statement that "we are now at a point where the function of the specific intellectual needs to be reconsidered" (p. 130). Here, Foucault alluded to the intellectual's participation in the construction and functioning of regimes of truth, and pointed to the "specific" as a way to minimize such participation.

Power, in Foucault's view, emerges from specific practices in local arenas of action. "Power is strictly relational and cannot exist other than as a function of multiple points of resistance. The play of power relations is complex, unstable, self-transforming, and never definitely sure of a particular global effect. . . . In short, . . . power must be analysed as a *microprocess* of social life, as an all-pervading phenomenon which emerges everywhere out of the infinitesimal violences of concrete, local transactions" (Knorr-Cetina, 1981, p. 22). While Foucault's (1978) references to "local centers" of power-knowledge provide further justification for my modification and application of "regime of truth" to the micro level of radical pedagogy discourse, the following caveat must shape such use of "regime of truth":

> No "local center," no "pattern of transformation" could function if, through a series of sequences, it did not eventually enter into an overall strategy. And inversely, no strategy could achieve comprehensive effects if [it] did not gain support from precise and tenuous relations serving, not as its point of application or final outcome, but as its prop and anchor point. There is no discontinuity between them, as if one were dealing with two different levels (one microscopic and the other macroscopic); but neither is there homogeneity (as if the one were only the enlarged projection or the miniaturization of the other); rather, one must conceive of the double conditioning of a strategy by the specificity of possible tactics, and of tactics by the strategic envelope that makes them work. (pp. 99–100)

Here, Foucault argues that it is important to be constantly conscious of the "double conditioning" of radical pedagogy whose tactics are conditioned by the overall strategy of modern disciplinary society at the same time as those specific tactics condition the overall strategy. In other words, while I analyze radical pedagogy discourses as regimes of truth I must acknowledge both the effects of these discourses on larger regimes of our present and the ways in which these larger regimes affect the construction and functioning of radical pedagogy discourses.

"REGIME OF TRUTH" AND PEDAGOGY

Although Foucault did not carry out a detailed analysis of schools, it is clear that he saw schools and formal education as playing a part in the growth of disciplinary power. In *Discipline and Punish*, in the chapter titled "Docile Bodies," Foucault (1977b) outlines early pedagogical innovations and the model they provided for eighteenth-century economics, medicine, and military theory. Later in the book he asks, "Is it surprising that prisons resemble factories, schools, barracks, hospitals, which all resemble prisons?" (Foucault, 1977b, p. 228). Hence, "regime of

truth" may be particularly relevant as a tool for the analysis of pedagogical discourse and practice inasmuch as disciplinary relations of
power-knowledge are fundamental to pedagogy. Furthermore, in defining pedagogy as the process of knowledge production we can say that
disciplinary power, exercised via normalizing technologies of the self, is
in part pedagogical.

In the search for techniques and practices which actualize a particular
regime of truth, *pedagogy* provides an important site. The pedagogical
process embodies *power relations* between and among teacher and learners (defined either narrowly to refer to the actors in institutionalized
education or broadly to refer to other pedagogical relations such as those
of parents and children, writers and readers, and so on) concerning issues
of *knowledge*: "What is valid knowledge?" "What knowledge is produced?" "Whose knowledge?" and so on.

Pedagogy relies on particular techniques of *government*, the development of which can be traced historically/archaeologically (e.g., Hamilton, 1989; Hunter, 1988; Jones and Williamson, 1979; Luke, 1989a),
and which produces, and reproduces at different moments, particular
rules and practices. Increasingly, pedagogy has emphasized self-disciplining whereby students keep themselves and each other in check. We
can call the specific techniques/practices which elicit such behavior *technologies of the self*. These technologies are enacted at the site of the body;
eyes, hands, mouths, movement. For example, in many classrooms students quickly learn to raise their hands before speaking in class, to keep
their eyes on their own work during a test, to keep their eyes on the
teacher and appear to be listening when the teacher is giving instructions,
to stay in their seats, and so on. As Corrigan (1991) puts it: "pedagogy
works on the mind and emotions, on the unconscious, and yes, on the
soul, the spirit, *through the work done on, to, by, with, and from the body*"
(p. 211). "They/we are the subjects who are taught, disciplined, mea-
sured, evaluated, examined, passed (or not), assessed, graded, hurt,
harmed, twisted, re-worked, applauded, praised, encouraged, enforced,
coerced, consensed" (p. 210). We can say that pedagogies produce particular political regimes of the body. Such technologies of the bodily self
can also be understood as manifestations of the internal (mental) self—
how people identify themselves. Pedagogies operate as regimes of truth.

This argument is pertinent not only in relation to pedagogies argued
for, that is, in relation to particular social visions and instructional practices enacted in the name of pedagogy, but also in relation to the pedagogy of the arguments which characterize the discourses of radical pedagogy. Thus, in the chapters that follow, my naming of regimes of truth

will focus on both of these discursive practices in critical and feminist pedagogies. Additionally, I will outline a methodology for this analysis. First, I want briefly to argue why "regime of truth" seems to have advantages over other tools and concepts for the analysis of discursive formations in radical pedagogy.

No other available concept seems as sufficient as "regime of truth" to enable such an analysis of the power relations in pedagogical practice and in pedagogical discourse. Consider other approaches to the analysis of power in pedagogy: Bernstein's (1975, 1986) sociolinguistic analysis of pedagogy in different class locations, and Bourdieu and Passeron's (1977) assertion of pedagogic authority both employ critique in an attempt to uncover ideologies in schooling and society. Holding on to the conventional conception of the relation of power and knowledge, these analyses are helpful only insofar as they locate power in macro-social relations. Furthermore, as their object is pedagogical practice rather than pedagogical discourse, they do not provide the means for self-criticism, unlike Foucault's construction of "regime of truth." Consequently this kind of analysis of pedagogy maintains the intellectual in the privileged position, "bearer of universal values" (Foucault, 1980b, p. 132).

Similarly, to employ other concepts in the analysis of power and/or domination, such as "hegemony," is to lose some of the complexity and multiplicity that Foucault's analyses of power-knowledge not only permit but demand. For example, while hegemony is considered to be dynamic and contested (Williams, 1976), the concept of hegemony tends toward identification of *the* dominant classes, groups, and so on. In contemporary Western society, feminism, in this view, would be an emergent social category in opposition to the existing hegemony. "Regime of truth" allows us to posit that feminism may have its own power-knowledge nexus which, in particular contexts and in particular historical moments, will operate in ways that are oppressive and repressive to people within and/or outside of the constituency of feminism. For example, many women of color have expressed anger at the alienation they have felt from what developed as a primarily white, middle class form of feminism in the academy (e.g. hooks, 1984; Lorde, 1984; Omolade, 1985). "Foucault's genealogical approach is antithetical to both forms of global or totalizing theory and conceptions of power as a product or possession of a class subject" (Smart, 1986, p. 162) implicit in most conceptions of hegemony. Instead, Foucault's view of power as fragmented and circulating "requires that the concept of hegemony be opened up, not . . . [just] vertically to make room for the local situation as well as the grand fact, but horizontally to make room for the multiple axes on which power in society inevitably turns" (Cocks, 1989, p. 50).

As should become clear in the following section, my use of "regime of truth" not only cautions against interpretations of discourses or practices as either inherently liberating or inherently oppressive, but also begins to identify the features of a particular regime which are potentially dangerous to that regime. Here, I find a space for optimism in Foucault's work. Shortly before his death he said "All my analyses are against the idea of universal necessities in human existence. They show the arbitrariness of institutions and show which space of freedom we can still enjoy and how many changes can still be made" (Foucault, 1988a, p. 153). However unsettling, positing a single or stable center of power against which to pose counter strategies of resistance, is an oversimplification of the realities of modern disciplinary society. While Foucault's alternative does not offer simple solutions or answers, it is, for me, a compelling analysis.

TOWARD A METHODOLOGY FOR IDENTIFYING REGIMES OF TRUTH

Some readers might feel uncomfortable with the implication of my argument, that everything can be related to regimes of truth. However, my point is not to argue whether or not radical pedagogy discourses *are* regimes of truth. My point is rather to emphasize the helpfulness of examining radical pedagogy discourses *as* regimes of truth. In order to do so, attention must first be given to how one is to proceed with such an analysis.

Michel Feher (1987)[5] who, following Foucault, was interested in political regimes of the body, is a helpful resource for the development of a methodology. He juxtaposed the "political" and the "ethical" aspects of Foucault's work, calling them the intertwined aspects of any regime: "On the one hand, there is the political question of the body as a battlefield of power relations; on the other hand, there is the ethical question of one's relation to one's own body and how that relation shifts. So intertwined with the political regime of the body is an ethical typology defined by the relationship of people to their bodies" (p. 162). Feher brings together power-knowledge and "technologies of the self" in ways consistent with my earlier discussion of "regime of truth." His brief paper proceeds with a mapping out of two sets of questions for the analysis of political regimes of the body. Feher's questions closely match Foucault's (1983b, 1983c) own explication of five points for the analysis of power relations (see pp. 223–224) and four aspects of ethics (see pp. 238–243). The following points then, borrowed from Foucault and Feher, provide the framework for the investigation of discourses of radical pedagogy as regimes of truth explored in Chapters 4, 5, and 6. In terms of the *political* aspects of the regime (the relations of power, what goes on between people), the following will be examined: (1) the system of differentiations that characterizes a given regime, permitting one to act upon the actions of another or to exercise power; (2) the functions and objectives pursued by those who act upon the actions of others within a given regime—the objectives of the relations of power; (3) the specific techniques and practices that actualize the relations of power; (4) the institutions which integrate these practices; (5) the formation of knowledge that describes the reality produced by a given regime of power and that raises problems immanent to that reality. The *ethical* aspects of the regime (the relation to one's self and the way that relation shifts) will be identified with attention to: (1) aspects of the self considered problematic in any given regime—the gestures, postures, and attitudes which are in need of disciplining or styling; (2) in the name of what the self is disciplined or styled—the "mode of subjection" (Foucault, 1983c); (3) the specific techniques that are developed to achieve a particular self-styling; (4) the assigned goals of these ethical practices of self-styling, the kind of being to which we aspire.

Drawing on this framework, I want to explore the usefulness of "regime of truth" as an analytical tool, through an attempt to identify regimes of truth at two different levels (both local in relation to society writ large), both which are pertinent to discourses of critical and feminist pedagogy. First, if I reconsider questions of academic culture and intellectual competition and the separation of strands of radical pedagogy, I can begin to name a regime of truth which produces, and is produced by, intellectual work in the university. To elaborate, differentiations are made within the academy about what constitutes scholarly/political/pedagogical work. Particular interests are served by these differentiations, usually the interests of those people and discourses already in dominant positions within the academy. There are specific practices which actualize the relations of power within the academy (e.g., blind review of manuscripts for publication and presentation at conferences, tenure demands, alienation from particular "in" groups, representation on committees, funding mechanisms, exile). Institutions which integrate these practices, such as the university, funding organizations, and "professional" associations, both facilitate and constrain, at different moments, academic work.

These power relations are linked to particular demands for disciplining the self. Certain gestures, postures, and attitudes are considered to be in need of styling (e.g., conference dress, oftentimes that which resists the "norm," not appearing too entrepreneurial, writing in a particular —often linear—style). Styling is conducted in the name of, for example, making a career, and/or being "politically correct." Specific techniques of disciplining the self include diplomatic speech when addressing the work of peers, controlling emotion, enduring endless meetings, making certain decisions about conferences to attend and colleagues with whom to work. The assigned goal of this kind of self-disciplining is to be a particular type of academic—feminist pedagogue, critical theorist, "transformative intellectual," and so on.

Given this characterization of academic work as a regime of truth, it is clear that every text of radical pedagogy is constructed within contexts of particular discourses which function through particular institutions. This characterization of the regime of truth of the academy helps frame the different manifestations of similar political and pedagogical projects, such as the different strands of critical pedagogy discourse and the different strands of feminist pedagogy discourse which are of central importance in my analysis.

Hence, at another micro or local level, I want to explore feminist and critical pedagogy discourses themselves as regimes of truth. Within the scope of this study, I limit the analysis to questions of authority and empowerment as they are constructed in feminist and critical pedagogy discourses. Before moving to that analysis I want to make some brief comments in anticipation of criticisms about the use of Foucault for a practical and political project such as the improvement of radical teacher education.

A RESPONSE TO FOUCAULT'S CRITICS IN ANTICIPATION OF MY OWN

Regimes of truth are not necessarily negative but, rather, necessary. Knowledge and power *are* linked, often in productive ways. Just as power can be productive, so, too, can the power-knowledge nexus in and through which one carries out one's work. The point of employing "regime of truth" to analyze radical pedagogy is not to engage in a "politics of the pointing finger" (Morris, 1988, p. 23). The relative lack of reflexivity among radical pedagogy discourses is hardly surprising, given the struggle to legitimate such discourses among "mainstream" educational discourses. I employ "regime of truth", therefore, as a "technology of self", one that requires greater humility and reflexivity in constructing claims for radical pedagogy, acknowledging that there is deconstructive work to be done within the domain itself as well as outside of it. Foucault's analyses of power-knowledge raise doubts about the possibility or desirability of reaching a final answer to the question, "Which pedagogical discourses and practices are liberating?" (Sawicki, 1988b). Foucault's politics, "designed to avoid dogmatism in our categories and politics as well as the silencing of difference to which such dogmatism can lead is a welcome alternative to polarized debate" (Sawicki, 1988b, p. 187).

But where does this kind of analysis leave us? There have been many criticisms of Foucault's work with regard to historical accuracy, methodological rigor, and political consequences: it is on the latter that I should like to focus. Some critics have argued that Foucault leaves us with gaps or aporias, with no way out of disciplinary power; that in his joining of power-knowledge, Foucault has removed the basis for the practical political linkage of the two (e.g., Anderson, 1983; Habermas, 1986; Taylor, 1986). Some claim that Foucault's analyses leave us only with pessimism; some argue that his work is antithetical to feminist projects (e.g., Balbus, 1988). A few readers of my work have expressed concerns that "regime of truth" does not substantively consider the gendered nature of knowledge, power, and possibilities for social transformation. While Foucault does not specifically address this question, I would argue that "regime of truth" does not itself exclude this possibility. Indeed, it leaves the empirical question open as to the ways in which power-knowledge has been, and continues to be, "gendered." The readings of Foucault which shape these criticisms stem from particular intellectual, political, and professional agendas (Bové, 1988). Bové (1988) argues that many leading humanistic intellectuals misread Foucault "to blunt the political consequences of his critique of their disciplines', their discourses', and their own positions within the knowledge/ power apparatus" (p. xi).

To the contrary, others have argued, "Foucault's own reluctance to be explicit about his ethical and political positions is attributable not to nihilism, relativism, or political irresponsibility, but rather to his sense of the dangers of political programs based on grand theory" (Sawicki, 1988b, p. 189). Foucault (1980a) wanted to leave questions of specific tactics, strategies, and goals to those directly involved in struggle and resistance, hence his notion of "specific" intellectuals working within specific sectors "at the precise points where their own conditions of life or work situate them" (Foucault, 1980b, p. 126). "To proceed in this manner does not signify 'indifference' or a lack of critical concern but rather that a political discourse promising 'emancipation' constitutes at best a form of rhetoric" (Smart, 1986, p. 169). As Foucault (1983b) argued:

> A society without power relations can only be an abstraction. . . . To say that there cannot be a society without power relations is not to say either that those which are established are necessary, or, in any case, that power constitutes a fatality at the heart of societies, such that it cannot be undermined. Instead I would say that the analysis, elaboration, and bringing into question of power relations and the "agonism"[6] between power relations and the intransitivity of freedom is a permanent political task inherent in all social existence. (pp. 222–223)

It is toward this political task, from the sector within which I work, that I now turn to a specific analysis of critical and feminist pedagogy discourses as regimes of truth.

FOUR

Authority and Empowerment in Feminist Pedagogy

This chapter marks the beginning of the second part of my book as the focus now shifts to an explication of critical and feminist pedagogy discourses as regimes of truth. Following the methodological framework outlined in the previous chapter, I will begin the identification of regimes of truth by examining the differentiations made (a political component of the regime) as well as the aspects of the self considered problematic (an ethical component), within the discourses of critical and feminist pedagogy.

I focus on differentiations and aspects of self around issues of authority and empowerment for several reasons. First, problems of "authority for empowerment" or "empowerment through authority" seemed central to my own struggles with radical pedagogy as a practicing teacher educator. Second, "authority" and "empowerment" are central issues in the discourses of critical and feminist pedagogy: "authority" is frequently acknowledged as problematic within each discourse; "empowerment" is frequently cited as a goal of each discourse. One need only examine the titles of publications and presentations to realize that these issues draw considerable attention and energy within these discourses.[1] Third, not only *are* these concepts central, but they *must be* central within the very modernist construction of power through which feminist and critical pedagogies have historically been framed. Concerned about structures of repressive power, and power as the property of some over others, authority is clearly at issue in these discourses. Moreover, such a notion of power is necessary if the idea of em-power-ment is to be plausible. Fourth, insofar as my focus on authority and empowerment addresses issues of central importance to the construction of radical pedagogy discourses, this analysis is offered in the name of the reflexivity for which I argued earlier. Finally, it is important to note that this detailed focus remains consistent with the micro-level analysis of relations of power Foucault called part of the work of the specific intellectual.

Such a task thus involves a close examination of radical pedagogy texts in an attempt to highlight central features and nuances of the "regimes" as they are constructed through the issues of "authority" and "empowerment." All regimes are dangerous, but perhaps less so to the extent that one becomes conscious of, sensitive to, the specific dangers of one's work. It is with this project in mind that I attempt to uncover specific dangers, normalizing tendencies, and effects of domination, of critical and feminist pedagogy discourses.

In the remainder of this chapter, I systematically engage the methodological framework outlined in Chapter 3 to begin to name the regime of truth of feminist pedagogy discourse as it functions around issues of authority and empowerment. In the process, I differentiate between the two strands of feminist pedagogy only where distinctions markedly separate the two. I consider authority and empowerment concurrently because they are presented as connected issues within the discourse. Put simplistically, the connection is articulated something like this: feminist educators attempt to exercise "authority-with" rather than "authority-over" in order to "empower" their students (and themselves). I now turn to an elaboration of this "regime."

POLITICAL ASPECTS OF THE REGIME

The Differentiations

Authority, in the construction of feminist pedagogies, is addressed in a number of ways including authority versus nurturance, authority as power, authority as authorship. While I will elaborate these aspects of authority in feminist pedagogy discourse in turn, I also acknowledge that they are often connected in a variety of different ways.

One common differentiation is found in the juxtaposition-as-contradiction of authority and nurturance.[2] The perceived contradiction is vividly captured by Kathryn Pauly Morgan (1987) in her discussion of "the paradox of the bearded mother." She argues that feminist teachers are expected to be "bearded" in the sense that they are expected to embody and display the forms of rationality, modes of cognition, and critical lucidity that have been said to be the monopoly of men (while questioning these very things) and, at the same moment, "mothers" in the sense that they are expected to offer unconditional maternal nurturance and support. Morgan's argument highlights several issues at stake in this particular construction of authority within feminist pedagogy discourse: first, that "authority" is connected with a particular form of reason or rationality;[3] second, reason-based authority is the "monopoly of men"; third, that the feminist teacher is a kind of mother.

By attributing authority to male or masculine reason, and to the patriarchy/"fathers," some feminist writers are concerned with the antithetical subject position of "mothers." In feminist discourse, the notion of mother is laden with the traditional functions of care-giver and nurturer, as well as with psychoanalytic conceptions of the mother-daughter relationship, e.g., dependence and autonomy, attachment and separation (Culley et al., 1985). Brought into the domain of feminist classrooms, the mother/teacher is considered to be in the difficult position of trying to reconcile her own and her students' desires for mothering with patriarchal constructions of the teacher, such that the female teacher "is a strange creature—neither father nor mother" (Pagano, 1990, p. 33).

Margo Culley et al.'s (1985) analysis of "The Politics of Nurturance" directly addresses some issues of the perceived contradiction of authority and nurturance. "In our culture, the role of nurturer and intellectual have been separated not just by gender, but by function; to try to recombine them [in the role of feminist teacher] is to create confusion" (p. 13). The implication is that the teacher/professor (male, but sometimes female), as intellectual, has not traditionally functioned in a nurturing capacity. Moreover, the suggestion is that teaching is a patriarchal enterprise and that the position of the feminist teacher is particularly difficult because she (a few writers would add "and occasionally he") must work within that system while trying to alter it: "To the extent that our goal within and outside the classroom is the overthrow of the institutionalized patriarchy which currently structures our knowledge and relationships, the contradictions we as teachers simultaneously represent are heightened" (Culley et al., 1985, p. 12).

This view leads to a second aspect of authority apparent within feminist pedagogy discourse; that is, the linking of authority with power, where power as the monopoly of men is connected to vice, and is then differentiated from such notions as innocence and powerlessness. The general argument is that patriarchal models of authority, based on power over students, are to be avoided by feminist teachers. Thus some feminist

educators struggle to alter, or at least not reproduce, perceived characteristics of patriarchal pedagogy such as its emphasis on hierarchy,
competition, control. In some cases it is implied, if not explicit, that
women can quite easily achieve a different sort of classroom (non-hierarchical, non-competitive) because women are essentially innocent and
good (e.g., Rich, 1979). As Jo Anne Pagano (1990) points out, this construction of authority as power and power as vice can be rather immobilizing if, as is sometimes the case, it is constructed within a bipolar
logic that leaves the teacher with only two options: to "speak the Name-
of-the-Father or fall silent" (p. 37). Susan Friedman (1985) describes
one such situation:

> I watched a bright colleague of mine teach a small and enthusiastic
> group of advanced Women's Studies students. Discussion went very
> well, up to a point, on a number of tough theoretical issues about
> female imagery in women's art. Although I knew my colleague knew
> perfectly well how to synthesize the disparate issues the students
> brought up, I watched her suppress her own capacity to conceptualize
> what the students had discussed. (p. 206)

In this view, any kind of authority is seen to be "incompatible with the
feminine" (Friedman, 1985, p. 206).

Many authors who attempt to theorize feminist pedagogy reject this
view and argue instead that the "silent" position of teacher as facilitator,
nurturing but not challenging, amounts to not "taking our students seriously" (Rich, 1979). They argue that patriarchy is accountable for denying women "the *authority* of their experiences, perspectives, emotions,
minds" (Friedman, 1985, p. 206).

This argument inscribes a third construction of authority within feminist pedagogy discourse; a call to reclaim authority, often linked to
authorship and authenticity. Such a reclamation enables Adrienne Rich
(1979) to argue for teachers to exercise a great deal of authority:

> We can refuse to accept passive, obedient learning and insist upon
> critical thinking. We can become harder on our women students, giving
> them the kinds of 'cultural prodding' that men receive, but on different
> terms and in a different style. . . . We need to keep our standards very
> high, not to accept a woman's preconceived sense of her limitations;
> we need to be hard to please, while supportive of risk-taking, because
> self-respect comes only when exacting standards have been met. . . . A
> romantic sloppiness, an inspired lack of rigor, a self-indulgent incoh-
> erence, are symptoms of female self-depreciation. (p. 244)

In this view, women are seen to be authorities of their own experiences.

Similarly, Friedman (1985) argues "We need a theory that first recognizes the androcentric denial of *all* authority to women and, second,
points out a way for us to speak with an authentic voice not based on
tyranny" (p. 207). Friedman continues:

> In our eagerness to be non-hierarchical and supportive instead of
> tyrannical and ruthlessly critical, we have sometimes participated in
> the patriarchal denial of the mind to women. . . . In our sensitivity to
> the psychology of oppression in our students' lives, we have often
> denied ourselves the authority we seek to nurture in our students. (p.
> 207)

Instead, she says "We must . . . develop a classroom based in the 'authority' radical feminism has granted to women in the process of sub-
verting and transforming patriarchal culture" (p. 207). In a similar vein,
Culley (1985) claims "The . . . feminist teacher . . . *has* power and must
claim her authority if her students are to claim their own. The power
she has resides precisely and paradoxically in the source of her stigma:
her gender or her race, or both" (p. 211). In this view, the authority of
women as teachers comes from precisely those differences that have
constructed the feminine (as the opposite of masculine), and have constructed woman as Other.

Pagano (1990) is wary of views that are sometimes "romanticized,
ritualized, sentimentalized, theatricalized, privatized claims of matriarchy
[which] wedge knowledge into the cramped corners of commodity relations. My knowledge, not yours" (p. 39). From a slightly different perspective, Pagano argues that feminist educators can approach questions
of authority by focusing on authorship; "authorship is warranted not by
truth but by truthfulness. Truthfulness can be judged only in a common
language" (p. 99) to be found in the connectedness of sharing stories,
and based on particular attachments or affiliations to the world and to
each other. Pagano argues that instead of wrestling with "the apparent
contradictions between activities such as testing, evaluating, grading and
syllabus control and the nurturing and empowering aims of feminist
pedagogy," or accepting mainstream educational discourse which conceives of issues of authority "within the bounds of management and
control and are read as gender neutral" (p. 102), feminist educators
might instead consider teaching to be an enactment of a narrative in
which "authority" "refers to the power to represent reality, to signify,
and to command compliance with one's acts of signification" (p. 103),
a power that both teacher and students can exercise.

Although not all writers of feminist pedagogy use the same termi-
nology, all of the concerns discussed (concerns with nurturing, with not

reproducing "tyrannical power," and with the authority of women's experiences) seem to fit with the view that "the authority the feminist
teacher seeks is authority with, not authority over" (Culley, 1985, p.
215), a form of authority that is not experienced as authoritarian but
based in caring and reciprocal relationships. That authority is not rejected altogether comes, in part, from an acknowledgment (rarely articulated in detail) of the exigencies of the teacher-student relationship, of
the regulative aspects of pedagogy. That is, as a teacher, the feminist
teacher has to, will be expected to, or needs to exercise some authority.
She should therefore exercise a "good" kind of authority.

For some writers, what I refer to as the exigencies of the teacher-
student relationship are explained by focusing more on power than on
teaching itself. For instance, as Clare Bright (1987) sees it:

> Discussion of the student/teacher relationship must include a frank
> look at the power of the teacher. Feminists have often avoided the
> topic of power, preferring structures and situations where power is
> shared. However, the educational system is not an egalitarian one, and
> regardless of the extent to which a teacher tries to minimize her power,
> it cannot be completely given away. When the institutional power of
> the instructor is not acknowledged, the situation is mystified; abuse of
> power may be obscured, rendering subjects incapable of naming their
> experience accurately. (p. 98)

I will elaborate the discussion of power later in the chapter in an analysis
of the institutions involved in the integration of feminist pedagogy.

A more common explanation given for discussion of authority and
power in feminist pedagogy discourse is the desire of feminist teachers
to empower their (most often women)[4] students and themselves. Carolyn
Shrewsbury (1987a), for instance, outlines for feminist teachers "empowering strategies" that "allow students to find their own voices, to
discover the power of authenticity" (p. 9). She elaborates:

> Empowering classrooms are places to practice visions of a feminist
> world, confronting differences to enrich all of us rather than belittle
> some of us. Empowering pedagogy does not dissolve the authority or
> power of the instructor. It does move from power as domination to
> power as creative energy. (p. 9)

The differentiation of power as domination from power as creative energy is central to the reclaiming of authority for feminist pedagogy. As
we have seen, strong notions of the evil power of patriarchy (what Joan
Cocks (1989) refers to as "power is horror") are central to many constructions of feminist pedagogy discourse; thus, differentiating kinds of

power gets feminist pedagogy out of the immobilizing bipolar logic of power/vice versus powerlessness/innocence. However, it enters it into another bipolar logic of power as *either* "domination" *or* "creative energy," either oppressive or productive. This logic is dangerous to the extent that feminist power is perceived as always "good," always empowering and so never an object of criticism. For example, Shrewsbury (1987a) states that "by focusing on empowerment, feminist pedagogy embodies a concept of power as energy, capacity, and potential rather than as domination" (p. 8) whereby "the goal is to increase the power of all actors, not to limit the power of some" (p. 8). Smithson (1990) proclaims " 'Empowerment' may not be written on the syllabi of most Women's Studies courses, but it is necessarily the result of courses that allow women to increase their information, hone their perceptions, and share with other women their ideas and feelings" (p. 6). How does one use or exercise one's own power in order to em-power others? And who is the appropriate agent? Culley (1985) says:

> No amount of knowledge, insight and sensitivity on the part of a male instructor can alter the deep structures of privilege mirrored in the male as teacher, female as student model. . . . One would not want to deny that many positive things can happen when a male is the instructor of female students. . . . But these teachers cannot be the agents of the deepest transformations in a culture where women have been schooled to look to male authority and to search for male approval at the basis of self-worth. (p. 211)

Morgan (1987) perceives problems for the feminist teacher as the agent of empowerment in what she calls the paradox of democratic pedagogy:

> If the feminist teacher actively assumes any of the forms of power available to her—expert, reward, legitimate, maternal/referent—she eliminates the possibility of educational democracy in the feminist classroom; if she dispenses with these in the name of preserving democracy, she suffers personal alienation, fails to function as a role model, and abandons the politically significant role of woman authority. In short, she stops functioning as a feminist teacher. (p. 51)

Where Shrewsbury argues that the goal is to increase the power of all actors (power as property), Morgan's statement (above) suggests a zero-sum conception of power in which, if power is "given" to students in order to empower them, then the teacher must "give up" some of her own power.

As I have argued elsewhere (Gore, 1990c), the notion of empowerment carries with it an agent of empowerment (someone, or something, doing the empowering), a notion of power as property (to *em*-power implies to give or confer power), and a vision or desired end state (some vision of what it is to be empowered and the possibility of a state of empowerment). It is because someone, some agent, is to do the empowering, that the teacher's authority as the agent of that empowerment seems to be so troubling within the discourse of feminist pedagogy.

It is evident that many of the differentiations around authority and empowerment in feminist pedagogy discourse are made via a rather totalizing logic which views the world of power and classroom practice in "either/or" terms. One can either act as an authority or nurture. Classrooms are either hierarchical or non-hierarchical. Power is either repressive or productive. Hence there is considerable reference to the "contradictions" of feminist pedagogy created, generally, by the location of feminist pedagogy in "patriarchal educational institutions." As James Ladwig (1990) has argued, the language of "contradiction" limits its proponents to a bipolar logic. For example, Friedman (1985) asks whether authority in the feminist classroom is a contradiction in terms, posing authority and feminism as opposites.

Some writers within feminist pedagogy articulate problems with this logic (Grumet, 1988a; Pagano, 1990): for example, Pagano (1990) states "while an interest in developing nonpatriarchal curricular and pedagogical forms is desirable, it is undesirable that the project be conceived within the limits of this logic" (p. 37). But with their own strong critiques of "patriarchy," these writers still carry (as I shall explain shortly) elements of bipolar logic. Implications of such logic for feminist pedagogy's "regime of truth" will be elaborated shortly.

Objectives of Differentiations/Relations of Power

In whose interest, in the interest of what, are these differentiations —of authority/nurturance, authority-over/authority-with, authority/authorship, power as domination/power as creative energy/power as property—central to constructions of authority and empowerment in the discourse of feminist pedagogy? As Foucault puts it, the system of differentiations that characterizes a regime permits some to act on the actions of others. The differentiations discussed above emerge from and set up a series of potential power relations within feminist pedagogy: relations of teacher and student, women and men, feminist and non-feminist, feminist and patriarch. "Every relationship of power puts into operation differentiations which are at the same time its conditions and its results" (Foucault, 1983b, p. 223). In this section I will consider the types of objectives pursued by those who act upon the actions of others in the name of feminist pedagogy.

Major objectives of feminist pedagogy with connection to the differentiations outlined above are (1) to counter patriarchy which "denies women the authority of their experiences, perspectives, emotions and minds" (Friedman, 1985, p. 206), and (2) to "transform feminism into lived educational experience" (Morgan, n.d., p. 2); i.e., to transform schools and/or the academy toward feminist politics/practices. Although related, I will consider these two objectives separately.

The objective of "countering patriarchy" is one around which several differentiations function. Underlying feminist pedagogy discourse's constructions of authority and power is a rigidly drawn differentiation between patriarchy and feminism. It is in the interests of feminist pedagogy theorists to continue to name and blame the patriarchy for the oppression of women. To do so is to have a very clear account of what feminist pedagogy is not and what it might be. Moreover, appealing to the patriarchy of traditional pedagogy (whether conducted by men or women as "surrogate[s] for absent fathers, reproducing their order, asserting patriarchal authority over the mistresses of misrule" [Pagano, 1990, p. 33]) is to help feminists create and/or claim a distinctly new and different form of pedagogy. Thus, for example, the suggestion that one cannot be both an authority (especially one who is authoritarian) and nurturing seems to enable feminists to define their own pedagogical terrain. The terrain of feminist pedagogy is to be occupied primarily (some would argue, solely) by women, often in a restructured relationship of teacher with other women. For example, Madeleine Grumet (1988a) argues, "We have been different too long . . . separated from each other, women in education have withheld recognition from our mothers and from each other" (p. 192).

The naming of patriarchy can also be seen to prevent the intrusion or, more insidiously, the appropriation of feminist pedagogy by men. Thus, many of the differentiations of feminist pedagogy function to keep men and women separate. However, as I shall elaborate in Chapter 6, following Joan Cocks' (1989) argument about the Masculine/feminine regime,[5] it may be that women who are actively at odds with the dictations of traditional pedagogy are closer in their sensibilities to the men who resist, for example, class, race, and gender oppressions of schooling (Cocks might name such men "traitors or rebels" in relation to the regime of traditional pedagogy), than to the many women who are "loyalists" to the current "regime."[6] As Cocks (1989) argues, it is odd to remain faithful to the "woman"/"man" distinction of the Masculine/feminine regime, especially when one is engaging feminism to show that regime's less-than-total triumph over life.

Naming "patriarchy" the object feminist pedagogy must resist is itself consistent with such differentiations as authority/nurturance, authority-over/authority-with, power as domination/power as energy inasmuch as they all are based on a totalizing conception of power. Cocks (1989) says of "The Patriarchy," "no other term so strongly conveys a sense of male power—indeed, of all power—as something wielded from a single center, in an absolutely monolithic and intentional way, working in the same interests for the same goal in every period and place" (p. 209). It is this view of power that Foucault challenges, arguing instead that power is inherently fractured, operating in a capillary way, and that freedom can only be provisional. As evidence that Foucault's notion of power can be helpful in avoiding such totalizing views of patriarchy, Cocks argues that despite the contemporary decay of patriarchal (if not phallic) rule,[7] the Masculine/feminine regime still functions strongly: hence, "what seems to emerge from the decay of patriarchal rule is not freedom along the axis of sex and gender or even the preconditions for that freedom" (p. 214).

Associated with a totalizing view of patriarchal power in much feminist pedagogy discourse is an essentialized view of "woman-ness," one which leaves that discourse open to philosophical charges of essentialism. Peter Taubman (1986) makes precisely this charge against feminist pedagogy:

> The practice and discourse of feminist pedagogy as presented in *Gendered Subjects* . . . is informed by essentialist and separatist arguments and assumptions, and therein lies the danger of a feminist pedagogy. The old dualities are preserved. The origin of truth is found in anatomy. . . . Feminist pedagogy loses its usefulness to the extent that it sees itself as synonymous with good teaching, having an exclusive claim on good teaching and controlling the discourse on good teaching. It loses its force to the extent that it locates the origin and horizon of pedagogy in and on the bodies of women. (p. 93)

Essentialist views clearly underlie those notions of authority as authorship in which pedagogy "brings out" the "authentic voices" located in the experiences of women. From this view, "in contrast with the patriarchal self, women are held to be relational and empathetic in their connection with the world, rather than egotistical and impersonal. . . . They look to care for, not master, the other and so lean in all relations towards harmony, not conflict" (Cocks, 1989, p. 10), towards authority-with, not authority-over. However, if, for a moment, I appeal to the "authority" of my experience, considered valid by many feminist pedagogues, I was both nurtured and disciplined (sometimes in authoritarian ways) by my parents and some teachers. Moreover, the nurturing sometimes occurred through the exercise of power over me.

The charge of essentialism is one worth considering in more detail. As Diana Fuss (1989) puts it, "Essentialism can be located in appeals to a pure or original femininity, a female essence, outside the boundaries of the social and thereby untainted (though perhaps repressed) by a patriarchal order. . . . Further, essentialism underwrites claims for the autonomy of a female voice and the potentiality of a feminine language" (p. 2). It has recently become theoretically and politically more common, particularly among some poststructuralist feminists, who have previously rejected essentialist positions, to argue that "the risk of essence may have to be taken" (Fuss, 1989, p. 18).[8] Fuss (1989), for instance, argues that there is an important distinction to be made between "falling into" or "lapsing into" essentialism, which implies that essentialism is inherently reactionary—inevitably and inescapably a problem or a mistake—and "deploying" or "activating" essentialism, which implies some strategic or interventionary value. Some claim that feminists need to "risk" essentialism in order to enact their political objective of countering the patriarchy that has constructed woman as Other.

Fuss (1989) argues that "the radicality or conservatism of essentialism depends, to a significant degree, on *who* is utilizing it, *how* it is deployed, and *where* its effects are concentrated" (p. 20). Clearly this view is in keeping with the argument made in Chapter 3 that no discourse or practice is inherently liberating or oppressive. In the classroom, says Fuss, essentialism can have both silencing and empowering effects, politicizing and de-politicizing. While, in feminist pedagogy, "the category of natural female experience is often held against (and posited as corrective to) the category of imposed masculinist ideology" (Fuss, 1989, p. 114), arguments based on the authority of experience become problems in the classroom "when those 'in the know' commerce only with others 'in the know', excluding and marginalizing those perceived to be outside the magic circle" (Fuss, 1989, p. 115). Fuss elaborates that such problems of essentialism can take several forms such as a tendency to "one-down" each other on the oppression scale and a tendency to see only one part of a subject's identity (usually the most visible part) such as "maleness" or "Asianness" or "lesbianness"; in short, "the paradoxical and questionable assumption [is made] that some essences are more *essential* than others" (p. 116).

I turn now to the related objective of feminist pedagogy to transform feminism into lived educational experience, to bring practices of feminist politics into the classroom, to transform education in the academy.[9] A fundamental requirement of attempts to transform and empower is an agent of that transformation or empowerment, hence the differentiation/power relation of teacher-student. Feminist pedagogy's goal to "replace hierarchical authority with shared leadership" (Schniedewind, 1987, p. 17) and its distinction between authority-over and authority-with function, in part, to justify the "contradictory" experience of feminist practice in a "patriarchal" institution. Attention given to questions of authority in feminist pedagogy is evidence of the extent to which this aspect of feminist practice is perceived to be a problem.

The difficulties in trying to reconstruct authority for feminist purposes are clear in statements like the following from Culley (1985): "The feminist teacher can be a potent agent of change who, through combinations of course content and process, has the power to replace self-hatred with self-love, incapacity with capacity, unfreedom with freedom, blindness with knowledge" (p. 21). This immense and hierarchical power and agency invested in Culley's feminist teacher is overwhelmingly inconsistent with feminist pedagogy's aims to "share leadership" and "replace hierarchical authority," though perhaps consistent with a discourse rooted in bipolar logic. Furthermore, the reliance on the "*feminist teacher*" as the agent of transformation sets up power relations between feminists and other women, and among different groups of feminists. The feminist teacher or feminist academic who writes about teaching is positioned, within feminist pedagogy discourse, to be able to define "correct" feminist pedagogy or feminist practice, in particular contexts for *all* women. In so doing, the feminist teacher is able to exercise power over others, at times replicating the authority-over denounced as patriarchal.

Techniques and Practices

There are two sets of specific techniques and practices that actualize the relations of power of feminist pedagogy: one set involves the practices advocated or reported in feminist classrooms, the ways feminist teachers attempt to share leadership and so on—the pedagogy that is argued for; a second set of practices can be identified in the literature of feminist pedagogy—the pedagogy of the argument.

In terms of the pedagogy argued for, the discourse of feminist pedagogy attends to aspects of content and aspects of classroom processes, with the emphasis on processes (especially among the Women's Studies writers). In terms of content, three main approaches (often used in conjunction) are evident: (1) presenting "new" texts, previously marginalized or overlooked within disciplinary knowledge; (2) engaging in "new readings" of old texts, (for example, Carol Gilligan's "readings" of Kohlberg's studies of moral development or feminist readings of Shakespeare); (3) drawing on the personal experiences of teacher and students as the basis of knowledge production.

In terms of process, the emphasis is on pedagogy which is "collaborative, cooperative and interactive" (Maher, 1985b, p. 30), on "teaching practices which stress cooperative rather than competitive participation" (Maher, 1985b, p. 33). Thus, non-didactic approaches are emphasized, with lots of discussion, role play, journal writing and storytelling, and alternative grading and evaluation approaches are explored. These practices are often aimed at forming connections—among class participants, between people with different experiences and different "subjectivities," between the private realm of mothering and the public, between the private and public worlds of each woman (Grumet, 1988b).

These classroom practices are consistent with the primary differentiations in feminist pedagogy discourse around authority and empowerment. For example, the emphasis on cooperation, connection, and personal experience is consistent with the attempt to exercise authority-with rather than authority-over—to nurture. The emphasis on feminist materials and readings is consistent with the notion of power as creative energy rather than as domination. That is, the feminist teacher needs to bring such readings to the attention of her students in order to empower them. The emphasis on participation and stories is consistent with the notion of authority as authorship.

Marilyn Boxer (1988) deems "collectivity in teaching and program governance" to be "the most radical and vital contribution of the women's movement to educational innovation" (p. 76). Like other writers of feminist pedagogy, claims are frequently made about the novelty of specific classroom processes. Consider the following examples:

—I teach in a *totally non-traditional way*. I use every trick in the book: lots of positive reinforcement, both oral and written; lots of one-on-one conferences. I network women with each other, refer them to professor friends who can help them; connect them to graduate students and/or former students who are already pursuing careers. In the classroom I force my students to come up in front of their classmates, explain concepts or read their essays aloud. I create panels presenting opposing viewpoints and hold debates—lots of oral participation, role-playing, reading their own texts. Their own writing and opinions become part of the course. On exams I ask them questions about their classmates' presentations. I meet with individual students in local coffeehouses or taverns: it's much easier to talk about personal pain over coffee or a beer or a glass of wine than in my office. (Castellano, 1990, p. 20) [emphasis added]

—strategies [feminist] teachers can adopt to reduce their classroom power and to allow students increased learning through cooperation: Relying on seating arrangements that encourage conversation, using eye contact and a tone of voice that invite participation, referring to students by name so as to authorize their comments, sharing class time among teacher, outspoken students, and quiet students, and encouraging informality and humor. (Smithson, 1990, citing Thorne, p. 15).

—[there were] widespread attempts to restructure the classroom experience of students and faculty. Circular arrangement of chairs, periodic small-group sessions, use of first names for instructors as well as students, assignments that required journal keeping, "reflection papers", cooperative projects, and collective modes of teaching with student participation all sought to transfer to women's studies the contemporary feminist criticism of authority and the validation of every woman's experience. (Boxer, 1988, pp. 75–76)

The extent to which these "pedagogies" are "non-traditional," let alone specifically "feminist," is questionable. That is, the pedagogy argued for in these passages is clearly *traditional* in progressive education.

Turning to a focus on the pedagogy of the argument, the potential for relations of power operating within feminist pedagogy to have dominating effects becomes clearer; for example, when feminist perspectives or "readings" become the only valid course content, we can see how the power relations of men and women, teacher and student, feminist and non-feminist become actualized. Nina Baym (1990) acknowledges this potential in one instance: "At the moment that the feminist teacher's readings become the content of the course, the woman student is in precisely the same relationship to that teacher as she stands to any other teacher. As feminism becomes another variety of interpretation, the feminist is overriden [*sic*] by the teacher" (p. 64). That is, the ever-present power relation is one of teacher able to exercise power over students. Friedman (1985) makes a similar point in her caution to her feminist peers that they resist "the temptation to impose a feminist orthodoxy that students do not feel free to critique" (p. 208). (I would broaden this not only to students, but to other educators and theorists).

As already indicated, one way in which the feminist attempt for authority-with is unsuccessful, becoming instead authority-over, lies in the language of the discourse. For instance, such essentialist notions as "authentic womanhood" (e.g., Friedman, 1985, p. 205), "the true knowledge of women" (e.g., Rich, 1979, p. 245), or "authentic voice" can silence some students even while others might feel empowered. The reliance within feminist pedagogy discourse on totalizing notions of power and "The Patriarchy" is paradoxically the source of inconsistencies within feminist pedagogy discourse. For instance, naming (almost) all non-feminist pedagogy patriarchal, contributes to the tendency to ignore the achievements of women in education (as teachers, scholars, administrators), despite feminist claims about validating women, listening to all voices, and so on.

I would also argue that more care in the pedagogy of the argument is needed; otherwise feminist pedagogy discourse such as this risks being dismissed as insufficiently developed within the broader educational field. The general suggestion I want to make is that the specific practices argued for in order to actualize feminist pedagogy might not be the practices that could make pedagogy *feminist*. There is a fundamental flaw in the pedagogy of the argument which, I will argue, is attributable to insufficient theoretical inquiry into questions of pedagogy itself. To introduce this argument, I cite Baym (1990) who remarks: "I take it that whenever there is teaching, there is a power relationship; the question is what is produced by and through that relation" (p. 66). In feminist pedagogy, there is a kind of attempt to override the "teacher" with the feminist; to override the traditional hierarchical authority of the teacher over students with a nurturant feminist practice. It might be better strategy for those concerned with constructing "feminist pedagogy" to engage less dismissively with the position of "the teacher," and to consider more carefully what it might mean to be a "feminist teacher." I propose that a feminist teacher is more than a feminist who teaches.

The lack of attention to the pedagogical context itself, by which I mean, the historical construction of "pedagogy" within the "machinery of cultural regulation" (Hunter, 1988), also manifests itself in what I have previously referred to as decontextualized accounts of feminist pedagogy. That is, while feminist pedagogy lends description to particular classes and events, it offers little analysis of the institutional conditions of feminist pedagogy. It is to these conditions that I now turn in this systematic exploration of "the regime of truth" of feminist pedagogy.

Institutions

Foucault (1983b) argues that while it is "perfectly legitimate" to analyze power relations by focusing on carefully defined institutions, "the fundamental point of anchorage of [power] relationships, even if they are embodied and crystallized in an institution, is to be found outside the institution" (p. 222). Therefore, he suggests, "one must analyze institutions from the standpoint of power relations, rather than vice versa" (p. 222). Feher (1987) makes the same point very directly: "institutions do not cause or create relations of power; they integrate them" (p. 161). In this section, I consider the two institutions which seem most important in the integration of the power relations of feminist pedagogy: the academy, and the school.

In some places, the university is integrating (perhaps, *slowly* integrating) feminist pedagogy, primarily through the mechanism of Women's Studies. Certainly, within the academy, efforts to practice feminist pedagogy can be expected to have better institutional support in Women's Studies than, for example, in Education, English, or other disciplines. The drawback is that while Women's Studies may be uniquely positioned to develop and practice feminist pedagogy, to do so in the separate sphere of Women's Studies (often deemed to be the territory of feminists alone) is to limit the potential for a broader transformation of university pedagogy—not to mention of pedagogy in general. To some extent, feminists have chosen this path, creating a separate and unique space, where a "new" form of pedagogy can take shape removed, as much as possible, from "the patriarchal institution." This "choice" also reflects "separatist" feminist politics outside of the academy whereby, in particular spaces, women create their own spheres and practices. On the other hand, some feminists would argue that they had no other choice, that they were forced by "The Patriarchy" to create separate spaces within and outside the academy. Unquestionably women have struggled, and still are struggling, in an academy historically governed largely by men and in an academy that often deliberately excludes women. A dilemma faced in constructing Women's Studies as something of a haven for women, is meeting the concomitant desire for legitimacy in and recognition from the academy.

Whether chosen or forced, one reason for the feminist construction and embrace of Women's Studies is, as discussed earlier, feminist pedagogy discourse's totalizing view that (non-feminist) schooling (at all levels) is patriarchal. From this view, the educational institution itself constrains feminist attempts to replace patriarchal pedagogy:

> We can clean out the male curriculum, banking education, the process/ product paradigm, the myth of objectivity. We can give the old furniture away to Goodwill or domesticate it, turning old school desks into planters and telephone tables. We can silence the clanging lockers,

period bells, "now-hear-this" loudspeakers. We can make [the school/
classroom] a demilitarized zone. But still we are not in an empty space.
(Grumet, 1988a, p. 186)

The space, according to Grumet, is a patriarchal one.

Such a view is common in the discourse of feminist pedagogy. As
additional examples, consider the following:

—Women are silenced, objectified and made passive through both the
course content and the pedagogical style of most college classrooms.
(Maher, 1985b, p. 31)

—The silencing, humiliating and devaluing of girls and women is the
outcome of patriarchal pedagogy regardless of how progressive or
authoritarian that pedagogy might be. It is built into the educational
establishment itself, operating as institutional sexism even when it is
not built into the deliberate assumptions and intentions of teachers in
patriarchy. (Morgan, n.d., p. 23)

If indeed patriarchal pedagogy is built into our schools and universities,
a question emerges as to whether feminist pedagogy, as articulated, *can*
exist within those institutions. Is it possible to relocate/revise/reclaim
authority when this would require us all, teachers and students alike, to
unlearn years of "patriarchal pedagogy"?

I neither want to deny the very real conditions of women's oppression
and of men's administration over schooling at all levels, but nor do I
want to reduce the exigencies of schooling to a simple or single dynamic.
As I shall elaborate in Chapter 6, the authority exercised by teachers
(men or women, feminist or not) over students might not be located
solely in some external power relation such as "patriarchy" or "feminism," but also in the "pedagogical device" (Bernstein, 1990) itself. Despite any differences related to "feminist process" or "feminist pedagogy," or to a student population consisting primarily of women,
teaching feminism in a Women's Studies classroom remains an act of
pedagogy in an educational institution. Arguments about the patriarchal
educational establishment enable feminists to continue to blame "The
Patriarchy" for all that is evil in education. Thus, if/when feminist pedagogues replicate aspects of authority-over, for instance, it can be attributed not to problems within feminist pedagogy but to the pervasive-
ness of "The Patriarchy". It is precisely such totalizing and polarizing
logic that can compel a discourse toward a lack of reflexivity.

While the academy is seen to constrain feminist pedagogy, it also plays
a role in structuring and supporting the discourse and practice of feminist pedagogy. Magda Lewis (1989) acknowledges this: "Educational

institutions are contradictorily both the site where reactionary and repressive ideologies are entrenched *and* the site where progressive, transformative possibilities are born" (p. 126), such as the "transformative possibility" of Women's Studies. Moreover, as mentioned in Chapter 2, the academic game has to be played to some extent, and there is always the risk of compromising oneself/one's project in order to survive in the institution. That feminists are surviving clearly indicates duplicity (Bourdieu, 1984; Foucault, 1977b) in the integration of feminist pedagogy in the university.

Although feminist pedagogy is often posed as a deliberate attempt to counter patriarchal pedagogy in all levels of schooling, the discourse of feminist pedagogy appears to be overwhelmingly concerned with transforming the academy rather than with transforming schools. There *is* academic feminist literature that gives considerable theoretical and empirical attention to issues of gender in schools. But the feminist *pedagogy* literature includes very few pieces on schools. Exceptions include Roy and Schen's (1987) discussion of high school teaching, some of Maher's work (especially Maher, 1987), Grumet's (1988a) analysis of women and teaching, and Pagano's (1990) and Miller's (1990) recent books that tangentially address schools via the authors' involvement in teacher education. Each of these authors is institutionally located within Education (high schools for Roy and Schen; Education Departments for the others). It seems writers from Women's Studies rarely advocate feminist pedagogy for schools, focusing instead on universities and particularly Women's Studies classrooms.

Why are schools so rarely posited as a site for the practice of feminist pedagogy? And does this exclusion have anything to do with the power relations of the "regime"? Perhaps teachers within state institutions such as elementary and secondary schools are perceived to have less autonomy. Perhaps schools, with a history of positing teaching as women's work that is regulated by male administrators, are seen to be more patriarchal than universities, thus leaving less space for feminists to intervene. It might be that schooling (at the elementary and secondary levels) is viewed as a cruder, coarser form of practical activity, not worthy of the intellectual attention of serious feminist scholars trying to assert themselves in the academy (and/or the world). Perhaps the feminist premise that the personal is political is interpreted to direct feminists to write and talk about their own experiences and practices in a connected way, which often amounts to their experiences as university teachers—in many cases, long since removed from schools. Perhaps the content of feminist pedagogy (sometimes referred to as "the new scholarship on women") which, one could argue, is what really distinguishes feminist from other forms of pedagogy, is considered more appropriate for women than for girls. Certainly, feminist pedagogy which is based on exposing and transcending women's experiences of oppression, and is deeply concerned with women's experiences of sexuality, mothering, the body, denial of opportunities, and so on, is likely to find more sympathizers and less resistance among older females. Young girls simply have fewer experiences to draw upon. Whatever the reasons, it seems odd (to this teacher educator) that a discourse which claims for itself the label "feminist pedagogy" is largely absent from schools. I am not suggesting that schools have a monopoly on pedagogy; but, there is a great deal of pedagogy which takes place in schools, much of which has profound effects on gender relations. I would expect that more feminists who advocate feminist pedagogy would want to intervene more directly in that sphere.

The Formation of Knowledge or "Rationalization"

"The exercise of power is not a naked fact, an institutional right, nor is it a structure which holds out or is smashed: it is elaborated, transformed, organized; it endows itself with processes which are more or less adjusted to the situation" (Foucault, 1983b, p. 224). In this section I examine how the regime of feminist pedagogy is elaborated, transformed, and organized; how the formation of its knowledge is more or less adjusted to its situation.

It seems that the central problem to be rationalized by feminist pedagogy, particularly around issues of authority and empowerment, is how to reconcile feminism (politics and theory) with the situation of the "patriarchal" institution. The result of this rationalization is that "feminist pedagogy" comes to mean something other than, or more than, a feminist form of pedagogy, or even feminism plus pedagogy.

In the discourse of feminist pedagogy, it seems, from the preceding analysis, that some of its central concepts create its major inconsistencies and problems. For example, the concept of authority-with is central to the knowledge-claims of feminist pedagogy. But to claim a non-hierarchical classroom and the possibility of "authority-with" is to deny the institutional location in which most feminist pedagogy (of the type discussed in the literature) takes place. Bringing feminism into the academy, primarily through the auspices of Women's Studies, positions the discourse of feminist pedagogy within the historically constituted relations of power and specific practices of institutionalized pedagogy. While feminist pedagogy discourse seeks to alter some of those relations and practices, and embraces a whole different set of power relations and practices—those which have come to constitute feminism(s)—paying more attention to the specific practices which constrain feminist pedagogy and which characterize the feminist *teacher* would help address the problems created by the institutional integration of feminist politics and practices through feminist pedagogy discourse. Those writers who have begun to acknowledge the complexity of relations of power and the "mythical" nature of some feminist pedagogy objectives, who recognize that knowledge is partial and contradictory, seem in a better position from which to create an alternative pedagogical form. To paraphrase Lewis (1988), it is not enough to dream of an alternative classroom; the vision needs to acknowledge what already exists and the specific constraints which confront it.

Feminist pedagogy is often equated with a feminist teacher, one who not only holds feminist ideas or perspectives but who "teaches" them to her students. Hence, content is of concern, despite the fact that feminist pedagogy writing tends to concentrate more on processes of instruction. Perhaps the inordinate attention to processes results from the disconcerting experience of feminist teachers who find themselves and their students caught up in the same kinds of power relations that are found in non-feminist classrooms. The way this experience is rationalized is often in an appeal to the overwhelming power of the evil patriarchy, an invocation that implies that women are innocent. But as Joan Cocks (1989) writes, the

> romanticization of women as essentially innocent or good may be more benign than the dominant culture's degradation of women . . . Still, it is absolutely infantilizing and embalming. It implies that women are not complex enough in desire, sophisticated enough in imagination, and dynamic enough in will to act in vicious as well as virtuous ways, out of passions, predilections and motive forces that are not men's but their own. It denies, in short, that women have the fundamental capacity for every possible emotion and desire and so for being able to think, will and try to do despicable things . . . Women's thoughts and actions are suspect, too, precisely because they are thoughts and actions. (pp. 181–82)

Proceeding from a beginning, perhaps safer, point from which to attempt to practice feminist pedagogy, Women's Studies classrooms seem to have become, for some feminist pedagogues, an ending point as well. This raises political questions about the "for whom" of feminist pedagogy. Despite claims about transforming the academy and schooling in general, if feminist pedagogy is largely restricted to Women's Studies, to what extent does it function as transformative—if it "empowers" only those women (and few men) who have enough openness to, or sympathy with, feminist concerns to elect to take Women's Studies classes? To the extent that feminist pedagogy imposes its own truth and requires conformity to that truth, it limits, perhaps deliberately, its constituency. Thus, while in Women's Studies, as in other pedagogical sites, there exists a struggle to alter the power relations of teacher-student, the particularity of feminist struggle seems to concentrate on altering the historically constituted power relations of men and women in a patriarchal culture, and thus assumes primacy in the discourse of feminist pedagogy. Subsequently, the gap between critical and feminist pedagogy discourses solidifies, marked by gender-specific terrain and techniques.

ETHICAL ASPECTS OF THE REGIME

Having discussed at length certain political aspects of the feminist pedagogy regime of truth, its relations of power, what goes on between people, I turn now to the ethical aspects of the regime; that is, what feminist pedagogy discourse says about the relationship one ought to have with oneself. In feminist pedagogy, the ethical can be seen to have two dimensions: the relationship students of feminist pedagogy ought to have with themselves and the relationship the teacher/theorist ought to have with herself.[10] To remain consistent with my discussion of the political, I refer to Foucault's (1983c) outline of the four aspects of a genealogy of ethics to organize my analysis. Using such sub-headings begins to illustrate how little is articulated in the discourse of feminist pedagogy about the relationships one ought to have with oneself. Hence, in addition to elaborating what is articulated and also what is implied, I explore, in a preliminary fashion, possible reasons for this limited attention to the ethical.

The Ethical Substance

The major aspect of self considered problematic by the regime of feminist pedagogy (what Foucault calls the "ethical substance") is that part of the self which has been colonized by patriarchy—mind, body, feelings, desires. Women are urged to be true to themselves, to break away from the prison of patriarchy, to free and empower themselves. They are to avoid acting, thinking, reading, writing "like a man"; hence the emphasis on reclaiming their authentic voices. While statements about the need for women to find their true selves are relatively common,

there is little articulated about precisely what is to be done, how women
are to act on themselves as woman and/or feminist teacher. The following
statement by Adrienne Rich (1979), in its plea for women to "take ourselves seriously," provides one example:

> Recognizing that central responsibility of a women to herself without
> which we remain always the Other, the defined, the object, the victim;
> believing that there is a unique quality of validation, affirmation, chal-
> lenge, support, that one woman can offer another. Believing in the
> value and significance of women's experience, traditions, perceptions.
> Thinking of ourselves seriously, not as one of the boys, not as neuters,
> or androgynes, but *as women*. (p. 240)

Perhaps because of the attempt to share leadership and exercise authority-with rather than authority-over, there is little in the rhetoric of
feminist pedagogy which addresses in any detail gestures, postures, or
attitudes in need of styling. Women are simply exhorted to be women;
to recognize, believe in, and think of themselves as women.

A reason for this rather general focus given to the ethical substance
might be that any demand for women to discipline/style themselves in
specific ways contradicts claims that feminist pedagogy provides a space/
place in which women can finally be themselves in classrooms; "the feminist classroom is the place to use what we know as women to appropriate
and transform, totally, a domain which has been men's" (Culley, et al.,
1985, p. 19). Hence, without empirical evidence of classroom interaction,
there is little documentation of the governing required in feminist classrooms. The rhetoric is of freedom, not of control. The discursive location
of much feminist pedagogy in liberal—and, especially, radical—feminist
thought, both of which attempt "to define women's nature once and for
all" (Weedon, 1987, p. 135), further explains this finding. The assumption is that women *are* cooperative, nurturing, sensitive to each other,
and so on.

Thus, until recently,[11] writers have ignored the difficulties of feminist
classrooms. Examples of such difficulties are reported by Gardner et al.
(1989) who share the following comments from students:

> —We are all on different levels with regard to feminism. Some of us
> have been into the movement for years, some since this class began.
> Sometimes I have a very difficult time understanding, let alone relating
> to, what is being said. I feel some women in the class are very con-
> demning of other women who aren't quite as "into" it as they are. It
> is turning me off from the movement (and the class) more than en-
> couraging me.

—I never feel like I belong. Even though we all talk about difference and diversity, I don't feel as if we act on it. Especially "the feminists" in the class. I'd often see them in the Union and they wouldn't even acknowledge me—they'd kind of look right past me. Well, so much for sisterhood.

Another of the difficulties of feminist classrooms lies in assumptions of "women" as a unified category. bell hooks (1990) shares her experiences of teaching courses from a feminist standpoint and the difficulties for "the black student with no previous background in feminist studies [who] usually finds that she or he is in a class that is predominantly white" (p. 29).

> When black students acknowledge that they are not familiar with the work of Audre Lorde and the rest of the class gasps as though this is unthinkable and reprehensible ignorance, they invariably get the feeling that feminism is a private white cult. Estranged and alienated, they may retreat into further scepticism about the relevance of feminism. Their fellow-students usually regard this scepticism with contempt. . . . And so suddenly the feminist classroom is no longer the safe haven many Women's Studies students imagined it would be. Instead, it presents conflict, tension, sometimes ongoing hostility. (p. 29)

Perhaps there is less of an inclination to articulate these kinds of difficulties and to address specific aspects that need self-styling because of the ongoing struggle for legitimacy which confronts women who write about, and practice, feminist pedagogy in the university.

I should emphasize that this limited articulation of the ethical substance does not mean that feminist discourses, including strands of feminist pedagogy discourse, do not attend to ethics in their own senses of "ethics."[12] For example, feminist discourses deconstruct dominant notions of ethics linked to individualism, and also construct a notion of responsibility to a group; the discourses contrast an ethic of rights and justice to one of care and concern for others, thereby conflating ethics and morality. Foucault's notion of ethics which deals with one's relationship to oneself is not directly addressed in the feminist pedagogy discourse. However, even if different notions of ethics are found in feminist pedagogy discourse, we can still attend to the technologies of self that may be exercised in the functioning of the regime of feminist pedagogy. I shall return to specific techniques of the self shortly.

The Mode of Subjection

Any disciplining which is necessary in the feminist classroom is performed in the name of authenticity: being true to oneself as women, as feminists, and in the name of solidarity to one's "sisters" and other oppressed people. This is what Foucault (1983c) calls "the mode of subjection"—"the way in which people are invited or incited to recognize their moral obligations [such as] divine law, . . . a cosmological order, . . . rational rule, [or] . . . the attempt to give your existence the most beautiful form possible" (p. 239). Given that there is so little written about the ethical substance of the feminist pedagogy regime, there is also little said about the mode of subjection (or the following aspects of the ethical component). Nevertheless, "*we* (women, feminists) don't behave like that" is the sort of message one might expect a non-conforming woman or man to receive in the feminist classroom.

Techniques of Self-Styling

Although specific techniques of self-styling—the means by which we can change ourselves in order to become ethical subjects—are not articulated, given feminist pedagogy's aims of authority-with and shared leadership, I would speculate that the feminist classroom demands that students rely less on the teacher and much more on themselves and each other, that they listen to each other, validate each other. Meanwhile, feminist teachers will need to be careful to construct practices consistent with their rhetoric, or else to confront themselves as hypocrites: "Is it not hypocritical, or at least ineffective, to teach about feminism but not utilize feminist process in teaching?" (Schniedewind, 1985, p. 84). Drawing from my own experience in such classrooms, there seems to pervade a tendency toward extreme politeness, attempts made to listen to and accept multiple viewpoints even when one is in strong disagreement. Again, empirical studies of classrooms would help to identify whether this is a common experience, and the specific techniques through which one forms one's relationship with oneself as a feminist teacher or student.

The kinds of techniques which might be identified will be as specific and taken-for-granted as the techniques Sandra Lee Bartky (1988) discusses in her analysis of embodied femininity:

> The woman who checks her makeup half a dozen times a day to see if her foundation has caked or her mascara has run, who worries that the wind or rain may spoil her hairdo, who looks frequently to see if her stockings have bagged at the ankle or who, feeling fat, monitors everything she eats, has become, just as surely as the inmate of the Panopticon, a self-policing subject, a self committed to a relentless self-surveillance. (p. 81)

Bartky's vivid elaboration of modern disciplinary power's "invasion" of the female body is an example of techniques of the self set forth by regimes within disciplinary society. Disciplinary power is dispersed and anonymous, invested in everyone and in no-one in particular (Bartky, 1988). However, resistance to this particular form of self-surveillance which, Bartky says, amounts to obeying The Patriarchy, does not free women from all forms of self-surveillance and self-disciplining. Even in the struggles of some feminist communities to reject hegemonic images of femininity and construct a new female aesthetic (Bartky, 1988), techniques of the self will be enacted. In attempting to better understand, and perhaps alter, the regime of feminist pedagogy, it would be helpful to continue to identify specific techniques of the self.

The Telos

Foucault's concern with ethics in the final phase of his work was premised on his view that individuals act on their own bodies, souls, thoughts, conduct, way of being, in order to transform themselves and attain a certain state of being (Martin, Gutman and Hutton, 1988). Which is the kind of being to which feminist pedagogues or students aspire, the *telos*, when they/we behave in a moral way? In the discourse of feminist pedagogy, participants are to act on their bodies, thoughts, ways of being, in order to reclaim themselves from patriarchal classrooms/structures and to work toward a more just world for women (and other oppressed groups). The being to which feminist pedagogy aspires is the woman free from patriarchy's dominating effects.

CONCLUDING COMMENTS

I want to emphasize that my aim has been to examine constructions of authority and empowerment in feminist pedagogy discourse. To that task I have selected, from materials published during the last decade or so, examples of some of the dangers of feminist pedagogy as a regime of truth. However, this analysis has not historically positioned the various cited works within feminist thought. For instance, while *Gendered Subjects* (Culley and Portuges, 1985), the text from which I have drawn many examples, is perhaps representative of feminist thought in the early 1980s and central to the feminist shaping of questions of pedagogy, it was only minimally influenced by poststructuralist and women of color (Third Wave) feminisms that are now more widely embraced. Such influences have resulted in contemporary challenges posed to essentializing and

totalizing arguments, even within radical feminist thought. Thus, some
of the arguments I make, as they pertain to feminist scholarship in general, have been addressed and revised to include Third Wave feminism's
impacts on feminist academic work.

However, feminist *pedagogy* discourse remains strongly influenced by
these earlier works (e.g., Weiler, 1991). To the extent that such works
are primarily celebrated as the basis for current constructions of feminist
pedagogy discourse, my critique highlights specific practices and conditions in the functioning of feminist pedagogy discourse as a regime of
truth. In particular, this chapter has highlighted (1) problematic conceptions of authority and empowerment; (2) the emphasis of much feminist pedagogy discourse on feminism, with a tendency to overlook specific conditions and practices of pedagogy; (3) the focus on university
classrooms as the primary site for the practice of feminist pedagogy, with
a relative neglect of schooling at elementary and secondary levels; (4)
the lack of attention to the ethical (in Foucault's sense of that term).
Before discussing some of these major "findings," I turn to an examination of constructions of authority and empowerment in critical pedagogy.

Authority and Empowerment in Critical Pedagogy

Using the same methodological framework as in the previous chapter, I turn now to an examination of constructions of authority and empowerment in the discourse of critical pedagogy. "Authority" and "empowerment" also exist as related concepts within the discourse of critical pedagogy whereby a particular kind of authority is deemed necessary for the empowerment or liberation of students. It will soon become apparent that I make more direct distinctions between the different strands of critical pedagogy in this analysis than I made between the different strands of feminist pedagogy in the previous chapter. I do so because the different strands of critical pedagogy approach aspects of authority and empowerment in significantly different ways. Moreover, the nature of the texts in critical pedagogy (outlined in Chapter 2) shifts the focus of the analysis from that in the previous chapter in at least two ways. First, as is consistent with my designation of these strands through their affiliation with key proponents, versus the more diffuse and communal constructions of feminist pedagogy, the focus will shift more directly to individuals' articulations of authority and empowerment. Second, the focus will shift to a level of greater theoretical and political abstraction. Similar to my discussion of feminist pedagogy discourse's constructions of authority and empowerment, I will deliberately select examples from the studied texts to highlight the potential dominating effects of critical pedagogy discourse.

POLITICAL ASPECTS OF THE REGIME

The Differentiations

In the discourse of critical pedagogy two basic "types" of authority are recognized: a "good" or "empowering" type of authority and a "bad" or repressive type. For Giroux and McLaren this differentiation translates into "emancipatory authority" versus "authoritarianism" while Freire and Shor differentiate between "liberating" (Freire) or "liberatory" (Shor) versus "domesticating" authority. Because of the similarities in the ways these terms are employed, I will use "liberating" and "emancipatory" authority as synonymous terms. The critical pedagogue/teacher is to make use of this authority in order to empower students and transform society.

Giroux (1988a) presents authority as a site of struggle for meaning. He pushes beyond the frequent association of authority "with an unprincipled authoritarianism," and freedom with "an escape from authority in general" (p. 75), such that authority "becomes a mediating referent for the ideal of democracy and its expression as a set of educational practices designed to empower students to be active and critical citizens" (p. 88). In short, Giroux claims that "the dominant meaning of authority must be redefined to include the concepts of freedom, equality, and democracy" (p. 89). Similarly, Freire argues that "without authority it is difficult for the liberties of the students to be shaped. Freedom needs authority to become free. It is a paradox but it is true" (Shor and Freire, 1987, p. 91). Indeed, the idea that authority is necessary for freedom runs contrary to common sense beliefs. In order to better understand this connection of authority with democracy and freedom, I want to further differentiate notions of authority, empowerment, and their connection in critical pedagogy.

First, if I begin with the conceptions of power that undergird constructions of authority and empowerment in critical pedagogy discourse, it is clear that, like much feminist pedagogy discourse, critical pedagogy discourse often conceives of power as property. Specifically, power is located in the hands of "the dominant classes" (which has come to include not just economic classes but also classes constructed by race and gender formations).[1] While Giroux (1988a) and McLaren (1989) have recently begun to refer to power as embodied in concrete practices (drawing on Foucauldian analyses of power), they still refer to dominant classes and cultures and discourses in ways which risk viewing power as property. For instance, "Giroux assumes that schools must be seen . . . as complexes of dominant and subordinate cultures, each ideologically linked to *the power they possess* to define and legitimate a particular construction of reality" (McLaren, 1989, p. 200) [emphasis added]. Furthermore, power as property can be seen as part of the notion of "empowerment" itself, inasmuch as to em-power suggests to give power, to confer power, to enable the use of power. Power is transferred much as property is.

Corresponding with this view of power, dualisms such as disempowerment (or powerlessness) and empowerment, silence and voice are frequently invoked within critical pedagogy discourse. The world is divided into dominant and subordinate (classes, cultures, discourses). For example, Giroux (1988a) states: "how teachers and students read the world is inextricably linked to forms of pedagogy that can function *either* to silence and marginalize students *or* to legitimate their voices in an effort to empower them as critical and active citizens" (p. 165) [emphasis added]. McLaren (1989) draws on Foucault to claim that "we can consider dominant [educational] discourses (those produced by the dominant culture) as 'regimes of truth,' as general economies of power/knowledge, or as multiple forms of constraint. . . . A critical discourse . . . is self-critical and deconstructs dominant discourses the moment they are ready to achieve hegemony" (p. 181). Analytically, these claims leave few shades of grey.

In addition to power being perceived as the property of the dominant "classes," the authors put forth a collective conception of social change. In this conception, critical pedagogy analyses of empowerment usually distinguish self from social empowerment where the former is seen as necessary, but not sufficient, for social transformation. Freire's position on this point is slightly different from the other theorists in that his concern has been explicitly that of social class empowerment; "*Not* individual, *not* community, *not* merely social empowerment, but a concept of 'social class empowerment' " (Shor and Freire, 1987, p. 111). As he argues "it is *one* thing to make a class analysis in Latin America, and it is something altogether different to make the same kind of analysis in the [United] States. . . . I recognize that this preoccupation I have with 'class' has to be recreated for the States" (p. 112). He makes the general point, however, that "even when you feel yourself *most* free, if this feeling is not a *social* feeling, if you are not able to use your *recent* freedom to help others to be free by transforming the totality of society, then you are exercising only an individualist attitude towards empowerment or freedom" (p. 109). "This *feeling* of being free . . . is still *not* enough for the transformation of society [even though] it is *absolutely necessary* for the process of social transformation. . . [Students'] curiosity, their critical perception of reality, is fundamental for social transformation but it is not enough by itself" (p. 110).

Giroux (1988a,1988b) and McLaren (1989) also speak frequently of "self and social empowerment," distinguishing between and connecting the empowerment of individuals and social positions. The following statement by McLaren (1989) provides an example: "Teachers must engage unyieldingly in their attempt to empower students both as individuals and as potential agents of social change by establishing a critical pedagogy that students can use in the classroom and in the streets" (p. 221). Similarly, Giroux (1988a) claims, "Students need to be introduced to a language of empowerment and radical ethics that permits them to think about how community life should be constructed around a project of possibility" (p. 166).

In the discourse of critical pedagogy, notions of opposition and empowerment are embedded in a self-proclaimed shift from "a language of critique" to "a language of possibility" (e.g., Aronowitz and Giroux, 1985; Simon, 1987). A second conception of power is found in this differentiation of critique and possibility—one which enables power to be used for productive purposes. That is, the proclamation of a language of possibility in critical pedagogy is connected to shifting conceptions of power—from power as repressive to power as productive (implied in the concept of emancipatory authority)—and shifting from emphases on ideology and structure to an emphasis on agency. Resistance theories of the "new sociology of education" can be located at the transition between the discursive foci on critique and possibility. Paul Willis' (1977) study, for example, pointed to a productive aspect of power but concluded with an elucidation of the oppressive structures which kept "the lads" in their class position. The development of a "language of possibility" seems to function in part to separate critical pedagogy from other critical educational scholarship. Hence, in critical pedagogy discourse "empowerment" has been constructed in ways that take the productive moment of power further, and so go "beyond resistance." This movement to a language of possibility is part of a general shift in critical educational discourse toward acknowledging that education has played a role in social movement and not just in social reproduction (Wexler, 1987). The language of possibility functions to highlight schooling practices as playing a part in social transformation. There has been movement from encouraging teachers to recognize the structural constraints under which they work, to having them also acknowledge "the potential inherent in teaching for transformative and political work" (Weiler, 1988, p. 52).

The strong sense of agency found in this language of empowerment can be connected to the language of possibility in which it is embedded.

The particular agents and actors who constitute the process of educational empowerment through critical pedagogy—the theorist, the teacher, and the student—are also clearly differentiated within this discourse. In the analysis of critical pedagogy's "agents," I return to questions of authority, because the teacher is constructed as a primary agent in the process of empowering students, and must use his or her authority to that end.

The ways in which the teacher (as agent of empowerment) uses authority differs among the various proponents of critical pedagogy. Shor (1980) speaks of the "withering away of the teacher" (p. 100), the handing over of authority. He says, "As I understand it, in a liberating classroom, the teacher seeks to withdraw as the director of learning, as the directive force . . . You can let go of authority too soon, just as you can let go too late. Making that calculation is precarious . . . when and how to pass on authority to the students" (Shor and Freire, 1987, p. 90). In this passage, both property (which can be "passed on") and zero-sum (handing authority over to students which requires the "withering away" of the teacher's authority) conceptions of power are evident.

Freire's stance on this issue is based on the claim that the teacher is always an authority,[2] that the teacher cannot get outside authority:

> For me the question is not for the teacher to have less and less authority. The issue is that the democratic teacher never, never transforms authority into authoritarianism. He or she can never stop being an authority or having authority. . . . The question nevertheless is for authority to know that it has its foundation in the freedom of others, and if the authority denies this freedom and cuts off this relationship, this *founding* relationship, with freedom, I think that it is no longer authority but has become *authoritarianism*. (Shor and Freire, 1987, p. 91)

Freire elaborates, "education always has a directive nature we can't deny. The teacher has a plan, a program, a goal for the study. But there is the directive *liberating* educator on the one hand, and the directive *domesticating* educator on the other. The liberating difference is a tension which the teacher tries to overcome by a democratic attitude to his or her directiveness" (Shor and Freire, 1987, p. 172). "For me education is always directive, always. The question is to know towards what and with whom it is directive" (p. 109).

While Shor is concerned with handing over authority and Freire emphasizes that the teacher is always an authority, McLaren (1989) argues that teachers must *choose* emancipatory authority:

> The challenge of critical pedagogy does not reside solely in the logical consistency or the empirical verification of its theories; rather, it resides in the moral choice put before us as teachers and citizens . . . We need to examine that choice: do we want our schools to create a passive, risk-free citizenry, or a politicized citizenry capable of fighting for various forms of public life and informed by a concern for equality and social justice? (p. 158)

This argument supports critical pedagogy's emphasis on agency—the teacher has the capacity to make a choice. Giroux (1988a) implores the critical pedagogue to make the latter choice, suggesting that it is the only defensible choice: "Educators have a moral and ethical responsibility to develop a view of radical authority that legitimates forms of critical pedagogy aimed at both interpreting reality and transforming it" (p. 68).

In the Giroux/McLaren strand of critical pedagogy, there is also a rather clear social differentiation between theory and practice, wherein, unlike the feminist pedagogy discourse or the other strand of critical pedagogy, the theorist is less explicitly concerned with his own practice than with the practice of others—large amorphous groups called teachers (or, occasionally, teacher educators). For example, Giroux (1988a) says: "For teachers to function as transformative intellectuals who legitimate their role through an emancipatory form of authority, they will have to do more than gain further control of their working conditions and teach critical pedagogy" (p. 108). While there is nothing in Giroux's words to preclude him from applying these arguments to himself, he tends to talk about a vaguely defined community of people known as teachers in a language which universalizes and generalizes and does not explicitly address his own work as a teacher (and member of that community). I'm inclined to argue that in this strand of critical pedagogy the leftist adage "pessimism of the intellect, optimism of the will" (usually attributed to Gramsci) takes the form of optimism for the will of others.

Before leaving this discussion of differentiations (among types of authority, between self and social empowerment, between critique and possibility, among theorist, teacher and student), I want to return to what it means to argue that authority is necessary for freedom or empowerment. There is a fundamental assertion, in critical pedagogy, that leadership is necessary in the process of liberation. This leadership comes from the direction provided by the theorist and from the agency and authority of the teacher.[3] As a logical consequence of their constructions of authority, a question emerges within critical pedagogy discourse: "To what extent is emancipatory or liberatory authority a different type of authority than that type usually exercised in pedagogical situations, namely teacher authority?" I shall explore this question when I turn to an analysis of the specific practices which actualize the relations of power of the critical pedagogy regime.

Objectives of Differentiations/Relations of Power

In whose interests, in the interest of what, are these differentiations central to constructions of authority and empowerment in the discourse of critical pedagogy? McLaren (1989) claims "critical theorists are united in their *objectives*: to empower the powerless and transform existing social inequalities and injustices" (McLaren, 1989, p. 160). Such can be seen as the interests around which the differentiations (among types of authority, between self and social empowerment, between critique and possibility, among theorist, teacher and student) are made. Two major power relations are recognized by the discourse (power relations which both construct and are constructed by the differentiations): the power relation of dominant and subordinate wherein critical pedagogy is "irrevocably committed to the side of the oppressed" (McLaren, 1989, p. 160), and the power relation of teacher and student which is necessary to the act of empowerment through emancipatory authority. There is also a third power relation, typically left unaddressed by critical pedagogy; the rhetorical relation of theorist and teacher/reader. For Giroux and McLaren, as implied in the following statement, theorists provide the direction *for* teachers: "Critical pedagogy . . . provides historical, cultural, political, and ethical direction for those in education who still dare to hope" (McLaren, 1989, p. 160). "Critical pedagogy," in this view, very much identifies itself as a social vision, a direction, toward which "those in education" (in this case, teachers) should act.

In whose interests is authority redefined as "emancipatory"? is empowerment viewed as social? is a "language of possibility" required? At one level, the rhetoric of critical pedagogy makes clear that "emancipatory" or "liberatory" authority is necessary for participatory democracy. Critical pedagogy is committed to "social justice." Historically grounded in discourses concerned about economic class oppression, critical pedagogy in the U.S. has broadened its scope to espouse a universalized concern for all oppressed people. Despite this broadening, critical pedagogy still demonstrates a primary concern for struggles against the evils of capitalism. For instance, Giroux (1991) claims that:

> central to [a radical democratic] politics and pedagogy is a notion of community developed around a shared conception of social justice, rights, entitlement. This is especially necessary at a time in our history

in which the value of such concerns have been subordinated to the priorities of the market and used to legitimate the interests of the rich at the expense of the poor, the unemployed, the homeless. (p. 56)

In its focus on this particular oppressive formation, critical pedagogy's emphasis on capitalism parallels feminist pedagogy's emphasis on patriarchy. At another level, when Giroux (1988a) states that emancipatory authority "might be used in the interests of a critical pedagogy" (p. 75), both a democratic intent and the potential for abuse are evident. Giroux (1988a) acknowledges that potential in the following comments on "teacher voice":

On the one hand teacher voice represents a basis in authority that can provide knowledge and forms of self-understanding allowing students to develop the power of critical consciousness. At the same time, regardless of how politically or ideologically correct a teacher may be, his or her "voice" may be destructive for students if it is used to silence them. (p. 144)

Giroux demonstrates a form of reflexivity here, directed at a generalized "teacher" (i.e., with no explicit application of the argument to Giroux himself).

Moreover, the notion of emancipatory authority can be seen to function in the interests of the teacher who is able to exercise a great deal of power in deciding who should "have a voice," which voices are in the interests of democracy, and so on. "The concept of emancipatory authority suggests that teachers are bearers of critical knowledge, rules, and values through which they consciously articulate and problematize their relationship to each other, to students, to subject matter, and to the wider community" (Giroux, 1988a, p. 90). Giroux (1988a) argues that emancipatory authority "provides the ontological grounding for teachers who are willing to assume the role of transformative intellectuals" (p. 90). Here, another objective of the teacher-student power relation constructed through the category of emancipatory authority is found: it "dignifies teachers' work by viewing it as a form of intellectual practice" (Giroux, 1988a, p. 90) rather than the work of technicians or public servants who implement rather than conceptualize pedagogical practice. As the agent of empowerment who uses emancipatory authority, the teacher, even when not viewed as a transformative intellectual, is placed at center stage in the discourse of critical pedagogy. For example, Shor (1980) states, "the teacher is the architect of this un-doing and re-doing. The extraordinary re-experience of the ordinary cannot begin without the teacher's counter-structures" (p. 97) and, "the dialogical teacher is more intellectually developed, more practiced in critical scrutiny, and more committed to a political dream of social change, than are the students. In fact these differences make the liberatory project possible" (p. 95). Shor (1980) does however emphasize that the teacher should be open to learning from the students: "the teacher who does not seek to learn from the class will not listen carefully to what students offer, and hence will condition students into non-speaking" (p. 105). Freire (1985) makes this point more strongly: "My emphasis is on our need to learn from others, the need we have to learn from learners in general . . . For this to happen it is necessary that we transcend the monotonous, arrogant, and elitist traditionalism where the teacher knows all and the student does not know anything" (p. 177). He continues, however, "this does not mean teachers and students are the same" (p. 177). Thus, although he may be humble about the teacher's authority, Freire recognizes inherent inequalities in the positions of teacher and student which justify the teacher's directiveness.

The differentiation between the languages of critique and possibility also functions to attribute a great deal of agency to the teacher, and thus contributes to the hierarchical conception of the teacher-student power relation. Without such a sense of possibility, the importance of the teacher as transformative intellectual, critical or dialogical pedagogue, would be greatly diminished; indeed, the whole notion of a critical pedagogy might then be inconceivable. Instead, teachers are exhorted to "take as their first concern the issue of empowerment"; empowerment which "depends on the ability of teachers in the future to struggle collectively in order to create those ideological and material conditions of work that enable them to share power, to shape policy, and to play an active role in structuring school/community relations" (Giroux, 1988a, p. 214). In short, this notion of empowerment *depends on* teachers using and actualizing the discourse of critical pedagogy.

Whose interests are served by these differentiations? For instance, "Whose interests are served by dignifying teachers' work?" "Dignifying," in whose eyes? A cynical reading might suggest that such a trajectory attempts more to dignify educational theorizing within the academy rather than teachers' work itself (a stance that was historically important in the U.S. as "education," and especially teacher education, moved into the universities).[4] Hence, we might ask whether the notion of teacher as "transformative intellectual" functions in the interests of students, teachers, "social change," and/or the theorist? While Giroux (1988b) argues strongly that this notion is beneficial to teachers, students, and the whole project of educational and social change through critical pedagogy, the fact that it does not seem to have been widely embraced by either teachers or other educational theorists suggests that its resonance with others in the educational community has been limited—or that few have heard of it.

However sincere in intention, it is possible that the concept of emancipatory authority, applied wherein the teacher is *an authority* on oppression or liberation, is dangerous in the extent to which it primarily functions to emancipate both the theorist and the teacher from worrying about inconsistent effects of their pedagogy, rather than smoothly functioning to emancipate students or others from oppression. Ellsworth (1989) is critical of this construction within critical pedagogy. In her experience as professor in a class working against racism, she admits:

> I did not understand racism better than my students did, especially those students of color coming into class after . . . months . . . of campus activism and whole lives of experience and struggle against racism—nor could I ever hope to. . . . My understanding and experience of racism will always be constrained by my white skin and middle class privilege. (p. 308)

For Ellsworth, the superior knowledge and/or commitment of the liberatory teacher is not a given. Although Ellsworth writes about her own experiences in a university classroom, the same argument could apply to many student populations.

The notion of political and ideological "correctness," and the implication that the teacher is central in either giving voice to or silencing his or her students, are indicative of the same bipolar logic found in the feminist pedagogy discourse, the same kind of logic which separates domination and liberation, powerlessness and empoweredness. As further evidence of critical pedagogy's universalizing or totalizing tendencies, consider again the language that asks teachers to "engage *unyieldingly* in their attempts to empower . . . ." Such words connote not only a refusal to compromise but also a certainty about the "proper" approach that leaves little space for tentativeness or openness. Bob Connell (1983) explains the danger of this tactic as follows:

> Of all the magnificent variety of ways to go wrong, the one that is most seductive for the left, and most destructive in the long run, is theoretical dogmatism. There is an endless temptation, when confronting power structures and trying to mobilise people who by definition tend to be powerless and poor, to seize on and solidify a dogma. It can be a genuine shield against cooptation, a means of guaranteeing at least a verbal militancy. It can also become a talisman, a magical guarantee

that right will triumph in the end if only one keeps the faith and rejects all modifications and alternatives. (p. 254)

In short, the "emancipatory authority" of critical pedagogy, exercised in the pursuit of justice and emancipation, may be dangerous (like any other discourse) to the extent that it sees itself as not requiring further justification or critique.

Moreover, within the theorist's discursive focus on Others/teachers, there lies a danger of overlooking one's own (or one's group's) implication in the very conditions one is attempting to ameliorate as a theorist of critical pedagogy. Consider, for example, the following statement made by Giroux (1988a):

Teachers' work has to be analyzed in terms of its social and political function within particular "regimes of truth". That is, teachers can no longer deceive themselves into believing they are serving on behalf of truth when, in fact, they are deeply involved in battles "about the status of truth and the political role it plays". (p. 212)

Despite his insistence, illustrated in this passage, that teachers are intellectuals who need to be conscious of the contradictory effects of their work, Giroux does not specifically reflect on the possibility that his own construction of critical pedagogy could be seen as a "regime of truth." It is possible that he has read Foucault (from whom he has borrowed the concept) in a way which costs him his critical openness (Bové, 1988). His generalized and globalized insight about teachers seems to double as his oversight when it comes to the particular and personal of his own work. In the (well-intentioned) focus on empowering others lies a paradoxical danger of overlooking the very reflexivity which, rhetorically,[5] is considered integral to critical practice.

The potential actualization of this oversightedness is a function of the pedagogy of the argument. The tendency to generalize and globalize carries with it the tendency of the author to overlook his or her own work as theorist or teacher, thus constructing an insinuation that *others* are to do the work of empowerment and transformation. Giroux and McLaren make several arguments about the potential dominating effects of critical pedagogy, but frequently in a general, unspecified way. For instance, McLaren (1988b) declares:

Nor must we ever give up becoming more theoretically vigilant on the basis that we are morally innocent. To claim immunity from our exercising domination over others on the basis that we have good intentions is to euphemistically dodge Michel Foucault's injunction that we

> judge truth by its effects and to deny our complicity in economies of
> oppression on the grounds of theoretical ignorance. (p. 70)

While this statement is resonant with my own thesis, it is not followed
by a specific examination of critical pedagogy. Consequently, the statement functions more as a rhetorical device that reveals theoretical ac-
complishment than as an injunction to place critical pedagogy under
scrutiny.

Such are the inconsistencies of a discourse which creates an image of
others doing the work of empowerment when there is similar work to
be done in the theorist's field as well (a field which claims to be about
pedagogy and which is itself pedagogical, if not in the classroom interactions of professor and students, then at least in the arguments it
makes).[6] These dangers loom more so in the strand of critical pedagogy
constructed by Giroux and McLaren than in the strand constructed by
Shor and Freire insofar as Shor and Freire explicitly apply and develop
their notion of critical pedagogy in relation to their own pedagogical
practice. Although, it should be noted, such applications do not, in themselves, guarantee reflexivity.

Furthermore, setting oneself apart as teacher or intellectual or leader,
via discursive strategy, can also foster an arrogant assumption of what
empowerment means for teachers and students. Bové (1986) writes:

> Leading intellectuals tend to assume responsibility for imagining al-
> ternatives and do so *within* a set of discourses and institutions burdened
> genealogically by multifaceted complicities with power that make them
> dangerous to people. As agencies of these discourses that greatly affect
> the lives of people one might say leading intellectuals are a tool of
> oppression and most so precisely when they arrogate the right and
> power to judge and imagine efficacious alternatives—a process that
> we might suspect, sustains leading intellectuals at the expense of others.
> (p. 227)

In the following discussion of techniques and practices which actualize
the relations of power of the critical pedagogy regime, I shall elaborate
how such "oppressive" effects can be produced by these emancipatory
discourses.

Techniques and Practices

As with the discourse of feminist pedagogy, practices which actualize
the power relations (dominant/subordinate, teacher/student, theorist/
reader) of critical pedagogy can be identified in the pedagogy argued

for and the pedagogy of the argument. It is in this aspect of the critical pedagogy regime—the specific practices which actualize the relations of power—that the two strands diverge most vividly. In terms of the critical pedagogies argued for, we must look to Freire and Shor for direction on specific classroom practices. Both provide detailed accounts of their own practice and make suggestions for other educators (see for example, *Education for Critical Consciousness* [Freire, 1973] and *Critical Teaching and Everyday Life* [Shor, 1980]).[7] Similar to the practices in feminist pedagogy, many of the techniques suggested for critical pedagogy are characteristic of progressive pedagogy in general; such as, students creating their own texts and media, collective and cooperative work styles, peer and group evaluation, self and mutual instruction, exchanging self-discipline for hand-raising (Shor, 1980). "The teacher needs to come to class with an agenda, but must be ready for anything, committed to letting go when the discussion is searching for an organic form" (Shor, 1980, p. 101). As well, the teacher must be ready to take on a range of roles including: initiator/coordinator, peer-discussant, convenor, facilitator, advocate, adversary, lecturer, recorder, mediator, librarian. Shor (1980) acknowledges that these practices are not new, explaining that his pedagogical ideas emerged from his own teaching experience and from his "familiarity with Freirian and progressive education practices" (p. 94).

Although these practices are aimed at altering the teacher-student power relation toward a more democratic, emancipatory/liberatory form, both Shor and Freire acknowledge the difficulties of achieving this new kind of relationship. For example, Freire describes students conditioned by "authoritarian" teachers, who, when confronted with a dialogical classroom in which they are told "we in this class are different, we have the right to think and to ask questions and to criticize" (Shor and Freire, 1987, p. 93), expect that they are in a position of equality with the dialogical teacher. According to Freire, these students challenge or "test" the teacher to find out whether what the teacher espouses is functioning. In these situations the teacher is advised to respond carefully so as not to reproduce the authoritarianism the students might expect, but also so as not to allow the "test" to pass without comment. Freire says "the student needs to know that in some moments freedom must be punished, when it goes beyond the limits of democratic authority. And the punishment has to be made by the authority" (p. 93). He adds however, that "you cannot accept the invitation to authoritarianism which the dominant ideology makes to you *through* the test of a student, who challenges you with the very freedom we believe in!" (pp. 93–4).

Similarly, Shor says "the student is the ironic messenger, inviting the liberatory teacher to fall back into rigid relations" (p. 94). He admits:

> all my reasoning and ingenuity and good intentions are not always enough, and I have to regularly ask students to leave the course. I can't let them wreck my work or the learning possible with the other students, so I tell them to drop the course if they don't change or else give them work to do outside the classroom. The other students are often relieved that I asserted my authority to expel such a disruptive person from the room. I do this because it has to be done. (Shor and Freire, 1987, p. 94)

In light of such examples, the "emancipatory authority" of critical pedagogy does not seem to significantly differentiate it from other progressive pedagogies.

However, in the discourse of critical pedagogy both "progressive" pedagogical practices and emancipatory authority are linked to particular "critical" content. Freire (1973) describes using "generative themes" in his attempt to integrate the lived experiences of the Brazilian peasants with whom he worked into his pedagogical process of dialogical empowerment. By studying the lives of his "students," Freire identified a number of terms central to the students' daily lives that could be used both to problematize experience and to teach literacy. The generative themes such as "brick," "rice," "slum," "wealth," "bicycle," and "land" were selected for their syllabic and phonetic structure, and for their connection to social themes around which consciousness could be raised. Similarly, Shor (1980) emphasizes "re-experiencing the ordinary," examining familiar situations in an unfamiliar way. One of the best known examples is Shor's problematization of hamburgers, which brought his classes into discussions and activities related to such topics as "health food" and "junk food," the production and distribution processes involved in delivering a burger to a consumer, and the largely invisible relations of commodity culture. Other examples provided by Shor (1980) of "re-experiencing" or "problematizing" everyday life include marriage contracts, work, and chairs. Shor outlines and illustrates a three-part, problem-solving method—description, diagnosis, and reconstruction.

In these examples it becomes apparent that what separates the emancipatory authority of critical pedagogy from other types of authority is not so much its form but its content.[8] Although there is acknowledgment that the content requires a democratic form, that students should experience a form of participatory democracy, democratic form is not seen as sufficient for a critical pedagogy. "Emancipatory authority" can thus be seen as amounting to the exercise of teacher authority for the development of critical consciousness necessary for self and social empowerment.

In what I call the pedagogy argued for by Giroux and McLaren, it appears that the goals of empowerment and transformation are considered of such importance that specific pedagogical practices are not addressed, are left for teachers to discern. Certainly, the dearth of attention to specific practices by Giroux and McLaren suggests that questions of how to practice critical pedagogy are not among their primary concerns even though, in an early paper written with Anthony Penna, Giroux claimed:

> Before changes in social education and in social studies development can be undertaken, . . . social studies educators will have to develop very specific classroom processes designed to promote values and beliefs which encourage democratic, critical modes of student-teacher participation and interaction. (Giroux and Penna, 1981, p. 221)

Since that paper, however, it is not uncommon to find such statements as "at this point we must forego a detailed specification of teaching practices and instead attempt to briefly sketch out particular areas of study" (Giroux and McLaren, 1986, p. 228); but, neither is there explanation of why they must forego the specification of practices, nor is there a detailed account of the areas of study. Thus, when content is addressed, the reader is often left with rather abstract analyses of such areas of study as "power, language, culture, and history" (Giroux and McLaren, 1986, p. 229).

The reluctance to articulate specific practices often emerges out of a concerted attempt to avoid prescriptive dogmatism by providing space for the democratic processes argued for in the discourse of critical pedagogy. In this way, there is tremendous concern for, and awareness of, the potential inconsistencies between the pedagogy argued for and the pedagogy of the argument. Specific practices have little meaning out of context. However, when so much critical pedagogy discourse takes the form of "teachers should . . . ," "teachers must . . . ," "teachers ought to . . . ," the failure to provide specific (versus universal) guidance can have effects which are just as immobilizing as dogmatic prescription. For instance:

> —Teachers must take active responsibility for raising serious questions about what they teach, how they are to teach, and what the larger goals are for which they are striving. This means that they must take a responsible role in shaping the purposes and conditions of schooling. (Giroux, 1988b, p. 126)

—The teacher's task must take the form of a critical pedagogy. That is, the teacher must do more than simply further legitimate shared assumptions, agreed upon proprieties, or established conventions. He or she must make classrooms into critical spaces that truly endanger the obviousness of culture . . . , must excavate the "subjugated knowledges" of those who have been marginalized or disaffected . . . , must function as more than [an agent] of social critique. (McLaren, 1989, p. 241)

—For critical pedagogy to become viable within our schools, teachers must learn to employ critical analysis and utopian thinking. (McLaren, 1989, p. 238)

—I want to conclude that teachers should become transformative intellectuals if they are to subscribe to a view of pedagogy that believes in educating students to be active, critical citizens. . . . Transformative intellectuals need to develop a discourse that unites the language of critique with the language of possibility, so that social educators recognize that they can make changes. In doing so, they must speak out against economic, political and social injustices both within and outside schools. At the same time they must work to create the conditions that give students the opportunity to become citizens who have the knowledge and courage to struggle in order to make despair unconvincing and hope practical. (Giroux, 1985, p. 379).

As Judith Williamson (1988) says of critical content, "these things . . . are easy to write about at a distance from actual, diverse, unconfident, recalcitrant kids; but the question which confronts the teacher, (and, as far as I can see, *only* the teacher, since no one will talk about it) is *how* to teach these things, literally how to get them across, how to make them make sense to actual, living individuals (sorry, but they *are* individuals)" (p. 90). To structure the relations of the teacher to critical pedagogy and social empowerment in this way, is to create conditions wherein the teacher will be blamed in those instances when the goals of critical pedagogy are not met.

Given that teachers already feel overburdened (as Giroux and McLaren acknowledge), and that this strand of critical pedagogy leaves them with the task of both conceptualizing and implementing critical pedagogical practice (in terms of specific content and form), it would not be surprising to find critical pedagogy neither widely embraced nor adopted by teachers. While Giroux and McLaren emphasize the need to understand and challenge conditions for teachers and students in schools and other institutions, the critical pedagogy they espouse almost relies on the *a priori* establishment of conditions that would allow teachers' work to be restructured as the work of intellectuals. That is, Giroux and McLaren argue that teachers as transformative intellectuals are to work toward altering conditions in schools and society, but also suggest that in order to be transformative intellectuals some "democratic" conditions are required. If the critical pedagogy regime is to break out of this circle of conditions needed for intellectuals who are needed to change conditions, it would be helpful to have specific suggestions for first steps in the process of bringing about change through critical pedagogy. This brings me to some of the specific practices of the pedagogy of the argument. The language of "emancipatory authority" and "transformative intellectual," indeed the language of critical pedagogy in general, can be seen to further distance teachers from the discourses of critical pedagogy. The language or style employed by Giroux and McLaren, and to a lesser extent, Freire and Shor, codes and mystifies. In short, the language of critical pedagogy with its concepts borrowed from Neo-Marxism, the Critical Theory of the Frankfurt School, and oppositional politics generally, can operate to assert the authority of the theorist in a way that is not emancipatory but rather separatist in its inaccessibility to people who are not familiar with that language (or in Schrag's [1988] words "not already members of the 'critical cult' " [p. 143]). As Giroux (1988c) correctly points out, it can be condescending to call for simplicity of language with the assumption "that teachers, students, and others are not intelligent enough to grapple with or unravel a complex thought or issue" (p. 146). It can be equally as condescending, however, to deny the complexity of teachers' realities, with the assumption that teachers can find time to unravel such complex thoughts and issues.

The pedagogy of the argument in the discourse of critical pedagogy is one that might benefit from a careful examination of the way in which we all have a tendency to refuse our own implication in relationships of power-knowledge and in particular discourses; we all participate in the construction and operation of regimes of truth even while working or arguing against dominance or authoritarianism, or for empowerment, democracy, and liberation. Cocks (1989) acknowledges these dangers in the following way:

> An emergent order will likely have much that is unruly and highly charged about it, an exuberance that comes in the absence of rules for how things must be thought about and so what can be thought to be done. But to the extent that it acquires any real coherence, complexity and strength, what began as an anarchic *melange* of shifting conceptions and practices will harden into a counter-cultural hegemony in its own right. This is only to say that every vigorous counter-culture is bound to end up exerting its own discipline over life. (p. 190)

The "counter-cultural" discourse of critical pedagogy can be seen to exert its own "discipline over life" in part though its use of language. For instance, Giroux (1988a) responds to the charge, "critical theorists have no right to impose their 'language constructs' on others" when he writes, "it is theoretically flawed because it confuses the ideological interests inherent in developing a critical (or any other) political project with the pedagogical strategy to be used in conjunction with it" (p. 68). In this passage (like the response to Schrag from which it is taken) Giroux asserts that criticisms of the language of critical pedagogy emerge from politically naive, conservative, or incorrect positions.

Moreover, the passage requires readers to separate the "pedagogical strategy" from the "critical political project" of critical pedagogy. But, given the discursive claim to be constructing "a critical pedagogy," it seems inconsistent to separate the "pedagogical strategy" from the political (pedagogical) project. On the other hand, this separation (of theory from practice) reflects the theorists' view that their role is to outline the political project for teachers, while the role of teachers, as transformative intellectuals, is to conceptualize and implement the pedagogical strategies or practices. While Giroux and McLaren might be attempting to overcome the theorist/practitioner dichotomy, especially with the notion of transformative intellectual, they not only risk failing, but they also risk exacerbating the dichotomy. Another aspect of the theorist-reader power relation is found in the production of the "grand theories" or the "grand narratives" of critical pedagogy. Giroux and McLaren frequently speak with voices of authority which, as Lusted (1986) observes vis-à-vis critical theory in general, imply "This is so, is it not?": "The mode of address of much critical theory . . . [suggests] that to be not so positioned is to be deviant—ignorant or foolish. The pedagogy, in other words, neither brooks dissent nor appeals to the possibility of dissent within it. . . . It is a pedagogy of closure and a politics, not of debate, but of direction" (p. 10). Recently, using postmodernist and feminist discourse, Giroux (1991) argued against "grand" or "master" narratives that make totalizing claims to emancipation and freedom and are monocausal. Instead, he called for "formative" or "large" narratives which "provide the basis for historically and relationally placing different groups or local narratives within some *common project*" (pp. 24–25) [emphasis added]. However, the line between grand and large seems quite fuzzy, and the effects of Giroux's distinction do not necessarily remove the theorist from the totalizing dangers of such regimes of truth. A major danger of this strand of critical pedagogy lies in the juxtaposition of its abstract metatheoretical analysis of schooling with its abstract dictates and declarations for what teachers should do. I do not wish to suggest that pedagogy discourses must offer concrete suggestions for classroom practice. The term pedagogy clearly can be employed for any number of purposes, such as claiming ground for a new articulation of critical educational theory—ground which is articulated in a language of possibility, and which thus addresses, at some level, what teachers should do (that is, the possibility only comes about through practice). I am concerned that—despite its many proclamations about what educators should do—this particular strand of critical pedagogy risks deluding itself insofar as it considers its proclamations to be sufficient guidance.

This strand of the discourse which expresses such optimism about what teachers might do, and which claims to function as a critical pedagogy for schools (and other institutions), seems limited by the extent to which it refuses to grapple with the details of pedagogical practice (content or process) with which teachers are expected to grapple. While there is some recognition of possible contradictory effects in the practice of individual teachers who might silence students, there is insufficient recognition of possible dangers in the *concepts* of emancipatory authority or empowerment, or (and especially) in the academic construction of the discourse of critical pedagogy. Some reasons for such a lack of reflexivity lie, I would argue, in the very institutions which attempt to integrate the discourse of critical pedagogy.

Institutions

The two institutions centrally involved in the integration of critical pedagogy are schools (elementary and secondary) and universities (or the academy). The academic discourse of critical pedagogy is premised on a critique of schooling. Schools are seen as failing to produce the active critical citizens necessary for the critical political project of social transformation toward greater equality, justice, and freedom. Schools are also criticized for failing to create the ideological and material conditions that would allow teachers to function as intellectuals which, for Aronowitz and Giroux (1985), means "conditions that will allow them to reflect, read, share their work with others, produce curriculum materials, publish their achievements for teachers and others outside of their local schools, etc." (p. 42). Aronowitz and Giroux (1985) point out:

> teachers labor in the public schools under organizational constraints and ideological conditions that leave them little room for collective work and critical pursuits. Their teaching hours are too long, they are generally isolated in cellular structures and have few opportunities to

teach with others, and they have little say over the selection, organization, and distribution of teaching materials. Moreover they operate
under class loads and numerous noncurricular tasks. . . . Intellectual
work needs to be supported by practical conditions buttressed by concomitant democratic ideologies. (p. 42)

However, beyond simply recognizing such oppressive conditions of
schools, critical pedagogy relies on what McLaren (1989) refers to as "a
dialectical understanding of schooling" which permits a view of schools
"as sites of *both* domination and liberation: this runs counter to the
overdeterministic orthodox Marxist view of schooling, which claims that
schools simply reproduce class relations and passively indoctrinate students into becoming greedy young capitalists" (p. 167). For instance, the
isolation of teachers in the "cellular structures" of classrooms, while
inhibiting collective pursuits among teachers, offers opportunities, as
many of us know from our own experiences, for a wide range of activities
outside of the institution's official curriculum. Giroux also views schools
as one of several democratic public spheres. "Radical education . . . has
a public mission of making society more democratic. . . . Most disciplines
don't have that [public sphere]" (*Journal of Education*, 1988, p. 92). This
view of schools as the site of both domination and liberation is clearly
in keeping with critical pedagogy's discursive emphasis on agency and
possibility.

Similarly, the institutional location for the production of the academic
discourse of critical pedagogy has both inhibiting and facilitating effects.
Certain universities have provided critical pedagogy theorists the opportunity to pursue their work while certain other institutions, even the
disciplinary communities themselves, continue to marginalize work which
is perceived to be radical (in any field), sometimes so much so that individuals have been forced to leave. For example, Giroux and McLaren's
location at Miami University clearly has afforded them the opportunity
to complete a tremendous amount of scholarly work. At the same time,
there are few references in their writings to their own teaching or to
"testing out" their theories of critical pedagogy. To what extent has their
political and theoretical project been shifted by their location in a small,
predominantly white, middle/upper middle class university? Similarly,
Freire's positions, political activist and teacher of adult literacy, and
Shor's position, teacher of English in a public university, might account
for their more detailed practical concerns. Like the two strands of feminist pedagogy, it is ironic that those theorists located within the practical/
professional discipline of Education should direct less attention to instructional matters than those outside of Education.

Freire's multiple institutional positions, given his experiences of exile and of many different countries and cultures, might contribute to his insights on the institution. He (1985) writes:

> I have been trying to think and teach by keeping one foot inside the system and the other foot outside. Of course, I cannot be totally outside the system if the system continues to exist. . . . Thus, to have an effect, I cannot live on the margins of the system. I have to be in it. . . . This is an ambiguity from which no one can escape, an ambiguity that is part of our existence as political beings. This ambiguity is risky. That's why many people keep both their feet squarely inside the system. (p. 178)

For Freire the institution must be negotiated. It constitutes the "apparatuses of our present" (Walkerdine, 1985) within which we must conduct our struggles for change.

Although much critical pedagogy rhetoric surrounds the empowerment of teachers and students—*as* teachers, *as* students, and *as* "critical citizens"—because the primary site of knowledge production is in the university, it is not surprising that critical pedagogy seems to have had little impact on the general educational community. For instance, while Giroux's work has been lauded as pedagogically "empowering" for many of us *in the academic field*, it has also been criticized for the inaccessibility of its language. (Bowers [1991a, 1991b], Miedema [1987], Schrag, [1988] point out that Giroux's work may not have been *as* pedagogically empowering at the sites of school and classroom). Of course, such criticisms need to be considered cautiously, given that they, too, are academic articulations, just as my own critique is positioned within the academic context of its construction.

Finally, the will to truth of academia cannot be overlooked in the formation of critical pedagogy discourse. The demands of the university, such as expected levels of productivity and the quest for academic expertise which often disdains "practice," do not encourage particularly reflexive work. Instead, academics are required to produce "new" materials for publication and presentation on a regular basis.

Formation of Knowledge or "Rationalization"

Like feminist pedagogy's approach to authority (one component of the framework of knowledge), the discourse of critical pedagogy seems to create problems internal to its discourse. Redefining authority such that it can be linked with freedom runs contrary to commonsense notions and cannot be "dreamed into existence" (Lewis, 1988). If this concept is to be accepted more widely within the educational community, I would argue that the discourse needs to rethink the pedagogy of its argument, become more aware of its own relations of power, its own regime of truth. McLaren (1989) states, "Critical educators argue that knowledge should be analyzed on the basis of whether it is oppressive and exploitative, and not on the basis of whether it is 'true' " (p. 182). This statement captures the voice of authority which undergirds this discourse of critical pedagogy: that is, while McLaren suggests that we cannot know what is "true," he also assumes that we can know whether something is "oppressive." The roots of critical pedagogy in the totalizing discourses of Neo-Marxism and the Critical Theory of the Frankfurt School also account for some of the authoritativeness of the discourse.

Cocks (1989) provides yet another insight which might be helpful in thinking about the regime of critical pedagogy:

> Political theory in general and critical political theory above all loses the source of its inspiration and vitality once it breaks its connection with practice. It cannot, after all, pull new ideas and the passion for criticism endlessly out of itself. (p. 218)

Some of Giroux's most recent work illustrates such a static, unchanging characteristic of critical pedagogy. That is, although Giroux (1991) has recently provided a lucid and thought-provoking account of modernist, postmodernist, and feminist traditions, the final section of his paper, which addresses implications of his analysis for critical pedagogy, shows little modification from earlier treatises "toward critical pedagogy." For example:

> Pedagogy is about the intellectual, emotional, and ethical investments we make as part of our attempt to negotiate, accomodate, and transform the world in which we find ourselves. The purpose and vision which drive such a pedagogy must be based on a politics and view of authority which links teaching and learning to forms of self and social empowerment, that argues for forms of community life which extend the principles of liberty, equality, justice, and freedom to the widest possible set of institutional and lived relations. (Giroux, 1991, p. 56)

One wonders whether a different conclusion wouldn't be reached if the discourse of critical pedagogy were to draw from contemporary classroom experiences in its ongoing struggles with the formation of knowledge.

ETHICAL ASPECTS OF THE REGIME

As in feminist pedagogy discourse, there is little direct address in critical pedagogy discourse to ways in which teachers, students, or especially the theorists themselves need to style their gestures, postures, attitudes, feelings, desires, or actions. Unlike the other theorists whose work has been discussed, Giroux (1988a) draws on Foucault to distinguish between morals and ethics, but in his reading of Foucault, Giroux is not led to directly discuss implications for critical pedagogy of Foucault's emphasis on the relationship to oneself. In Giroux's reading, "moral" refers to the prescriptive codes or rules one follows to live in a particular society and culture—regulations which are enforced externally, and which have also been internalized. "Ethical," in Giroux's reading, refers to the kind of person and life one aspires to attain. From this perspective, Giroux (1988a) argues for the development of an "ethical grounding and set of interests upon which to construct a public philosophy that takes seriously the relationship between schooling and a democratic public life" (p. 37). In so asserting, Giroux retracts from discussion of "relationship to self," focusing instead (consistently) on the articulation of a social vision. Nevertheless, in this social vision, as in the social visions of other critical pedagogy theorists, we can find implications for the disciplining of the self.

The Ethical Substance

Students are to discipline themselves in the critical or democratic classroom, relying on each other rather than the teacher. Shor (1980) explicitly argues that the goal of liberatory pedagogy is "self-regulation of the students" (p. 100), and Giroux (1988a) promotes "the democratic imperative that students learn to make choices, organize, and act on their own beliefs" (p. 69). In both of these cases the student is considered to be both capable, and in need, of self-styling. Notions of self and social empowerment suggest the need for students to change themselves in ways that give them greater control over their own lives while enhancing equality and justice for all.

Teachers are to discipline themselves in relation to theorists/theory and in relation to their students. For instance, teachers are to resist what Giroux and McLaren might label the "anti-intellectualism" at the root of claims that the language of critical pedagogy is too difficult—teachers should discipline themselves to grasp the language of the discourse. Furthermore, teachers are to resist temptations to revert to authoritarianism in their classrooms. They are also exhorted to be involved in politically progressive social movements outside of the school. In general, teachers are to engage in "the task of making the pedagogical more political and the political more pedagogical" (Aronowitz and Giroux, 1985, p. 36).

The general neglect of the ethical in relation to the theorist points
to a general lack of reflexivity about the theorists' own practices, the
pedagogies of their own arguments (except in the broad, unspecified
terms already mentioned). These two conditions go hand in hand: lack
of attention to the ethical both produces and is produced by a lack of
reflexivity.

The Mode of Subjection

Teachers and students discipline themselves in the name of rational
and moral choice. The lack of specific attention to this rational and moral
choice in the critical pedagogy discourse is indicative of a structuring
absence. That is, the reliance on an abstract and universalized notion of
making correct choices might be precisely the point at which this discourse functions most clearly to discipline and normalize in relation to
its regime of truth. Despite the claims about multiple voices and perspectives, this discourse functions through a general assumption that the
right choices will be clear, that the teacher will/should know which voices
to affirm and which to silence, which social movements to support and
which to fight, and so on.

Techniques of Self-Styling

Again, given that generally there is little in this literature about the
ethical substance, we find even less said about specific techniques of self-
styling. While in the Freire/Shor strand of critical pedagogy we find some
attention to self-styling and self-disciplining, specific techniques for self-
regulation are not detailed. Shor (1980) states: "The object-subject
switch involves a turn away from authority dependence toward self-regulation . . . not simply a person-centered turn-to-yourself. Because disempowerment is social, empowerment has to be social" (p. 109). It has
been argued (Foucault, 1977b; Walkerdine, 1986) that the move toward
greater self regulation, can have the contradictory effect of increasing
the teacher's surveillance and control. Posing the need for self-regulation
in abstract terms perhaps also increases its effectiveness because individuals are not entirely sure which of their postures, attitudes, desires,
and so on, should be regulated.

The teacher is not immune from this kind of disciplining (King, 1990).
Shor (1980) provides one example of refusing to make eye contact with
students who begin to address their remarks exclusively to him, even
though it goes against "usual" teacher practice. No doubt both teachers

and students have to restrain some of their impulses to speak and act in ways contrary to the democratic classroom which this discourse espouses. However, the construction of the teacher as one who "knows" in this discourse leaves the teacher relatively unfettered. If the teacher had to listen to all voices, this would require some self-styling in relation to one's students, but the category of emancipatory authority seems to legitimate the making of unilateral decisions by the teacher about all classroom activity; it risks reducing the self-styling the teacher might need. Again, we are confronted with the essentializing of the critical pedagogy regime which poses the critical pedagogue as all-knowing, beyond racism, sexism, and all other oppressions. Its roots in Neo-Marxism correspond to some of the essentializing tendencies of this discourse.

In terms of the theorist, we can note Freire's recent attempts to demasculinize his own language (Stanage, n.d.), and Giroux and McLaren's attempts to integrate feminist and postmodernist discourses, as efforts to style themselves toward different kinds of beings.

The Telos

In critical pedagogy the being to which theorists and teachers aspire is the transformative intellectual, the critical pedagogue, the critical and active citizen. Especially in the Giroux/McLaren strand of critical pedagogy, the "critical pedagogue" to which the theorist aspires also is one who has also integrated successfully the most recent shifts in political and social theory. For instance, their recent work has addressed, among others, Lyotard, Baudrillard, Rorty, Habermas, Hartsock, Kellner, Fraser, Huyssen, McCarthy, Spivak, Minh-ha, Poster, Said, Clifford, Marcus, Derrida, Foucault, Lacan, hooks, Morris, Haraway, de Lauretis, Alcoff, Flax, Kristeva, Bartky. While such efforts suggest reflexivity, without reassembling the already-articulated discourse of critical pedagogy, they might instead have the effect of repositioning the theorist in his own interest.

CONCLUDING COMMENTS

As in my analysis of feminist pedagogy discourse, I have selected examples from critical pedagogy discourse which illuminate questions about authority and empowerment, but I have only minimally accounted for the shifts that allow a historical positioning of the works to which I have referred. However, my aim is still to illustrate problematic aspects of each discourse that could potentially function in a mode of domi-

nation. In particular, this analysis has highlighted (1) problematic constructions of authority and empowerment, (2) the emphasis on social
vision, (3) the problematic relation of theorist to reader/teacher, (4) the
relative lack of attention to the ethical (in Foucault's sense of "relationship to self"). Many of these findings coincide with the findings from
the previous chapter. In the next chapter I will elaborate and summarize
some of these points.

Regimes of Pedagogy

When the tools of opposition, useful to a point and in a specific local struggle against a particular form of power, lose their negative edge—when their critical effect makes no difference and they simply permit the creation of new texts, new documents recording the successful placement of the previously "oppositional" within the considerably unchanged institutional structures of the discipline—at that point criticism must turn skeptical again and genealogically recall how the heretical became orthodox. (Paul Bové, 1990, p. 64)

In this chapter I will focus on three findings from the preceding analysis of critical and feminist pedagogy discourses as regimes of truth (Chapters 4 and 5), each of which will return me to themes introduced in the opening chapter, each of which will point to the "orthodox" functioning of these "heretical" discourses. Briefly outlined, findings are: (1) critical and feminist pedagogy discourses are grounded in conceptions of "power-as-property," and "power-as-dominance," while also maintaining a notion of "power-as-productive," "power-as-creative energy"; (2) these discourses of radical pedagogy have difficulty escaping or altering regulative aspects of pedagogy; (3) in both critical and feminist pedagogy discourses, there is minimal attention to the ethical, in Foucault's sense of that term. In the first part of this chapter I will elaborate and discuss each of these findings. Then I will consider implications of these findings for the current fragmentation of the field of radical pedagogy. Finally, I will step back from the analysis in order to reflect on my use of the concept, and tool, "regime of truth," and will then consider where it leaves us.

CRITICAL AND FEMINIST PEDAGOGIES AS REGIMES OF TRUTH

Thus far, I have emphasized the differences between what I term the various strands of radical pedagogy discourse. In this chapter, I want to focus on some of the points of coincidence between critical and feminist pedagogy. In each of the findings that will be discussed, I will focus on the similarities between the two discourses. As I shall elaborate later in this chapter, identifying similarities does not mean, or even imply, that critical and feminist pedagogy discourses are the same.

Conceptions of Power

Critical and feminist pedagogy discourses conceive power to be both repressive and productive. As discourses constructed in opposition to the totalizing forces of Patriarchy and Capitalism,[1] feminist and critical pedagogies are grounded in conceptions of power as (a) the possession of dominant forces (e.g., the Patriarchy, the bourgeoisie), and (b) repressive: used to dominate, oppress, coerce, deny. Such is the power that has marginalized and silenced women, the poor, people of color, and others. Such is the power to be resisted, to be overcome. In order to oppose these oppressive forces, both critical and feminist pedagogy discourses reclaim power for their own productive, creative, democratic purposes. From this perspective, power does not always repress—it can also liberate.

It is this productive conception of power that undergirds notions of empowerment and notions of emancipatory or liberatory authority, authority-*with* rather than *over* others. With acknowledged educational roots in the dialogical pedagogy of Freire and hence a concern for "horizontal" rather than "vertical" relationships, each of the strands of radical pedagogy holds a notion of power as productive, allowing the reclamation of power for use by the critical or feminist teacher; power to be exercised *with* rather than *over* students and exercised for self and social empowerment. For most of the strands of radical pedagogy this productive conception of power is exemplified not only in the pedagogy argued for but also, by focusing on their own pedagogical practice as the basis for their pedagogical theories, in the pedagogy of their arguments: the theorist is to exercise power with and not over his or her readers. Giroux and McLaren stand out differently in this regard with their explicit attempts to provide a theoretical basis, moral and political direction for a critical pedagogy *for* teachers/Others. Despite their explicit claims to the contrary, they both employ a "power as property" conception rather than a relational conception of power. I suggest that, when directly addressing pedagogies, Giroux and McLaren fail to maintain the relational conception of power for which they explicitly argue precisely because their construction of critical pedagogy is "decontextualized." Nevertheless, their work is still situated within a productive conception of power.

As I have demonstrated in Chapters 4 and 5, radical pedagogy's dual conception of power—power as repressive, but reclaimable for productive and democratic purposes (in part, because power is understood as property)—is not exempt from repressive potential. As mentioned earlier, "em-power-ment" implies (1) a notion of power-as-property (to empower is to give, confer), (2) an agent of empowerment (someone or something to do the empowering), and (3) a vision or desired end state (a state of empower*ment*). From this perspective the theorist and/or teacher is viewed as the one who "has the power" to be "given" to readers/students. Hence, a great deal of agency is attributed to the theorist/teacher. In this view, the liberatory theorist/teacher is assumed not to oppress or repress by virtue of his or her liberatory intent. Furthermore, the theorist/teacher is assumed to know what is empowering, and, in such capacity, is thus positioned as the constructor and conveyer of truth.

Such conceptions of empowerment are all the more dangerous to the extent that they are grounded in philosophical assertions about, for example, "female experience" and/or "authentic womanhood," rather than in a discourse of the social realities, for example, of the historical marginalization of women in the construction of academic discourses and practices. To the extent that truth is thus constructed on the basis of abstract philosophical arguments, rather than on empirically-developed and contextually-specific evidence (Ladwig, 1992), it is likely that the regimes of critical and feminist pedagogy will be dangerous. (No discourses or practices are inherently liberating or oppressive). These dangers can be seen in a number of ways: in the closure that comes from the, "This is so, is it not?" tone which silences other viewpoints; in the limits such assertions place on reflexivity; in what becomes a "strategy of mystification" to which only a select few are given recourse; in the potentially limited impact of the argument, and of the discourse in general. Critical and feminist pedagogy discourses face these dangers inasmuch as they rely on philosophically-based essentialist arguments, and in the extent to which they claim to empower and emancipate others.

Placed within a broader discursive context, I would argue, moreover, that all of the strands of radical pedagogy share connection to what is known as "the Enlightenment," or "modernity,"[2] and consequently maintain notions of progress within an "onward and upward" view of the world in which change and improvement, freedom and autonomy, are not only favored, but expected. While some feminist discourses explicitly oppose aspects of modernism, particularly its constructions of rationality, *telos*, truth, and subjectivity, feminist *pedagogy* discourse is, in part at least, a modernist political project rooted in a view that individuals can be moved to recognize ideological and material domination (by the Patriarchy), and, in so recognizing, can then struggle toward conditions and relations which give meaning to the principles of equality, liberty, and justice. As I shall argue shortly, "the modernism of" feminist pedagogy should not be surprising, however, given the historicity of mass education and pedagogy in "the Enlightenment," and of discourses of progress in general. Put simply, no matter what one's political position, it is difficult to conceptualize educating others without also adhering to a certain conception of change or progress.

Within such notions of progress-through-education and/or consciousness-raising, are also found notions of leadership. The theorist/teacher of radical pedagogy, as the necessary agent of transformation, provides both moral and intellectual leadership through, for example, bringing critical and feminist materials to the classroom (university and school); imploring teachers/students to make the "right" choices (for example, Giroux's plea for teachers to choose to be "transformative intellectuals"); deconstructing grand narratives (such as the totalizing dominance of the Patriarchy). The kind of leadership necessary to pursue such political projects helps explain the location of authority in radical pedagogy. How is one to lead (as authority) a project founded on democracy and freedom away from specific conceptions of authority-as-domination?[3]

I am not suggesting that "modernity" and "the Enlightenment" be rejected because of their reliance on notions of progress and leadership, or even because, in discourses of radical pedagogy, such notions have merely transformed into the language of emancipatory authority and empowerment. Rather, my point is to highlight particular dangers (in terms of "effects of domination") that directly stem from radical pedagogy discourses' modernist roots. To reiterate, these dangers include tendencies to create grand narratives, to conceive of leadership in unreflexive ways, i.e. the liberating theorist/teacher *is*, by definition, liberating, good, true, to essentialize and to simplify. As I shall argue in the following section, these dangers are intensified by "pedagogy's" entrenchment within "modernity" (as "modernity" is presently constructed). Examining such larger regimes is an integral part of the reflexivity for which I am arguing. With this goal in mind, I turn to an analysis of pedagogical discourse, located somewhere between the micro, or local regimes of critical and feminist pedagogy, and the macro regime of "modernity," or modern disciplinary society.

Pedagogy as Regulation

In Chapter 1, I referred to the difficulties critical and feminist pedagogies encounter in their attempts to escape the regulative aspects of pedagogy. The analysis undertaken in Chapters 4 and 5 identified two specific instances of this. First, I recall the acknowledgments made within both critical and feminist pedagogy discourses that "the teacher is always an authority," from which recognition arise pressing/urgent questions of that authority concerning the ways in which, and the ends toward which, such authority could and should be exercised. Second, while the specific pedagogical practices argued for, in the name of either critical or feminist pedagogy, are remarkably similar to each other, and to those advanced in other progressive pedagogies, in certain ways, the practices also remain remarkably similar to, reminiscent of, mainstream or traditional pedagogies. In this section I reconsider these findings by elaborating connections among authority, empowerment, power, knowledge, and ethics within "pedagogical discourse."

Certainly, concern about the authority of the teacher is neither new nor unique to discourses of radical pedagogy. As Pagano (1990) identifies, "the moral nature of [the pedagogical] enterprise . . . renders our authority problematic" (p. 53). From the very beginning, mass, popular education has been centrally concerned with teacher-authority. For example, the position of teacher, as well as such lofty positions as school inspector or superintendent, were deemed only appropriate for those "cultivated men" who could set the correct moral example (Hunter, 1988). Similarly, the claim in feminist pedagogy that, "women (specifically, *feminist* women) are the singular agents of the deepest transformation of women students," resonates with such a discursive emphasis on the moral, political authority of the teacher. In addition, the primacy of the "transformative intellectual" or critical teacher in critical pedagogy reinforces traditional notions of teacher-authority: the teacher should provide a model to which the students might aspire.

Ian Hunter (1988) provides a provocative account of the development of "popular education" and its pedagogical imperatives which helps illuminate, in more detail, how "the teacher" came to be positioned as such an authority and model. I will use Hunter's work to elaborate my earlier claim that teaching feminism in a Women's Studies classroom remains an act of pedagogy in an educational institution.

Hunter explains that "the apparatus of popular education" derives its shape from a form of moral supervision and correction in the sphere of "social welfare"—"a sphere formed when traditional techniques of individual pastoral surveillance were redeployed in a new machinery of government aimed at the 'moral and physical' well-being of whole populations" (p. ix). Hunter argues that religious and moral norms entered the schools "not as ideology but as popular cultural practices [and techniques] connected to the formation of personal attributes" (p. 47):

> techniques for distributing individuals in supervisable spaces like the playground and the classroom; for passing all their activities through a grid of normalising observation; for making them responsible for their own conduct, sentiments and use of time; and, above all, techniques which embody new "social" norms in the purpose-built relation to the teacher in whose "moral observation" each individual finds his [*sic*] own conscience. (p. 268)

Hence, the techniques David Stow developed in the 1820s (Stow, 1850) that placed emphasis "on self-discovery and 'individual growth', on the techniques of 'learning through play', and on the non-coercive moral observation of the teacher" (Hunter, 1988, pp. 35–6), are not so different from the techniques of the critical and feminist pedagogies of the 1980s and early 1990s. Institutionalized pedagogy, it would seem, proceeds through a rather limited set of basic techniques.

The importance of the teacher-student differentiation in the "machinery of supervision" cannot be overemphasized. Hunter argues that it is in the "teacher-student couple" that the relation to the self—formerly acknowledged as a concern specific to the "cultivated elite," and enacted through the minority practice of ethical self-shaping—recalls the kind of relation to the exemplar, through which the populace would internalize new norms of social life. The teacher-student couple was based on relations of identification (with the teacher as friend, guide, exemplar), and correction (often self-imposed in trying to model the teacher). Thus, when Hunter speaks of the relation to the teacher, "in whose moral observation each individual finds his own conscience," I am reminded of the radical classrooms in which, despite efforts of the teacher to "de-center" him or herself, students still look to the teacher for approval and guidance, and of situations when grades are either minimized in importance or not given at all and yet, for many students, what matters most is the teacher's assessment.

While "the positive sciences of philology, economics or biology are not by nature pedagogical . . . [which] is to say that they form their objects of knowledge independently of any imperative to transform those individuals who will be bearers of this knowledge" (Hunter, 1988, p. 211), the human sciences are, by nature, pedagogical. The human sciences with which I am concerned are those which have been applied to education. To the extent that radical pedagogy discourses are positioned within these discourses of the human sciences, they carry this kind of transformative intent. Hunter argues, and I think Foucault would agree, that the transformation to "the good" and "the true" (however specified) is the achievement "of a special ethical practice and a local intellectual action" (p. 212). From this perspective, feminists can become "good" and "true" women/feminists only through particular ethical and intellectual practices, not simply by the fact of being women. "The good" and "the true" of radical pedagogies cannot be realized without directing attention to their practical circumstances—namely, that they are located within the system of institutional education, and, more precisely, within the disciplinary organization of the school.

When I apply this perspective on the construction of pedagogical discourse/practice to the regimes of critical and feminist pedagogy, I gain a new perspective on the proper object of a critique of these discourses. The mere givenness of a pedagogical apparatus that imposes norms for capacities and conduct, or is organized around techniques of moral supervision, or embodies these techniques in unequal relations between the differentially constructed social agents of teacher and student, does not, *ipso facto*, provide the grounds for critique. These features of critical and feminist pedagogies simply indicate that they are, indeed, pedagogies. Hence, if a critique of critical and feminist pedagogies as regimes of truth is to be made, the motivation lies (a) in the failure of these discourses to see and acknowledge their location within the disciplinary power of institutionalized pedagogy, and (b) in the as-yet-unrealized, alternative modes of deploying the disciplines of radical pedagogy—ways that are more contextualized, more reflexive, and more honest.

As Hunter (1988) argues "authority . . . is the inescapable product of the pedagogical imperatives and techniques and the purpose-built relations of supervision and correction deployed in the teacher-student couple" (p. 281). Strategies to modify current radical pedagogies must be formed on the basis of calculations made within the irreducible and ineluctable aspects of pedagogy: its location within the machinery of social/cultural regulation; the continuing importance of the teacher in the machinery of moral supervision; and its location in the field of human sciences.

The teacher cannot simply attempt to abolish his or her authority by maintaining an experiential realm in which "shared" narratives are assumed to equalize participants, and which, because the teacher and students learn from each other, is assumed to be a reciprocal enterprise. Nor can the teacher simply do away with the repressive potentials of his or her authority within a rhetoric of commitment to democratic relations both inside the classroom and outside. Attempts to do so are indicative of conceptions of power-as-property (which can simply be done away with), and power as *either* repressive *or* productive.

Given this perspective on pedagogy, the teacher might do better to acknowledge and admit his or her exercise of authority vis-à-vis specific intentions—sometimes emancipatory, sometimes repressive, sometimes both, sometimes neither. In developing a procedure whereby students facilitate classes, for example, the teacher's intention might be an emancipatory attempt to alter the power relations of the classroom. At the same time, however, this technique might be employed by the teacher with a regulative intention of controlling classroom interactions. That students participate in this practice via the directive of the teacher could be considered regulatory; that, in so doing, some students might feel "emancipated" could be considered emancipatory. Hence, in this specific pedagogical technique, the circulation of power is, potentially, *both* repressive and emancipatory.

As I will more closely examine the second instance of the regulative nature of pedagogy—that is, the "partial equivalences" (Bourdieu, 1984), the "overwhelming and staggering uniformity" (Bernstein, 1990), of pedagogical principles and practices (independent of the espoused philosophical or political approach)—it seems appropriate to consider pedagogy as having its own "regime of truth".

Employing the framework used earlier, differentiations are made within all pedagogy discourses between teacher and student, right and wrong, true and false. The main objective pursued in relation to these differentiations is the transformation of individuals and populations. The specific practices which actualize the power relations of teacher and student include surveillance, labeling, "supervised freedom" (Hunter, 1988). Schools and universities integrate these relations of power, as does the state by governing through modern disciplinary power (Foucault, 1979). The hierarchical relationship between teacher and student is rationalized as necessary, and inescapable. Within the ethical component, various aspects of the self (for both teacher and student) are considered in need of styling or disciplining, in the name of education or learning. Specific techniques of this self-styling include modeling ethical others, listening to one's conscience. The goal of such self-styling is to become an ethical and knowledgeable being. It is perhaps most helpful to think of specific pedagogy discourses in their intersection with this broader regime of pedagogy.

While discourses of radical pedagogy have concerned themselves with some aspects of the larger pedagogical regime, such as the power relations of teacher and student, and the institutions involved in the integration of pedagogies, as Bernstein (1990) argues, "there is no fundamental analysis of the internal logic (in the sense of regulating principles)" (p. 180) of pedagogical discourse. Pedagogy is most often considered a carrier or relay for power relations external to itself (Bernstein, 1990). Bernstein (1990) argues that we need also to consider the carrier, the relay, the specific practices of pedagogy; the fact that, much like hi-fi equipment, "the system carrying the signal has already regulated the signal" (p. 169).[4]

Bernstein's argument for an analysis of the "pedagogic device" entails a detailed analysis of the specific practices which actualize the power relations of the pedagogy regime. Without attention to this "internal logic" (or, I would argue, "the specific practices") of pedagogy, students can leave feminist or critical pedagogy classes more deeply entrenched in an unsympathetic relation to the material presented than when they entered. That is, it is not just the relation of the subject to the text, but the who (agent), the what (content), and the how (process), that influence what is learned or acquired. As examples, recall the "regimented reflective stuff" Scott experienced in one of my teacher education courses, or consider Gardner et al.'s (1989) student, in a feminist classroom, who concluded "so much for sisterhood."

In Bernstein's elaboration of the "pedagogic device," he argues that transformations of a text occur in the pedagogical process as the text is "recontextualized" from producer to teacher and from teacher to student. The pedagogy of the argument is important in that it links the intention of the radical pedagogue with the "texts"[5] produced, through the recontextualizing moments of pedagogy. As examples in teacher education, we need only consider the appropriation from critical discourses of practices such as action research or reflective teaching for other purposes. One reason for which no practice is inherently liberating or oppressive is precisely because of the recontextualizing that is always possible. For the purposes of my thesis, Bernstein's elaboration of this process is important in its support of the call for greater reflexivity about both the pedagogies argued for and the pedagogies of arguments made.

Neglect of the "Ethical"

The "regime of truth" analysis of critical and feminist pedagogies also revealed a remarkable lack of attention within these discourses to the ethical, to what Foucault calls our relationships to ourselves. Foucault (1983c) cautions/explains that analyzing techniques of the self is difficult:

> First, the techniques of the self do not require the same material apparatus as the production of objects, therefore they are often invisible techniques. Second, they are frequently linked to the techniques for the direction of others. For example, if we take educational institutions, we realize that one is managing others and teaching them to manage themselves. (p. 250)

In teacher education, such analysis is further complicated by the situation in which we also teach our students to manage others. Certainly, it was difficult to identify techniques of the self in radical pedagogy discourses when there is so little articulated in the texts about the ways in which teachers, students, or theorists might "manage themselves." This reluctance to articulate techniques of the self might also result from the opposition of radical pedagogy discourses to those educational discourses which advocate or directly effect social control. With such minimal articulation available in radical pedagogy discourse, there is no doubt that classroom observations would prove fruitful for mapping techniques of the self.

Nevertheless, I believe we can reasonably claim that discourses of critical and feminist pedagogy pay little attention to the ethical (in Foucault's sense of the term). There is even a sense in which these discourses could be called un-ethical; not in the commonsense use of the term which is often conflated with morality, but in the sense of one's relation to oneself. Through foregrounding what to say and do for others, what to say and do for ourselves, as theorists/teachers of radical pedagogy, has generally been neglected.

As introduced in Chapter 3, Foucault's (1983b) notion of ethics is separate from, and located within, the broader realm of morals: "in what we call morals there is the effective behavior of people, there are the codes and there is this kind of relationship to oneself" (pp. 239–240). Foucault (1985) was concerned "with the models proposed for setting up and developing relationships with the self, for self-reflection, self-knowledge, self-examination, for the decipherment of the self by oneself, for the transformations that one seeks to accomplish with oneself as object" (p. 29). Foucault's notion of ethics is captured in the expression "care of the self." "Care of the self" "does not mean simply being interested in oneself, nor does it mean having a certain tendency to self-attachment or self-fascination" (p. 243). Foucault explains that the Greco-Roman practice of the self, conception of the self, (from which he developed the notion) is "diametrically opposed" to "what you might call the California cult of the self" (p. 245). Instead, Foucault's "care of the self" suggests an ethic of self-disentanglement and self-invention. Because ethics operate somewhat independently of "moral code," constitution of oneself as a moral being is possible. Our ethical self-styling is not the result of our moral duties, but of our moral choices. Hence, Foucault (1985) demonstrates that while the moral code remained largely unchanged from the Greek period through the development of Christianity, the techniques through which people formed themselves changed from a care of the self to an "accounting" and confessing of oneself.

This notion of ethics—most likely considered idiosyncratic by many Anglo-American philosophers (Davidson, 1986)—is important for at least two reasons in better understanding critical and feminist pedagogies. First, identifying the specific techniques and practices with which we constitute ourselves will help elucidate the micro workings of ethical behavior in much the same way as attending to the pedagogic device draws attention to the micro dynamics of pedagogic discourse. That is, in this argument, ethics is to morality what the pedagogic device is to pedagogy. Ethics allows us to identify the "micro-practices" through which power and knowledge circulate. As Foucault (1983c) emphasizes, we constitute ourselves through real practices—"historically analysable practices" (p. 250).

Second, because ethics operate somewhat independently of moral codes, we are dealing not with duties but with *choices*; choices about the ways in which we act on ourselves, about the relationships we form with ourselves. Even when there is little change in moral codes—for example, in the moral codes of pedagogy with its themes of goodness and truth, and its operation through supervision and correction—we can change the ways in which we encourage students to discipline themselves, and we can change the ways in which we discipline ourselves. The ethical substance, the modes of subjection, the specific practices, and the goals of our ethical behavior are not dictated by moral code. For instance, within the domain of radical pedagogies, I can choose to constitute myself as a transformative intellectual or as a feminist teacher, or I can practice radical pedagogy without attempting to constitute myself as either one of these particular beings.

In Foucault's studies of the Greek period (1983b, 1985, 1986), he discusses some of the techniques employed by the Greeks in the constitution of themselves. The most famous of these techniques was the Greek *hypomnemata*—notebooks in which there was not an account of oneself (as in the later Christian mode of confession with purifying value), but a *constitution* of oneself—wherein "the point is not to pursue the indescribable, not to reveal the hidden, not to say the nonsaid, but on the contrary, to collect the already-said, to reassemble that which one could hear or read, and this to an end which is nothing less than the constitution of oneself" (Foucault, 1983b, p. 247). The objective of the *hypomnemata* was "to make of the recollection of the fragmentary *logos* transmitted by teaching, listening, or reading a means to establish as adequate and as perfect a relationship of oneself to oneself as possible" (p. 247).[6] This technique is in stark contrast to *the confessional diary* of seventeenth-century Puritans, which was an account book of one's sins, "a mirror of one's sinfulness, . . . a mirror one held oneself" (Rose, 1990, p. 220).

It is interesting to compare these techniques of the self with the current exigencies of academic work. With the will to truth, the general competitiveness of the environment, the emphasis on originality and innovation, we tend to be much more interested in pursuing the indescribable, revealing the hidden, saying the un-said (all historical tendencies of the Enlightenment). It is rare that we take or make the time, or are rewarded for efforts that are primarily a collecting of the already-said, or a re-assembling of what we have read or heard. But it seems to me that there would be much to be gained using this kind of technique or task in the process of constituting ourselves as radical pedagogues. Indeed, the process of collecting and re-assembling leaves open the possibility for rupture, for interrupting our current regimes and practices, perhaps even more so than the constant attempts to innovate beyond what we "know." That is, in always looking forward, it is easy to accept what is behind as given. My project, in large part, is a re-assembling of what has already been said, of what I have already read, heard, and done toward constituting myself as radical teacher educator—not just individually, but with the community whose general commitments and theories I share—the community of radical pedagogues (theorists and teachers). My aim as a radical teacher educator attempting to practice critical and feminist pedagogies, has been to better understand those discourses through a detailed examination of their discursive practices.[7]

Foucault's notion of ethics should not be interpreted as an individual's self-absorption. His project of self-understanding deals with the life of the collective (Moore, 1987). In radical pedagogy, it is possible that individual and small group efforts to institutionalize their own discourses and practices may have inhibited the development of a collective ethic. Such an ethic would need to attend to the four aspects of ethics Foucault (1983c) outlined (part of the methodological framework used in the analysis in Chapters 4 and 5): (1) the ethical substance, the part of the self to be worked over by ethics; (2) the mode of subjection, the way in which people are invited or incited to recognize their moral obligations (e.g., divine law, rational rule, political power, glory, beauty); (3) the self-forming activity, the means by which we change ourselves in order to become ethical subjects; (4) the kind of being to which we aspire when we behave in a moral way.

As a starting point for my analysis I want briefly to re-assemble radical pedagogy through the lens of Foucault's three domains of genealogy. Foucault (1983c) argues that three domains of genealogy are possible:

> First, an historical ontology of ourselves in relation to truth through which we constitute ourselves as subjects of knowledge; second, an historical ontology of ourselves in relation to a field of power through which we constitute ourselves as subjects acting on others; third, an historical ontology in relation to ethics through which we constitute ourselves as moral agents. (p. 237)

Consider in radical pedagogy the ways by which we have constituted ourselves as subjects of knowledge, as subjects acting on others, and as moral agents. As subjects of knowledge, we have constituted ourselves more often as bearers or holders of knowledge, as pedagogues or intellectuals able to use knowledge as revenge, than as agents subjected to knowledge, caught up in various regimes. As subjects acting on others we have constituted ourselves through particular (modernist) conceptions of the role and function of the intellectual.[8] As moral agents, we have constituted ourselves primarily in relation to the ways in which we act on others rather than in relation to the ways we act on ourselves. Attention to the regimes of truth within which we operate, and which we perpetuate, would help identify the current ways in which we act on ourselves and hence, point the way toward acting differently.

"Foucault suggests a version of the ethical goal which involves a collective's dwelling within the relation between its theories or commitments and the institutionalization of these commitments as the life of the collective" (Moore, 1987, p. 89). Radical pedagogues dwell within the relation between their theories and commitments, and the exigencies of the academy and/or schools. Features of academic work shift and modify commitments; for example, the exigencies of academia militate *against* reflexivity to the *promotion* of self-interested career advancement and complicity with the regimes one resists, and separate groups of us whose pedagogical and political commitments are perhaps not so different. However, attending more to the ethical, to the relationships we have to ourselves, should help develop reflexivity that will (1) keep our commitments clearly in view while helping us to see how we have excluded or oppressed others with those commitments, (2) avoid focusing on "Others" in ways that sustain arrogant constructions of the role of the intellectual as leader of the oppressed and means (or catalyst) of emancipation, and (3) direct attention to our micro-practices of pedagogy and our broader social visions.

FRAGMENTATION OF THE FIELD: REGIMES WITHOUT MASTERS

While pedagogy has developed as a regime of "moral supervision and correction" and while critical and feminist pedagogies have developed, in part, as regimes of specific forms of supervision and correction (macro and micro manifestations of modern disciplinary power), it is important to avoid the simple blaming of any particular group or groups for the construction of these regimes. In this section, I adapt Joan Cocks' (1989) analysis of the Masculine/feminine regime to argue that the self-identity and self-understanding of those assigned to the positions of teacher, feminist teacher, critical pedagogue, are generated out of the regime(s) rather than the other way around. "This notion has, as its preliminary truth, the point that any individual always begins to think, desire, and act in terms specified for it by an established order of things, elaborated for it by past generations of individuals who began their thinking, desiring, and acting in the same way" (pp. 186–187).

Insofar as pedagogy is an apparatus of cultural regulation, and the teacher is positioned as an authority, we all (men and women, teachers, students and theorists, dominant and subordinate populations) inhabit the particular order of things called "pedagogy." Cocks argues that consciousness is not the result of indoctrination, by the dominant, of its subordinates who would otherwise be free, "unhinged from any givenness and objective determination" (p. 189). Rather, when we disentangle discursive from social power, we can pose questions about how consciousness is determined in a different way:

> What, one can ask, are the dominant culture's basic classifications and assignments of identity, its range of conceivable practices, its encouraged sensibilities, its prohibited trains of thought? That is, what is the nature of the order of things both dominant and subordinate populations [teachers and students (and theorists)] inhabit? What are the stances towards that order it is possible to take? Which of these stances are most likely to lead the way out, and which populations are most likely to be led, not to some free zone of thought and action, but from

the hegemonic set of specifications through their subversion into some other, different sort? How is the dominant culture kept alive, reproduced, and expanded? To what extent is instrumentalism correct when it claims that it is the subordinate population that must be, in normal times, most thoroughly captivated by hegemonic ideas, or that it is the dominant group that always plays the pre-eminent part in keeping the given order intact? (pp. 189–90)

As Cocks emphasizes "the perpetuation of any order of things through the absence of reflection about it, its refinement through the extension and embellishment of lines of thought and permissions of practice already firmly and unnoticeably in place, does not mean that any of its individual figures cannot be more rather than less self-conscious and calculating in helping things to continue on in the same vein" (p. 188).

Against this background, I return to questions of fragmentation, lack of engagement, insularity, and internal conflict in the field of radical pedagogy. Given that both critical and feminist pedagogies partially inhabit the same order of things—the pedagogical regime and its institutionalization—and seek to disrupt aspects of that order, less fragmented efforts are likely to be more supportive of the construction of radical pedagogies. For example, because of its participation in pedagogy, Women's Studies has inherited some of the very dangers or repressive elements that it rejects as "patriarchal schooling." Its rejection of most Educational theory and practice, whether male, female, or feminist, is inconsistent with its participation in schooling. As Nina Baym (1990) simply states it: "feminist teachers are teachers" (p. 62).

Similarly, a new perspective on the separation of strands of radical pedagogy over contexts for practice is gained. University and school contexts might not be as different as they appear, and academics might stand to learn a great deal from non-academic practitioners of radical pedagogy in schools and other sites. Moreover, neither Education (as a discipline) nor educational institutions have a monopoly on pedagogy. Those of us in Education might benefit from an examination of pedagogical discourses and techniques in other fields (such as medicine and counseling).

As stated in Chapter 2, I am neither arguing for the eradication nor for the minimization of the differences through which I have designated the strands of radical pedagogy. These differences can contribute to the vibrancy and dynamism of the field, especially if we engage in discussion and debate with each other. By analyzing the discourses consecutively in Chapters 4 and 5, and by highlighting their similarities in this chapter, I intend to systematically substantiate a major implication of viewing critical and feminist pedagogy discourses as regimes of truth: in order for the discourses' respective political commitments to be more reflexively actualized in classrooms, greater attention must be given to the particularities of pedagogy, in the specificities of context.

Hence, I simply argue for a greater acknowledgment of "the order of things" we all inhabit, for what Michel Feher (1987) calls a " 'thick perception' of the present—to see what are the weak and strong points of the current regime—so that when we resist we can at least make little holes or little scratches in the right spots" (p. 169). Is this where "regime of truth" leaves us?

WHERE DOES "REGIME OF TRUTH" LEAVE US?

In this section I will argue that "regime of truth" points us toward a powerful methodology (Feher's thick perception) and a compelling epistemological framework; that the concept can mobilize us in its identification of previously unrecognized workings of power, and, because Foucault's analysis offers little guidance toward "the right spots," that the concept could, in a sense, immobilize us. I will conclude this chapter by suggesting a way out of the pessimism and immobilization with which some readers of Foucault are left; a suggestion which will then be elaborated in Chapter 7.

"Regime of truth" provides us with a helpful methodology with which to identify specific practices in the formation and operation of political *and* ethical dimensions of the power-knowledge nexus. With its methodological frame, "regime of truth" could be applied to any discourse. Therefore, while I elected to focus on only those discourses and texts wherein the authors claim the label, "pedagogy," the same kind of framework could well be applied to discourses within the broader fields of critical or feminist educational scholarship, and to mainstream educational discourses. I would argue, however, that pedagogical discourse provides a special case because of its centrality in the construction of modern disciplinary power. Although Foucault (1973, 1977b) chose to analyze the birth of the clinic and the birth of the prison, for their formative role in disciplinary power, he might have made the same kind of arguments about the birth of the schoolroom. That students, even in progressive and radical classrooms, continue to proclaim, "This school is like a prison," is testimony to the point.

Some readers might wonder why I have chosen to spend all this time and intellectual energy "attacking" or investigating critical and feminist discourses when there is "more urgent work" to be done to counter the "dominant educational discourses" of our time. "Why not investigate mainstream and patriarchal pedagogies as regimes of truth?" "Why target some of the most progressive work that is being done?" I have three responses to such questions. First, such questions conceive of power in precisely those terms that Foucault questions—power as possession, power as repression/domination, rather than power as circulating, power as productive. Thus, to pose such questions is to deny Foucault's fundamental challenge to standard notions of power. It is to deny the possibility that we are all implicated in relations of power and that as Cocks (1989) puts it, even "counterhegemonic" discourses can end up exercising their own discipline over life. Second, I chose to focus on these discourses precisely because of my commitments to their projects (my work as a specific intellectual), and because I maintain that in order to facilitate their forward movement, the details of the discourses must be taken into consideration. Third, by centering these marginalized discourses, I have been able to address aspects of the functioning of pedagogy in general.

Arguing that to engage the notion "regime of truth," one should also accept Foucault's analyses of power, also highlights how "regime of truth" leaves us not only with a methodological structure, but with an epistemological framework. Hence, I would argue for the analysis of other discourses as regimes of truth, but only insofar as they are located within the framework of Foucault's analyses of power, knowledge, and ethics. This is not to suggest that all of Foucault's analyses should be accepted without question or criticism. Such a suggestion would advocate yet another regime of truth. What I mean, instead, to suggest, is that "regime of truth" is more adequately deployed as an analytical tool when it seriously engages Foucault's ideas.

"Regime of truth" thus provides us with both an epistemological and a methodological framework for investigating relations of power-knowledge and ethics. While I have been referring to "regime of truth" as a "tool," it is much more. Indeed, "regime of truth" is part of a framework through which to understand modern society; but, in addition to providing the means for a particular critique of existing pedagogies, it is itself pedagogical in its illumination of processes of knowledge production. As such, "regime of truth" can be seen as having entered into the struggle for pedagogies.

In pointing to its particular pedagogical/revealing moment and effect, I am proclaiming "regime of truth," like other pedagogies, part of a modernist project of Enlightenment. I make no apologies for, nor harbor any pretensions about, this. Nor does Foucault (1984b), who explicitly admits that he cannot claim to stand outside the Enlightenment tradition itself. If "regime of truth" functions to reveal, the questions are: "To what ends?" "For what purposes?" "With what consequences?" For Foucault (1984b), the response is to continually question "the contemporary limits of the necessary," pushing ourselves to think about "what is not or is no longer indispensable for the constitution of ourselves as autonomous subjects" (p. 43).

"Regime of truth" therefore mobilizes us. Foucault (1983c), himself, states: "If everything is dangerous, then we always have something to do. So my position leads not to apathy but to a hyper- and pessimistic activism" (pp. 231–232). Joan Cocks (1989) is again helpful. She states:

> The chasm between absolute domination and absolute emancipation surely is too wide to make one's way across. . . . This brings us back to the question . . . of whether theory can attend to the shades of grey in social life without contributing to a depoliticization of practical interests. . . . What effect must critical theoretical thinking have on the passion to oppose a given order of things? Surely it must have a mobilizing effect through its analysis of the hidden workings of power, its exploration of the possible forces and avenues of resistance, its development of appropriate strategies of subversion and transformation, and its insistence on the possibility of a dramatically different kind of life. (p. 220)

Certainly, naming a regime of truth is liberating. It liberates us (in thought at least) from within the regime. "The recognition of a regime of truth as deceptive . . . by definition occurs outside the pale of that regime. There it can precipitate all sorts of iconoclastic adventures or it can stop with itself, but in either case it is a fundamentally heretical recognition. . . . Any master of a regime of truth thus would be its first heretic at least in an intellectual sense" (Cocks, 1989, pp. 183–184). But, as Cocks also points out, "regime of truth" just as surely immobilizes:

> It does so first of all by obscuring any clear-cut line between enemies and friends in its insistence on the complexity of the present situation. It does so, second, by calling into question the point of any special effort to wrench a new situation out of the old one, through its warning that the very best that can be hoped for as a consequence is the surpassing of actual inequities but not all possible ones. (pp. 220–221)

If critical and feminist pedagogues can be friends with each other (intellectually and politically), and even friends with non-radical pedagogues, and if men and women are not necessarily enemies, we are forced to rethink the boundaries of our current work and affiliations. If our radical pedagogies can function as repressively as those we seek to surpass, what are we to do? The immobilization that could result from such pessimistic conclusions is perhaps the major limitation of "regime of truth."

Indeed, what is one to do when one accepts that no practices or discourses are inherently liberating or oppressive, that our most liberatory intentions have no guaranteed effects? A simplistic example would be the realization that the circle in which one has placed one's students might be more oppressive than the desks from which they were freed: such awareness could easily leave one paralyzed, unable to act at all. Such a pessimism, and paralysis, is not the least bit surprising, especially if one wishes to think in general and broad terms (to construct grand narratives). As Cocks (1989) recommends, we can guard "against a too-avid fixing and freezing of things" (p. 222), keeping radical discourses open to critique and alternative viewpoints. I shall argue and attempt to demonstrate in the following chapter that "regime of truth" need not lead to such paralysis if one thinks more locally, in terms of specific contexts. As all teachers, who, like myself, have attempted to practice critical and feminist pedagogies, know, we *have* to act. There is no other choice if one is resolved to meet the class for its scheduled hours (and more) each week. In the following chapter, I will consider where "regime of truth" directs my particular work as a teacher educator.

SEVEN

A Re-assembling for Practice
in "Radical" Teacher Education

What is in question returns in the question . . . [but it is] a disturbed return,
one fraught with worry, a sense of danger, ambiguity, and . . . mourning.
(Charles Scott, 1990, p. 8)

I want to return to the point at which I began this book, to the question
of practice in "radical" teacher education, a question made more visibly
urgent when a student termed my radical pedagogical practice, "regimented reflective stuff." In the previous chapter I outlined ways in which
the "heretical" discourses of critical and feminist pedagogy have become
orthodox, or, more precisely, have functioned in orthodox ways. The
central purpose of this concluding chapter is to return to the question
of practice in "radical" teacher education and to consider possibilities
and limitations of critical and feminist pedagogy discourses suggested by
the preceding analysis for my own practice in this more specific context.

Some readers may consider it ironic that my concerns with teacher
education practice should manifest themselves in the form of a theoretical study. Focusing on discursive constructions of pedagogy, authority
and empowerment, power and knowledge, and ethics—constructions
which do not even fit the common meanings attributed these terms—
might seem inappropriate, unnecessarily esoteric. However, as I asserted
in Chapter 1, in order to reflect on the discourses of critical and feminist
pedagogy that shaped my practices I have had to position myself, at least
partially, at least temporarily, outside of them. Foucault's work, not for-
tuitously, offered such a position. In particular, Foucault's declaration,
"everything is dangerous," resonates with my own experiences in critical
and feminist pedagogy. At the same time, although Foucault is frequently
faulted for his lack of political and normative prescription (e.g., Fraser,
1989), his commitment to particular struggles against human suffering

—for example, in asylums and prisons—seems to have provided a position from which I can critically investigate critical and feminist discourses without feeling paralyzed in my work as a "specific intellectual" in teacher education. Having named the order of things we all inhabit, and having identified disciplinary power as characteristic of modern society, Foucault seems to have provided a perspective which helps explain some of the problems I have experienced during my own attempts to practice radical pedagogy.

In order to move beyond the immobilization that could result from the awareness that we are all caught within various regimes, I concluded Chapter 6 by suggesting that we focus on specific and local contexts. In this, the final chapter, I will return to the context of radical teacher education (from which this book has emerged), and discuss how I might continue to work in this context in ways that address and alter "my" regimes. I am not attempting to generalize or prescribe for all applications of critical and feminist pedagogy. Critical and feminist pedagogy discourses function as regimes of truth only in their connection to specific practices within local contexts. To summarize the dangers and alternatives for critical and feminist pedagogy discourses *in general* would be to participate in the very construction of de-contextualized grand narratives of which I have been critical. Indeed, although I have begun a textual analysis of constructions of authority and empowerment in the discourses of critical and feminist pedagogy in general, there is no such thing as a functioning of these constructions or discourses *in general*. My aim, instead, is to test my own discourses of radical teacher education against my awareness of the regimes of truth elaborated in this book in order to understand my own involvement in those regimes, and, in so doing, I will attempt to find weak spots in them (Bové, 1986). I attempt to heed Bové's (1986) conclusion that "intellectuals must theorize their own past and present roles in modern and postmodern society in more restrictive, local, and less aggrandizing ways" (p. 237).

I begin this chapter with a brief elaboration of the specific context of radical teacher education in which critical and feminist pedagogies are recognized, namely the tradition of "social reconstructionist" teacher education. Then I will consider specific ways in which the regimes of critical and feminist pedagogy (outlined in Chapters 4 and 5) and the regime of institutionalized pedagogy (outlined in Chapter 6) function, and the ways in which they might be altered within their contexts. In particular, I will consider the institutional location of radical teacher education, some of the specific practices through which radical teacher education functions, and what it might mean to be more reflexive in Foucault's sense of "care of the self."

THE CONTEXT OF "RADICAL" TEACHER EDUCATION

The contemporary discourses of critical and feminist pedagogy that guided my work—prior to commencing this study, I spent four years as a teacher educator in Australia and one year as a student teaching supervisor at the University of Wisconsin-Madison—have influenced teacher education via what Liston and Zeichner (1991) refer to as the "social reconstructionist tradition" of teacher education.[1] This tradition, which is primarily concerned with "the preparation of teachers who can play a positive role in the making of a more just, equitable, and humane society" (Liston and Zeichner, 1991, p. 154), has held marginal status, throughout most of the twentieth century, in relation to teacher education programs in the U.S. (and other countries, including Australia), while "academic", "developmentalist" and "social efficiency" traditions have held dominant status.[2] Although social reconstructionism has a long-standing tradition in teacher education, for example in the efforts of John Dewey, I will focus in this chapter on the contemporary context of social reconstructionist teacher education as it has been influenced by critical and feminist pedagogy discourses.

Critical pedagogy discourse's impact on social reconstructionist teacher education has mainly taken the form of conceptual proposals. As Liston and Zeichner (1991) argue, the marginal status of the social reconstructionist tradition is indicated, in part, by a general lack of examples of teacher education programs which translate these conceptual proposals into either feasible programmatic components or teaching strategies. From critical pedagogy discourse they use for examples the prominent teacher education proposals of Giroux and McLaren (1986) and Shor (1987), and observe that there are few references to existing programmatic examples of the authors' proposals. This lack of articulation of specific practices for teacher education shaped by critical pedagogy discourse is not at all surprising, given critical pedagogy discourse's emphasis on the articulation of what I have referred to as a social vision, its level of abstraction, its global rather than local object, (in some cases) its strong theorist-practitioner dichotomy, and its lack of consideration of the ethical.

Until very recently, feminist pedagogy discourse has had even less impact on social reconstructionist teacher education. Where feminist pedagogy discourse has been integrated into social reconstructionist

teacher education it has highlighted gender issues in schooling and society, introduced "an ethic of care" to complement and sometimes challenge the social reconstructionist tradition's primary emphasis on social
justice, and has begun to develop specific programmatic practices as well
as conceptual proposals (e.g., Laird, 1988; Maher, 1991; Miller, 1990;
Tetreault, 1987). Given its emphasis on local contexts and its lack of
differentiation between theorist and practitioner, these effects of feminist
pedagogy discourse on teacher education are not surprising. The slower
impact of feminist (compared to critical) pedagogy discourse might be
explained, in part, by its more diffuse circulation and its less visible
location in such publications as the *Journal of Teacher Education*. Also,
the slower integration of feminist pedagogy work within teacher education discourse might be explained by the demographics of teacher
education wherein men comprise the majority, especially vis-à-vis the
most prominent and high-status positions (Ducharme and Agne, 1989).[3]
Moreover, feminists in teacher education might have been "listened to
without being heard" (Ellsworth, 1990).

Similar to my critiques of feminist and critical pedagogy discourses,
my turn to specific practices affiliated with the social reconstructionist
tradition in teacher education emerges from a position of having employed such practices. Hence, in focusing on aspects of the social reconstructionist tradition, my aim is not to destroy that tradition but to
contribute to it by (1) elaborating the local functioning of regimes of
critical and feminist pedagogy and the regime of institutionalized pedagogy in social reconstructionist teacher education, and (2) identifying
ways in which teacher educators might alter those regimes, using my own
practices to arrive at suggestions.

Questioning the traditions and discourses with which I have been
affiliated, and in which I still participate, does not mean abandoning
them. In Charles Scott's (1990) view, "questioning . . . is not a matter
of indifference or ignorance, but a way of relating to something that
holds its fascination or importance while it loses a measure of its authority" (p. 8). Foucault's notions of power-knowledge, regimes of truth,
and ethics assist me raising questions concerning aspects of my own, as
well as others', practices in teacher education, concerns which now seem
as important and revealing as ideology-critique once seemed.

This chapter, in the manner of the *hypomnemata* (see Chapter 6), presents a re-assembling of what I have read, thought, and said, as I have
begun to rethink critical and feminist pedagogy discourses in terms of
the specific instance of my own practice in social reconstructionist
teacher education, both as teacher and as researcher. I should emphasize

that, when referring to "practice" in teacher education, I include the entire range of pedagogical practices (in the broad sense of practices as processes of knowledge production). That is, I am not only concerned with what I do in university or school classrooms as lecturer or supervisor, or in my interactions with students, teachers, faculty, administrators, school board members and so on, but also with my practices as researcher and as scholar. Put another way, I want to question the pedagogies I argue for and the pedagogies of my arguments as a teacher educator, as well as the pedagogies in which I participate. I begin this analysis by focusing on the regime of institutionalized pedagogy as it functions in teacher education.

INSTITUTIONALIZED PEDAGOGY AS REGULATION

As asserted in Chapter 6, institutionalized pedagogy (including critical and feminist pedagogies) is located within the machinery of social/cultural regulation. The teacher *is* an authority, and, by mode of moral supervision, is central to this machinery. Pedagogy deploys a limited set of techniques through which to distribute and observe individuals in order to make them responsible for their own conduct.

One implication of recognizing the regulative function of pedagogy is that I have ceased trying to relinquish my authority, in search of "the *non*-hierarchical classroom." As an example of my regulative participation in pedagogy consider that the specific classroom practices with which I actualize my critical and feminist pedagogies (in teacher education and elsewhere) are frequently constructed in advance of meetings with students. For instance, I have arranged the classroom furniture into circles and have asked the students to do the same; I have included journals on course syllabi as a requirement over which there is little space for negotiation; I have included readings and topics that specifically address feminist, critical, anti-racist, and other perspectives *I* value. Such changes in traditional classroom pedagogy are often made by me alone. Not only will it be unlikely that students would call for these changes, but they might even resist the changes once made. In order to disrupt this aspect of the regime of pedagogy, I could explore with my students in teacher education the construction and effects of my own pedagogical practices. Such explorations might be genealogical investigations of particular pedagogical discourses and practices, not unlike this study, or they might be ongoing explications of why I have framed and conducted classes in the ways in which I have, or they might entail detailed and systematic scrutiny with students of the effects of certain practices.

Given the institutional charter for teacher education—to deal explicitly and directly with pedagogy—teacher education provides a site in which to engage more systematically in explorations of pedagogy as both teacher and researcher. Especially because teacher education is concerned with teaching people how to teach, providing/creating space in which to directly engage students over "the pedagogies of our pedagogies" might create greater spaces for freedom within institutionalized pedagogy. That is, if pedagogy is not just received *by* students, but is "unpacked" *with* students, the work of unpacking will occur at least partly "outside the pale of the regime" (Cocks, 1989). Hence, I consider teacher education to be a prime site for this kind of pedagogical investigation. I am not simply suggesting the "progressive" pedagogical practice of "negotiating" with students. Those kinds of negotiations are frequently much less open than we pretend or believe. Instead, I am suggesting that I use my authority as a teacher educator to engage my students in explorations of pedagogy. I suggest that I try to be more explicit, try to reveal my own regimes of institutionalized pedagogy and critical and/or feminist pedagogy as they are enacted in my own practices of teacher education. Such a commitment to explicating pedagogies and their related regimes requires a great deal of re-assembling on my part. However, such work might help both to disrupt the current regimes and to correct the reportedly weak effects of teacher education programs on teacher development. Of course, the dangers and responsibilities will increase as effects become apparent, and there is no guarantee that the effects would be consistent with those I desire.

The example of working through pedagogies with students highlights two aspects of institutionalized teacher education: first, the institutions in which teacher education is conducted pose limits *and* possibilities for the integration of critical and feminist pedagogies, as well as for the kinds of tasks outlined in this book; second, teacher education, *as institutionalized pedagogy,* is unique in its function as "meta" pedagogy—pedagogy about institutionalized pedagogy, through institutionalized pedagogy, for institutionalized pedagogy. I elaborate these points below.

If we consider the institutions in which specific practices, such as reflective journal keeping and action research, are implemented by social reconstructionist teacher educators, certain limitations of those institutions will be confronted. Given the distribution and organization of individuals in schools and universities, and given the demands on teachers and teacher educators to observe and assess, a number of questions arise: "How are teachers in schools to regularly keep a journal when many complain that there is no time to think?" "How could 'journal keeping' or 'action research' become a priority for practicing teachers?" Similarly, "How can we expect journals to be of priority for student teachers who must, for example, prepare lessons for the following day, grade students' work, work an evening job, and prepare assignments for other classes (McCarthy, 1986)?"

Thus, even if the practices of "reflective teaching" and "action research" (as they are constructed in social reconstructionist perspectives) were widely accepted among the general community of teacher educators, there are limitations that restrict their functioning within the pedagogical relations and conditions of schools and universities. It is precisely in an attempt to alter such conditions that Liston and Zeichner (1991) and others declare the need for teacher educators to act in spheres wider than, but related to, their own curricula and pedagogy. They argue, in order for social reconstructionist teacher education to make a difference, actions to alter the position of teacher education within universities, relations between universities and schools, conditions for schooling, social and political conditions of society will need to be implemented. It is certainly insufficient to alter curricula and pedagogy.

At the same time, however, possibilities exist within teacher education. As already suggested, in its function as "meta"-pedagogy, teacher education offers a unique site for genealogical and ethical investigations of pedagogy that could use a Foucauldian framework. In disrupting the general function of the "regime of pedagogy" that is usually imposed un-named, and often unquestioned by students, a space might open within which to alter that regime. Teacher education is supported by institutional resources, has been sanctioned to explore such spaces, to explore "the pedagogies of pedagogies," and hence garners unique potential for altering the regime of pedagogy.

In order to elaborate this point, I want to return to the "limited set of specific techniques" through which the regime of institutionalized pedagogy is enacted. If, currently, little work is being done to directly alter the *regime of pedagogy*, then any strategies imagined within this regime will necessarily have limited effects.

> Not to struggle against [a] regime and its affiliations is inevitably to reproduce and extend it and the misery it causes. To imagine alternatives within it without at the same time struggling against it—by, for example, calling into question the seemingly highest ideals we have and desire—is not critical at all. Critique is practiced only when the appropriation of truth itself is at stake, not simply morals or attitudes. (Bové, 1986, p. 233–34)

Certainly, I would argue, critical and feminist pedagogy discourses have had little impact on the regime of pedagogy, the specific techniques of pedagogy, the authority of the teacher, or the functioning of pedagogy in the machinery of social or cultural regulation. The specific classroom or instructional practices of schools and (most places within) universities have been remarkably *un*changed. As argued in Chapters 4 and 5, what really distinguishes critical pedagogy from feminist pedagogy, and from any other pedagogy, is the social vision that undergirds pedagogy, and, by extension, the curricula its discourse would support.

I do not want to underemphasize the importance of social vision. Just because their regimes of pedagogy are similar (critical, feminist, etc.) does not mean that these radical discourses have had no effects toward social reconstruction. Although the authoritative relation, teacher-student, may have changed little, in the particular character of that relation, and in the relations promoted between student teachers and schools and a range of social groups, the social vision might be seen to have disrupted certain morals and attitudes and certain claims to truth. For example, if students are exposed to a discourse that questions the labeling of students in schools (for instance, "learning disabled"), rather than a discourse that takes these labels for granted, the students' relationships to those labels might change when they enter schools as student teachers and teachers. But, the social visions of critical and feminist pedagogies remain, by and large, *within* the regime of pedagogy. The social visions of these discourses have been articulated through critiques of existing institutions and ideologies rather than through investigations of the specific techniques and practices which give concrete form to those institutions and ideologies. Insofar as the regime of pedagogy proceeds through a limited set of techniques, and the extent to which radical pedagogy discourses have not focussed on altering those techniques (such as techniques of surveillance, labeling, classification, and "supervised freedom"), it is not surprising that my implementation of radical pedagogies in teacher education reproduced many of the same techniques and had similar effects of domination.

From *within* the regime of pedagogy, the greatest space for freedom might well appear to lie in the articulation of critical and feminist social visions. In this regard, I would argue that those strands of critical and feminist pedagogy discourse which have emphasized the social vision are struggling in a "fruitful" direction. But their constructions of "new" "pedagogies" do not alter the regime of pedagogy. Here I find support for my claim that pedagogy as the process of knowledge production requires attention to both the social visions and their related instructional practices. The social vision is insufficient. Any regime of truth is enacted or functions only through specific practices.

The strand of feminist pedagogy discourse that has very directly concerned itself with instructional processes and changing relationships and interactions among class members, may be closer to altering the regime of pedagogy. This feminist pedagogy has primarily challenged the regime of pedagogy by rejecting its traditional institutionalization and by situating pedagogy within the new ("nonpatriarchal," "cooperative," "interactive") space of Women's Studies. The extent to which this challenge to the regime of pedagogy has been successful is debatable and would require empirical investigation. In some respects at least, Women's Studies remains institutionalized pedagogy.

From this analysis of the regime of pedagogy and the construction of critical and feminist pedagogy discourses I want to elaborate three points. First, if indeed the institutionalization of pedagogy in schools and universities constrains attempts at radical pedagogies, then investigations of disciplinary power in various institutionalized and non- institutionalized pedagogical sites might identify specific alternative pedagogical practices which teacher educators could attempt to integrate. Pedagogical sites outside of schooling institutions, such as voluntary women's groups and parenting, might successfully employ different practices and, at the same time, avoid effects of domination. Indeed, I would argue that the importance of identifying spaces for rupture in the regime of pedagogy lies in the attempt to understand pedagogical practices in non- or differently- institutionalized sites. Such studies represent the kind of research that I have recently begun, attempting to investigate institutionalized pedagogy as a site of modernist disciplinary power.

Second, given that the institutional practices of teacher education have inherited, and seem to perpetuate what I call the "regime of pedagogy," it might prove beneficial to modify the goals for critical and/or feminist work in teacher education. That is, certain specific struggles of critical and feminist discourses might be better pursued outside of school and university grounds if we would more realistically acknowledge the limitations of our work in teacher education. This is not to suggest that we give up hope and give in to despair, but that we begin to address, more specifically, the practices in our current and future work, attending to the details of the possibilities. It is not enough to dream of alternative classrooms (Lewis, 1988). Third, and related, I want to engage in studies that investigate specific pedagogical techniques, so that I can begin to identify the weak spots in my own practice through which to begin to chip away its regime of pedagogy. Given that pedagogy is one of the major techniques through which modern disciplinary power functions, such work within and against pedagogy would be consistent with Foucault's insistence that we work as "specific intellectuals." Altering the regime of pedagogy requires more than analyzing the institutions and ideologies in which and through which schooling occurs. Specific practices also require attention. Focusing more locally on the work of altering "the order of things we all inhabit" also provides a way to move beyond the immobilization with which Foucault's analysis leaves some readers. At the local level, there is always something to be done. The following section provides a preliminary analysis of specific practices of social reconstructionist teacher education, and considers how these practices function within the regime of pedagogy, in general, and within the regimes of critical and feminist pedagogy, more specifically. I begin this analysis with a return to questions of power-knowledge.

POWER-KNOWLEDGE, REFLECTIVE TEACHING, ACTION RESEARCH

Foucault's analysis of power, outlined in Chapter 3, adds a new dimension to conceptions of social reconstructionist teacher education. Contemporary social reconstructionist positions draw on critical, and, to a lesser extent, feminist discourses in which totalizing and essentializing views of power and the oppressor prevail. Indeed, social reconstructionism itself is a globalizing and universalizing discourse which seeks to improve "The World". Foucault's challenge to such conceptions of power does not deny the existence of massive inequalities in terms of gender, race, class, religion, with respect to educational opportunities and possibilities for students, and so does not paralyze the fundamental commitments of social reconstructionist teacher education: to change the social order toward a more just, equitable, and humane world for "everybody's children" (The Holmes Group, 1990). These and other inequalities and injustices exist and can easily be documented.

Foucault's analysis of power primarily alters conceptions of actions within social contexts. In social reconstructionist teacher education, therefore, instead of blazing forward toward liberation and change with the "intellectual" as leader, Foucault (1988a) asks that we look back in an attempt to understand "what we are today" (p. 145). This task does not imply that, in the meantime, we should simply continue to watch the horrors of schools, the "rotten outcomes" (Schorr, 1988). Nor does this task undermine action or prevent attempts to intervene. Foucault (1988b) explicitly makes this point about schooling when he explains:

> Power is not an evil. . . . Let us . . . take something that has been the object of criticism, often justified: the pedagogical institution. I don't see where evil is in the practice of someone who, in a given game of truth, knowing more than another, tells him [sic] what he must do, teaches him, transmits knowledge to him, communicates skills to him. The problem is rather to know how you are to avoid in these practices—where power cannot not play and where it is not evil in itself—the effects of domination which will make a child subject to the arbitrary and useless authority of a teacher, or put a student under the power of an abusively authoritarian professor, and so forth. (p. 18)

Hence, Foucault's analysis of power should not prevent educators from continuing pedagogical work. Rather, his arguments suggest that we attribute importance to reflecting on what we are as particular kinds of educators (such as social reconstructionist teacher educators), how we have come to be this way, and the ramifications and, especially, dangers of our actions—not just reflecting on our reality but on how our reality has come to exist.[4] Reflection is not a new concept to social reconstructionist teacher education, especially reflection on social and political conditions; but this tradition has been less vigilant about reflecting on its own functions and effects. Even when theorists/teacher educators have reflected on their own proposals they have tended to do so within the kinds of notions of power and knowledge that Foucault challenged.

Power as exercised, as circulating, as capillary, as produced in discourses, challenges "the what" and "the how" of my work as a teacher educator. In particular, Foucault's analysis of power relations draws attention to my own local implication and participation in regimes of truth. For instance, I am better able to understand Scott's resistance to the journal requirement in a new way. In my first analysis of the class in which Scott participated, I labeled him a "recalcitrant" student in relation to his "acquiescent" and "committed" peers (Gore and Bartlett, 1987). Foucault's analysis of power enables me to see Scott not simply as ideologically mistaken or ignorant but, as possibly resisting the technologies imposed by the regime of truth embodied in my teacher education practices. Whatever his reasons, Scott refused to engage in the self-disciplining my regime demanded.

Foucault's analysis of power in conjunction with my specific analyses of critical and feminist pedagogies as regimes of truth enable me to question power relations and "games of truth" (Foucault, 1988b) in the functioning of discourses and practices in social reconstructionist teacher education. As specific examples, I will focus on the currently popular emphases within teacher education on "reflective teaching" and "action research." I have selected these issues primarily because, due to the scarcity of "programmatic instances" of social reconstructionist teacher education, these were two of the few "techniques" with which I was able to actualize critical and feminist pedagogies, and which, therefore, constituted a significant part of my own work in teacher education (e.g., Gore 1987, 1990a, 1991a, 1991b; Gore and Zeichner, 1991).

Reflective Teaching

The term "reflective teaching" has been widely adopted across contemporary traditions in teacher education. In itself, this phenomenon provides an interesting case of the politics of truth. Three of the leading intellectuals who have advocated contemporary manifestations of reflective teaching—Ken Zeichner, Donald Schon, and Donald Cruickshank —although primarily affiliated with different teacher education traditions, draw on John Dewey's (1933) distinction between routine and reflective action to make their individual cases.[5] In this instance the "will to truth" functions in such a way that the same language is used to make vastly different claims about the "truth" of reflective teaching. The wide acceptance of the term "reflective teaching" is not surprising because, within the context of the bipolar logic that dominates much modernist thinking, it would be virtually inconceivable to find a teacher educator who would advocate *un*reflective teaching. Moreover, teacher education's avowed involvement in and commitment to practice might render reflective teaching appealing.

My own work in teacher education formed its goals from the reflective teaching outlined by Ken Zeichner and his colleagues, which in turn drew on Dewey and on van Manen's (1977) three "levels of reflectivity" (the technical, the practical, and the critical). From this perspective, "reflective teaching" refers to teaching which attends, mindfully, to the social and political context of schooling, as well as to technical and practical aspects, and which also assesses classroom actions on the basis of their abilities to contribute toward greater equity and social justice, and more humane conditions in schooling and society (Beyer, 1988). Specific practices which actualize this form of reflective teaching include journal-keeping, autobiographies, ethnographic studies, case methods, action research, collaborative learning, and seminars in association with student teaching (Tabachnick and Zeichner, 1991). I turn now to more closely examine the functioning of this/my reflective teaching approach within relations of power-knowledge.

I want to reconsider van Manen's (1977) differentiations between technical, practical, and critical levels of reflectivity which guided some of the early work on reflective teaching in teacher education at the University of Wisconsin (and which guided my early experiences as a teacher educator).[6] There has been some debate about the hierarchical privileging of the critical suggested by van Manen's account. Some (e.g., Noffke and Brennan, 1991) have argued that the technical and practical might be just as important as the critical (in some instances even more important) in pedagogical practice. Others, including myself, have tended to privilege the critical—even when disclaimers are made about concerns for all three. How does this debate function? In part, it emphasizes the practical demands of teaching and reminds teacher educators/theorists to stay attuned to the pragmatics of school teaching. In part, it functions strategically to persuade other teacher educators that one does not have to proclaim oneself a radical in order to embrace (this version) of reflective teaching. An ironic consequence of this "back door" or "underhand" persuasion technique—perhaps an important strategy given the marginalized status of social reconstructionist teacher education— might be "the wider embrace" but concomitant appropriation of "reflective teaching" by other teacher education traditions. In part, this debate over levels of reflectivity functions to disguise social reconstructionists' primary concern for social, political, and ethical issues. If these issues indeed distinguish social reconstructionism from other teacher education traditions, what might be the effects of a more open acknowledgment and embrace of its difference?

With its own use of critical (and recently feminist) pedagogy discourses, this form of reflective teaching embodies some of the same dangers outlined in Chapters 4 and 5: totalizing views of power; the intellectual-as-leader in social reconstruction; inconsistencies between the pedagogy argued for and the pedagogy of the argument; inattention to technologies of self. For example, consider the common reflective teaching practice of requiring students to keep journals. Sometimes students are required to "share" their journals with the teacher educator for such varied reasons as promoting dialogue, keeping abreast of students' progress, and holding students accountable. While journal-writing is considered a valuable experience for both teacher educators and their students, it can also have negative consequences. For instance, journals can function as a form of confession and/or therapy. Foucault wrote about both of these modern practices as epitomizing disciplinary power whereby the individual participates in her or his own subjectification through a form of rationality that emphasizes the need to disclose oneself.

When these practices are positioned within relations of authority, as in pedagogy, "one confesses in the actual or imagined presence of a figure who prescribes the form of the confession, the words and rituals through which it should be made, who appreciates, judges, consoles, or understands" (Rose, 1990, p. 240).

In Foucault's presentation of the *hypomnemata*, we find an alternative form for journals, one that emphasizes a constituting, rather than a confessing, of oneself. Exploring implications and effects of such an approach to journal-keeping vis-à-vis radical pedagogical practice might result in a more thoughtful usage of journals in teacher education. What I envision is more an historical tracing of what it means to be a teacher in specific contexts than a personal or biographical account. Furthermore, asking students to "re-assemble who they are" might also confront and challenge the conservative backgrounds from which many students in teacher education programs come. No matter the form of the journal, given the authority of the teacher who requires, or even requests, that a journal be kept, it is important to be attuned to the likelihood that our students, in part, will write what they think we want to hear. How do we "encourage [our] students to say what [we do] not expect them to say and perhaps would rather not hear" (Baym, 1990, p. 75)? Or at least, how is it possible within institutionalized pedagogy to have the journal function, as it is frequently intended, as a place in which students can explore their own thoughts and feelings? Making the journal an option among other assessment possibilities or other course requirements does not alter this aspect of its functioning, except perhaps to the extent that the teacher can exercise *more* authority, expecting "better work" because the student has "chosen" to keep a journal. The dangers and difficulties multiply. Even in cases where teacher educators exempt journals from the possibility of assessment, to advocate or even suggest journal-keeping is an exercise of the teacher educator's authority.

While Foucault's analysis of power-knowledge problematizes practices like journal-writing in the context of teacher education, it also enables us to understand the macro location of such practices within the regime of modern disciplinary society. Foucault (1988a) suggests that the failure of our pedagogical theories is neither due to our pedagogies nor to our theories "but to the type of rationality in which they are rooted" (p. 161). This rationality is characterized by the integration of individuals in a community or totality that results from a constant correlation between increasing individualization and the reinforcement of the totality (Foucault, 1988a). For instance, we attempt to integrate students into the community of radical teachers through practices which simultane-

ously individualize the students and reinforce the goals of social reconstructionist teacher education. "Action research," another specific practice that is often linked to reflective teaching, provides another instance
of this rationality.

Action Research

"Action research," like "reflective teaching," has been widely adopted
across teacher education traditions. The form of action research I
adopted was that which has been articulated within critical educational
thought (particularly as expressed by Carr and Kemmis, 1986), and which
is embraced by the social reconstructionist tradition. The appropriation
of this "emancipatory" action research by other traditions can be seen
as another instance of a politics of truth. Some borrow the "observe,
reflect, plan, and act" moments of emancipatory action research cycles
(see Kemmis and McTaggart, 1982), perhaps linking these moments to
stages in Tyler's model of curriculum development, and then completely
set aside the emancipatory intentions espoused by Carr and Kemmis,
and others.[7]

Despite the "emancipatory" intentions of those who employ action
research as a technique within the social reconstructionist tradition in
teacher education, it, too, (naturally) functions within regimes of truth.
For instance, some theorists, in a clear demonstration of the will to truth
declare that unless research is conducted by the entire group of participants in the given social situation affected by the research, it is not
worthy of the name action research (McTaggart and Singh, 1986). In
part, this declaration functions to discipline us all into acceptance of a
singular definition of action research, a singular view of truth. It polices
the discursive boundaries of action research. But when action research
is conducted by preservice student teachers, and rarely meets the participation requirement, are we to abandon action research in this context?

Any intervention by student teachers in the name of action research
is artificial and temporary. As one of my students at the University of
Wisconsin-Madison wrote in her action research report:

> No matter what, I was always aware that this still was not *my* classroom,
> nor were these *my* students. Worse still, was always knowing that the
> changes I made were only temporary influences in the lives of these
> students, as was I. That awareness had a discouraging effect on me,
> at times. (Kelly Larsen, action research report, 1989)

This statement is indicative of the operative power relations in student teaching insofar as the student teacher "accepted" her lowly position. Students' action research is situated within the power relations of student teaching, such as relations between university, school, supervisor, co-operating teacher, student teacher, and pupils. To what extent can action research by student teachers function as outlined in accounts of emancipatory action research? Does this matter? How has action research been brought into historical play in teacher education? On what grounds can/would one choose to include action research (however practiced) in social reconstructionist teacher education? How do we confront the limitations of institutionalized pedagogy, this time at the level of teacher education? These questions do not suggest that we should not introduce preservice teachers to action research, or any other pedagogical practices. Rather, these questions suggest that we investigate, acknowledge, and articulate the limitations of our practices (Gore, 1991b).

As most teacher educators would admit, "action research" conducted by student teachers is not likely to have immediate or widely-felt effects on the problems of schools and society. However, if action research is emphasized during a semester of student teaching, it is worth considering the pedagogy of that pedagogy. For instance, how does our pedagogy function if we direct students' selection of topics (e.g., Robottom, 1988)? How does our pedagogy function if we do or do not intervene when, after telling students to research something that *they* feel or perceive as problematic, they choose some aspect of teaching that is at odds with our own perceptions of what social reconstructionist work is?[8] What technologies of power and surveillance are operating in the requirement of students to conduct action research, and what technologies in my common practice of asking them to include in their report some reflective thoughts on the process of conducting action research? Again we confront a rationality that at once individualizes and integrates. Students conduct their own action research projects that integrate into a particular vision of teaching situated within the regime of disciplinary power.

Furthermore, what happens to the reports produced by student teachers in the name of action research? How often, and how, are students asked to read the knowledge productions of their former peers? To what extent does action research remain another hurdle in the process of becoming certified as a teacher? Again, I do not want to suggest that reflective teaching and action research should not be part of teacher education programs. Studies at the University of Wisconsin-Madison (some in which I have participated) and elsewhere, have suggested that these techniques can have very positive/beneficial effects (Maas, 1991). But, as Foucault tells us, and as I continue to repeat, *everything* is dangerous.

As this discussion of reflective teaching and action research illustrates, drawing on Foucault's analyses of power-knowledge, and ethics facilitates a more specific identification of regulative effects of particular pedagogical practices. Perhaps more importantly, using these Foucauldian techniques allows us to identify possible ways to disrupt the regimes and effects of domination actualized through specific practices. For instance, Foucault's notion of ethics suggests an alternative use of journals and an alternative goal for reflective teaching which is premised on attempting to understand who we are today and how we have come to be that way. Similarly, in the use of action research, we might investigate the effects of asking students to do more re-assembling work as part of their efforts to change conditions or practices. For example, instead of only exploring different classroom management techniques in an attempt to create more democratic classroom relations, a student teacher might also explore how it is that certain practices are taken for granted in classrooms, and how, positioned not quite as a teacher but no longer as a student in that classroom, the student teacher must choose from among a limited set of already-constituted management techniques.

In order to engage in the work of identifying potential dangers of social reconstructionist teacher education practices, and in order to alter those practices, a general attitude of reflexivity or what Foucault calls "care of the self" is needed.

ETHICS, CARE OF THE SELF, AND REFLEXIVITY

As Chapters 4 and 5 revealed so vividly, critical and feminist pedagogy discourses have tended to neglect the ethical. There has been a tendency to emphasize what we do and say for others rather than what we do to ourselves or ask others to do to themselves. In our efforts to move forward beyond (specific forms of) oppression or, recently, to work "across differences" in specific contexts, there has been a tendency toward a lack of reflexivity. Methodologies such as those oriented at ideology-critique tend to overlook the relations to one's self that emerge from particular practices or discourses, perhaps because they focus on ideologies as socially constructed. As suggested in Chapter 6, however, collecting and re-assembling—work that could help reveal technologies of self—opens the possibility for rupture. For instance, by identifying a particular regime of pedagogy through which radical pedagogy discourses function, my own re-assembling work has departed from previous conceptions of "important work for critical and feminist discourses"—work that has primarily focused on articulating social visions which are oppositionally posed to mainstream educational discourses.

With Foucault's notion of ethics, we confront the technologies through which we make ourselves into subjects, through which we participate in our own subjectification. Consider, for instance why it is that, despite our most emancipatory intentions, many of us, as teachers, have found ourselves repeating the very expressions and practices that typified the kinds of teachers we vowed we would never be. An explanation is that we have internalized the technologies that have constituted us as particular kinds of beings, "teachers," working with another kind of being, "students." If there is a space for freedom in the technologies of self because we make choices about the specific practices with which we will regulate our own actions, then it may be in the realm of the ethical that we have the greatest capacity to make alterations to dangerous aspects of our regimes. The more aware we are of the practices *of self*, the greater the space for altering those practices.

This work on "relations to ourselves" might best proceed via the kind of re-assembling task about which I wrote in Chapter 6, and which I have begun in this book by looking at specific institutional conditions and specific practices of radical pedagogies. In order to guard against the possibility that our own critical, feminist, social reconstructionist, or poststructuralist discourses would simply replace earlier discourses within the same institutions and disciplines, it is important to continuously and vigilantly carry out the work of re-assembling, recommencement, critical renewal. As Paul Bové (1990) has written about "discourse" (in his poststructuralist use of the term) and, as I have presented "regime of truth":

> Of course, it is, in itself, no panacea of critical opposition; it is no talisman—although many newer critics chant its terms as if they were a magical charm. It, too, can become a new disciplinary technique— some would argue it already has—within our regulated society, one that enables the production of new texts, new discourses, whose "contents" may be different and whose politics may be oppositional but whose effects on given power relations may be either minimal or unpredictable and undesired. Criticism must always watchfully resist the promotional powers of the disciplined discourse in which it is placed. (p. 64)

CONCLUSION

Some readers will be disappointed with this concluding chapter because of its lack of prescriptive guidance. The changes I suggest for my own teacher education practice are small in magnitude, and I am aware of the possibility that they too are dangerous. Charles Scott (1990) accurately captures and explains my own disappointment through his claim that "what is in question returns in the question . . . [but it is] a disturbed return, one fraught with worry, a sense of danger, ambiguity, and . . . mourning" (p. 8). The mourning comes from the "the doubtfulness as to whether we truly are the selves we seem to be" (p. 57). It is a mourning of selfhood, the loss of my own innocence as an emancipatory teacher educator.

However, I find that there is also exhilaration in the recognition of regimes and the new spaces of freedom suggested by this analysis. Understanding my work in teacher education, through aspects of Foucault's work, also clarifies some of the difficulties I experienced in my attempts to use critical and feminist pedagogies, and, moreover, promotes a greater understanding of my *self*.

Foucault (1988a) wanted to identify "spaces of freedom" we can still enjoy. According to Foucault's analyses, there will always be regimes of truth and technologies of self. The point of identifying spaces of freedom is not to escape all regimes and technologies, only current ones; to increase awareness of current regimes and technologies; to recognize that current regimes need not be as they are; to continually identify and squeeze into those spaces of freedom. This is the task I have begun in this analysis. At this particular historical moment, I would argue that a Foucauldian perspective establishes the instructional practices of pedagogy as an important site of investigation for radical educators, points to ways out of the pessimism often associated with poststructuralist positions (especially vis-à-vis its focus on specific power relations and technologies of the self in local contexts), and (despite arguments to the contrary) does not mandate rejecting visions of different societies, but proposes that they get worked out locally.

The clarity I now feel about ways in which to proceed with my practice in teacher education comes, in part, from having arrived at a different understanding of pedagogy. The "neglect of pedagogy" which at once troubled me and propelled me toward this study, seems even more poignant in light of the ways in which regimes function through *practices,* and the ways in which the regime of modern disciplinary power, through localized mechanisms of enticement, regulation, surveillance, and classification, functions, in part, through *pedagogy.* Without paying particular attention to our specific practices of pedagogy—those which have constructed what we are today *and* those toward which we aim in our educational and political dreams of different societies—we might altogether overlook the ways in which pedagogy operates, and, furthermore, the pedagogies for which we argue so earnestly and sincerely will remain inconsistent with the pedagogies of our arguments.

Notes

1. INTRODUCTION

1. Moreover, unlike those approaches to "discourse" which equate it with language and a purely textual form of analysis, and separate it from other social contexts and practices, this view of discourse is much more than an abstract politics of language games. Rather, this view focuses on the materiality of discourse. "That is, 'discourse' makes possible disciplines and institutions which, in turn, sustain and distribute those discourses" (Bové, 1990, p. 57). Discourses and their related disciplines and institutions are functions of power: they distribute the effects of power. Bové (1990) argues that the study of "discourse," in describing the surface linkages between power, knowledge, institutions, intellectuals, the control of populations, and the modern state, as these intersect in the functions of systems of thought, leads inevitably to a study of institutions, disciplines, and intellectuals. See Bové (1990) for a clear and very helpful account of the poststructuralist notion of "discourse" upon which this book draws.

2. See Popkewitz (1991) for a discussion of such constructions of pedagogy.

3. See, for example, Dewey (1897) and Kohl (1976).

4. Elizabeth Ellsworth's (1989) paper, "Why doesn't this feel empowering?", first presented at the Bergamo conference of 1988, precipitated a number of commentaries (e.g., Giroux, 1988e; Lather, 1991; McLaren, 1988b). Even here, many of the references to other theorists' work are couched in generalities.

5. This is not to suggest that pedagogy can only be seen as regulatory, nor that all desires for, or discourses of, social regulation are evil.

6. Foucault's writings on "the will to knowledge" have their source in Nietzsche's formulations. See, for example, Foucault's (1984a) essay "Nietzsche, Genealogy, History."

7. Interestingly, the French phrase *vouloir-savoir* means both "the will to knowledge" and "knowledge as revenge" (Rabinow, 1984, p. 100). I shall return to the notion of knowledge as revenge as I introduce Foucault's analyses of power in Chapter 3.

2. CRITICAL PEDAGOGIES AND FEMINIST PEDAGOGIES: ADVERSARIES, ALLIES, OTHER?

1. I am using "discourses," rather than "literatures" or "areas of work," to highlight the ways in which language, subjectivity, social institutions, intellectuals, and power are related. To minimize confusion I use three levels of radical pedagogy—(1) a *field* of radical pedagogy, (2) *discourses* of critical and feminist pedagogy, (3) *strands* within these discourses—even though one could argue that the various strands function as discourses.

2. This study was first reported in 1990 and revised in 1991. I note the rapid pace of publication in the areas of education and pedagogy, and the time lag between the production of manuscripts and publication.

3. For example, Simon has written with Giroux, but Simon's writing is not centrally focused on constructing a critical pedagogy; Smyth's work tends to synthesize and apply critical pedagogies to other domains; Liston has written critiques of the Giroux/McLaren strand; Zeichner has used the language of critical pedagogy to explicate "critical reflectivity".

4. Claims made around this differentiation are based on institutional affiliations given in notes identifying authors together with their place of publication.

5. I use these labels at the risk of under-emphasizing the anonymity of discourses. "The function of discourse and the realities it constructs are fundamentally anonymous. This does not mean that no individuals hold these perspectives nor that no individuals effect them. It means that their effective realities depend upon no particular subject in history" (Bové, 1990, p. 56). Thus, while fewer individuals can clearly be named as constructing critical pedagogy discourse compared to feminist pedagogy discourse, neither discourse depends solely upon the individuals who can be named. It is this construction of "discourse-as-anonymous" that leads me to use the passive form (e.g., "discourses themselves" . . .) throughout much of this text.

6. I am using the label "Education" to refer to the academic discipline as it has been constructed in Departments of Curriculum and Instruction, or Departments of Education. Women's Studies is, of course, also concerned with education. I use the labels of the "disciplines" to highlight the institutional location and to avoid more cumbersome nomenclature.

7. As an example of an explicit attempt to avoid the creation of new canons, see Patricia Hill Collins' (1990) *Black Feminist Thought: Knowledge, Consciousness and the Politics of Empowerment* in which she says:

> I deliberately include numerous quotations from a range of African American women thinkers, some well known and others rarely heard from. Explicitly grounding my analysis in multiple voices highlights the diversity, richness, and power of Black women's ideas as part of a long-standing African American women's intellectual community. Moreover, this approach counteracts the tendency of mainstream scholarship to canonize a few Black women as spokespersons for the group and then refuse to listen to any but these select few. (p. xiii)

8. Sandra Acker (1987) summarizes the three main Western feminist theoretical frameworks—liberal, socialist and radical—and their educational applications as follows:

> Liberal feminists writing about education use concepts of equal opportunities, socialization, sex roles and discrimination. Their strategies involve altering so-

cialization practices, changing attitudes and making use of relevant legislation. Critics of the liberal school point to conceptual limitations and the liberal reluctance to confront power and patriarchy. Socialist feminists analyze the role of the school in the perpetuation of gender divisions under capitalism. Major concepts are socio-cultural reproduction and to a lesser extent acceptance of and resistance to gender-based patterns of behaviour. So far socialist-feminist educational writing is mainly theoretical rather than practical and has therefore been criticized for its over-determinism and insufficient empiric foundation. Radical feminists in education have concentrated mainly on the male monopolization of knowledge and culture and on sexual politics in schools. Strategies involve putting women's and girls' concerns first, through separate-sex groups when necessary. Critics argue that radical feminism tends towards biological reductionism, description rather than explanation and also contains methodological weaknesses. (p. 419)

9. For example, Magda Lewis's (1988, 1990a, 1990b) work on feminist pedagogy, although increasingly aligned with poststructuralist feminism, continues to draw upon radical feminist categories. As one example, Lewis (1990b) states:

Women don't need to be taught what we already know: fundamentally, that women are exempted from a culture to which our productive and reproductive labor is essential. The power of phallocentrism may undermine our initiative, it may shake the foundations of our self-respect and self-worth, it may even force us into complicity with violence. But it cannot prevent us from knowing. . . . Rather, the challenge of feminist teaching is in finding ways to make speakable and legitimate the personal/political *investments* we all make in the meanings we ascribe to our historically contingent experiences. (p. 484)

In this passage are references both to contingency and to essentialized characteristics of women.

10. In one exception, Margo Culley (1985) states:

In all the important material written about teaching in the 1960s and 1970s —liberal, progressive, even radical; from Carl Rogers to Paulo Freire, Kozol to Katz—one crucial dimension is missing. None of the discussion of teacher, student, facilitator or learner is gender- or race-specific. (p. 209)

I see three problems with this statement: first, it speaks as *the* authorized voice on "what is important material" on teaching; second, it ignores "radical" approaches to education that have emerged since the 1970s (including critical pedagogy); third, it is inaccurate—Kozol (1968, 1975) explicitly addresses race and, to some extent, gender, with respect to the socialization of young boys into soldiers.

11. See Schneider (1987) for an empirical study of the status of Schools of Education.

12. See also Haywoode and Scanlon (1987).

13. Some recent work by feminists in Education, rather than advocates of feminist pedagogy *per se*, has, however, directly engaged critical pedagogy literature (e.g., Ellsworth, 1989; Gore, 1989, 1990b, 1990c; Kenway and Modra, 1989; Lather, 1991; Luke, 1989b)—perhaps in an attempt to illustrate the need for critical pedagogues to rethink their work.

14. See Kenway and Modra (1989), Orner (1989), and my own work (Gore 1989, 1990b, 1990c) for direct critiques of aspects of feminist pedagogy. See also Laird

(1988) for a less direct but important analysis of different views on the notion of teaching as "woman's true profession."

15. See, for example, Spelman (1988) and Ellsworth (1990).

16. In an apparent exception, McLaren (1989) recounts and reflects on his inner-city school teaching experiences:

> In my own situation as an inner-city teacher, I was unequipped to examine many of the ideological assumptions that informed my own pedagogy. My "authoritative discourse" was immune to its own hidden biases and prejudices. When I was too caught up with my role as teacher, I failed to learn more from my students. (p. 228)

As a call "for practitioners to appropriate critical theory into their own work" (p. 157), this demonstrates McLaren's own growth and might be intended to convince other teachers of the need for "critical tools," rather than to help articulate what it is that practitioners might do in their classrooms.

17. See, for example, Kenway and Modra (1989) and Luke (1989b).

18. I will more closely address this recent work at the end of this section on the critical pedagogy represented by Giroux and McLaren.

19. An article by Giroux and Penna (1981) is something of an exception, but the attention given to classroom practice in this paper is still rather abstract. See my discussion of this paper in Chapter 5.

20. McLaren reproduces the Simon statement inaccurately. I present it here in its entirety.

21. That is, while Simon has written with Giroux, his interest in the construction of critical pedagogies seems tangential.

22. See Chapter 5 for an elaboration and demonstration of this point.

23. For example, Erica Southgate, one of my undergraduate students, recently wrote in response to Giroux's (1988e) essay "Border pedagogy in the age of postmodernism":

> There is an irony in Giroux's claim to be developing a "power-sensitive discourse" which does not silence "Others" but stimulates interaction. The style of Giroux's own writing is hardly conducive to opening up dialogue. His language is inaccessible; it is not "power-sensitive", rather, it serves to alienate all those who do not understand the vocabulary of the postmodern or theoretical/philosophical (e.g. dialectical, Others, multiple positions, discourses, pedagogical and methodological boundaries, absolutes). It seems as though a reasonably extensive vocabulary and theoretical/intellectual framework is required if this is to be intelligible and capable of application.

24. For example, see "The Discovery Card" (in the final chapter) and the Appendix to Freire's (1973) *Education for Critical Consciousness*.

25. Although Giroux and Freire are co-editors of a "Critical Studies in Education" series, and have written complimentary introductions to each other's books, it is unclear how the two discourses have interacted.

26. I thank James Ladwig for both suggesting the utility of such a diagram and highlighting Bourdieu's (1984, p. 126) discussion of effects of such diagrams.

27. I want to emphasize that this diagram is not intended to provide a schemata for the categorization of all extant or possible pedagogy discourses. To attempt to create a grand scheme for all radical discourses that can be related to pedagogy would be contradictory with my emphasis here on the functioning of discourses in context

and time. Different types of delineations will be applicable in different temporal, geographic, and intellectual sites.

28. I am deliberately using the ambiguous "US," rather than "USA" or "United States," to enable the concomitant consideration of an us/them differentiation.

29. As an example, see Zeichner (1990a) for a powerful statement of the oversights of much teacher education research in relation to Third World contributions and perspectives.

30. See, for example, Alice Jardine and Paul Smith's (1987) *Men in Feminism*.

31. Kathleen Weiler's (1988) work provides a good example. She locates her study of women teaching for change in the critical pedagogy of her adviser, Henry Giroux, but brings a feminist perspective to that work. Had she been elsewhere, she might have approached the critical work rather differently. Likewise, my having been at the University of Wisconsin, at the time of Elizabeth Ellsworth's powerful and apparently wide-reaching critique of critical pedagogy, was highly influential in the development of my own work.

32. I elaborate this argument in Chapter 4.

33. As Ladwig (1992) points out, the affinity of earlier radical educational discourses to phenomenological and interpretive work can also be seen in this light.

3. REGIMES OF TRUTH

1. It should be noted that French is a highly gendered language. The "individual in his subjection" is a literal, but not faithful, translation. "*L'individu*" has no feminine equivalent.

2. Foucault died in 1984 at the age of 57 with his multi-volume *History of Sexuality*, unfinished.

3. This statement should not be read to imply only physical actions. Power exists and is actualized in both discursive (writing, publishing, speaking, reading) and non-discursive practices.

4. See, for example, McLaren (1989, p. 181).

5. I thank Elizabeth Ellsworth for bringing Feher's paper to my attention.

6. Foucault (1983b) explains "agonism" as "a relationship which is at the same time reciprocal incitation and struggle; less of a face-to-face confrontation which paralyzes both sides than a permanent provocation" (p. 222).

4. AUTHORITY AND EMPOWERMENT IN CRITICAL PEDAGOGY

1. See for example: "Authority, ethics and the politics of schooling" (Chapter 3, Giroux, 1988a); "Literacy, critical pedagogy and empowerment" (Chapter 5, Giroux, 1988a); "Authority in the feminist classroom: A contradiction in terms" (Friedman, 1985); "The nature and sources of teacher authority" (Chapter 3, Pagano, 1990); "Creating spaces and finding voices: Teachers collaborating for empowerment" (Miller, 1990); "Structure against structure: Liberating classrooms transform traditional authority" (Chapter 3, Shor and Freire, 1987).

2. I acknowledge that a number of feminist writers have been critical of "essentializing" tendencies within discourses that emphasize "women's nurturing capacities." Nevertheless, much of feminist pedagogy writing refers to a conflict between nurtur-

ance and authority (e.g., Culley et al., 1985; Friedman, 1985; Grumet, 1988a; Pagano, 1990).

3. Other feminist pedagogues have argued that it is a disservice to women to suggest that reason is not feminist (e.g., Cocks, 1985).

4. Some writers focus on women as a broad, and sometimes unitary, category. Others focus on particular groups of women such as "black" women (e.g., Butler, 1985; Davis, 1985; Omolade, 1987; Russell, 1985; Spelman, 1985) or lesbians (e.g., Crumpacker and Vander Haegen, 1987). Very few articulate a concern for empowering male students, not surprising given views of power as a male preserve and the historical struggles of women against patriarchal exercises of power.

5. Cocks (1989) refers to the specific cultural order that rules over the sexed body as "the regime of Masculine/feminine." She uses this phrase "to signify a system of power that operates by declaring the natural, foundational truth of two separate and complementary figures, the masculine self and the feminine self; but that actually creates these truths one as the reverse of the other and imposes them on the sexed body" (p. 233). She uses an upper case letter for the "M" alone to remind us that the masculine and feminine are in fact contradictory, internal aspects of a single whole; and to underscore the positive constitution of the masculine as opposed to the feminine self.

6. As I will clarify in Chapter 6, a question emerges regarding the relative concern of feminist pedagogy discourse for changing what I will call the "regime of pedagogy" or for changing the Masculine/feminine regime.

7. The distinction Cocks (1989) makes here is between a rule which claims to be based on familial position, which in turn rests on the possession of a particular kind of body (patriarchal rule), and a rule which rests on the possession of the particular body alone (phallic rule).

8. An explanation for this is perhaps found in the very category of *feminist* post-structuralism: As Fuss (1989) argues, "essentialism emerges perhaps most strongly within the very discourse of feminism, a discourse which presumes upon the unity of its object of inquiry (women) *even* when it is at pains to demonstrate the differences within this admittedly generalizing and imprecise category" (p. 2).

9. As will be elaborated in the analysis of the institutions which integrate feminist pedagogy, the discourse is primarily concerned with education at the university level, often in Women's Studies courses, rather than with elementary or secondary schooling.

10. Feminist teachers and theorists are often the same person because the site of the espoused feminist pedagogy is the university classrooms in which the theorists teach, whether in Women's Studies, Education, or other disciplines/departments. Hence the theorists are teachers, the teachers theorists.

11. See for example, Gardner, et al. (1989), Mahony (1988), and Mumford (1985), who acknowledge that "students need to learn how to *be* in a feminist classroom as much as we need to learn how to create one" (p.93).

12. See, for example, Shapiro and Smith-Rosenberg (1989).

5. AUTHORITY AND EMPOWERMENT IN CRITICAL PEDAGOGY

1. See, for example, the references to gender and race in Giroux (1988a, 1991) and McLaren (1988b). Indeed, even some of the early critical pedagogy literature referred to race and gender formations (for example, Shor [1980]) while the emphasis remained on class concerns.

2. This theme will be elaborated at length in Chapter 6.

3. In the critical pedagogy of Shor and Freire, the teacher and the theorist are often the same person. This is not clearly the case in the critical pedagogy of Giroux and McLaren, except to the extent that they argue for "educators" to conceptualize, and not just implement, pedagogical strategies. These authors do not explicitly address their own teaching practices—although they do consider their writing to be pedagogical.

4. See Labaree (1990) for a genealogical analysis of teacher professionalization in which he argues that current efforts to professionalize teaching have roots in efforts by teacher educators to raise their own professional status and develop a science of teaching. See also Gitlin (1990) and Herbst (1989).

5. Consider, for example, McLaren's (1989) statement cited earlier in this chapter, that critical discourses are "self-critical."

6. Michael Apple (1986) makes this point also. He says "the way we [academics] talk to others in education and the language we use to describe and criticize the workings of educational institutions constitute our audience as subjects. The language we use embodies a politics in and of itself . . . and a set of social relationships between author and reader" (p. 199).

7. Giroux and McLaren rarely address specific classroom practices. The most notable exceptions are Giroux and Penna's (1981) article in which they argue for the elimination of tracking, for processes which give students some control over grading, for self-paced and group work, and consequently for a change in the hierarchical social relationships of the classroom, and McLaren's (1989) *Life in Schools*.

8. This form/content dichotomy is not tenable in terms of Foucault's notions of power-knowledge and regimes of truth. For Foucault, form and content are not separable. One implies the other. I make the distinction here within the terms of the critical pedagogy discourse, and to highlight the lack of distinctiveness about the specific processes of emancipatory authority.

6. REGIMES OF PEDAGOGY

1. Although critical pedagogy is less singularly opposed to capitalism than feminist pedagogy is opposed to patriarchy, critical pedagogy's roots in and ongoing concern with Marxist and democratic socialist politics enables naming this force the central ideological/material concern of critical pedagogies.

2. The Enlightenment refers to Western philosophical traditions founded on the view that truth could be brought into light, the hidden could be revealed, through rational argument. Hence "man" could control nature and other "men," primarily through scientific endeavors. The human sciences and the institutions of social regulation and correction (e.g., hospitals, prisons, schools) find their origins in the Enlightenment, as does "the modern state"—no longer based on the sovereignty of the king, but on the government of populations.

3. I should clarify that the Modernism I describe, with its emphases on progress and leadership, is not the only possible form of modernism. While these characteristics are part of the modernist projects of critical and feminist pedagogy as presently constructed, other modernist discourses are possible. Habermas (1987), for example, has reclaimed (philosophically, if not yet empirically) a modernist discourse without the view of leadership outlined here.

4. While Bernstein's criticism of many of his contemporaries for treating pedagogy as a relay may be overstated, his argument that there has been no systematic analysis of the principles that regulate pedagogic discourse seems indisputable.

5. "Text," as I use it, does not only refer to written documents, but also to the whole range of social signs which can be read. See Gore (1990a) for one attempt to apply this broad conception of "text" to an analysis of pedagogy.

6. *Hypomnemata* entries can be considered analogous to footnotes—underlying messages, to oneself about oneself.

7. Of course, given that this study was first written as a doctoral dissertation, it also conforms to mandates for "original contributions" and so, if it is indeed a re-assembling, it is also one that reveals.

8. See Popkewitz (1991), Chapter 8, for an analysis of different constructions of the role of the intellectual.

7. A RE-ASSEMBLING FOR PRACTICE IN "RADICAL" TEACHER EDUCATION

1. For the remainder of this chapter I will use "social reconstructionist" rather than "radical" teacher education, because such a term is more descriptive of the kind of approach to teacher education upon which I focus.

2. See Liston and Zeichner (1991) for a detailed account of work within the social reconstructionist tradition, and an outline of other traditions in teacher education.

3. Ducharme and Agne (1989) report: "survey after survey shows the education professorate [*sic*] to be more than 65% male . . . [with] clear differences in gender distribution across professorial ranks" (p. 74). Their own study found that only 14% of full professors were female, with 86% male. At the assistant professor level, there was a more even distribution: 46% female; 54% male.

4. I can only provide a preliminary outline of some aspects of this task here. See Liston and Zeichner (1991) and Labaree (1990) for example contributions to this task. I focus on dangers of existing, prominent discourses and practices within social re-constructionist teacher education.

5. See for example, Zeichner (1987, 1990b), Zeichner and Teitelbaum (1982), Schon (1983, 1987), and Cruickshank (1987). Tabachnick and Zeichner (1991) provide a helpful account of these different approaches to reflective teaching.

6. Wisconsin faculty members no longer refer to "levels" of reflective teaching.

7. See Noffke (1989), for a detailed account of the historical development of action research as a technique within educational discourse.

8. See Gore and Zeichner (1991) for an elaboration of this issue.

References

Acker, S. (1987). "Feminist Theory and the Study of Gender and Education." *International Review of Education 33*(4): 419–35.

Anderson, P. (1983). *In the Tracks of Historical Materialism*. London: Verso Editions.

Apple, M. (1979). *Ideology and Curriculum*. Boston and London: Routledge and Kegan Paul.

———. (1986). *Teachers and Texts: A Political Economy of Class and Gender Relations in Education*. New York and London: Routledge and Kegan Paul.

———. (1987). "Gendered Teaching, Gendered Labor." In T. S. Popkewitz, ed. *Critical Studies in Teacher Education: Its Folklore, Theory and Practice*, (pp. 57–83). London, New York and Philadelphia: Falmer Press.

Aronowitz, S. and Giroux, H. (1985). *Education Under Siege*. Massachusetts: Bergin and Garvey.

Aronowitz, S. and Giroux, H. (1991). *Postmodern Education*. Minneapolis: University of Minnesota Press.

Balbus, I. (1988). "Disciplining Women: Michel Foucault and the Power of Feminist Discourse." In J. Arac, ed. *After Foucault: Humanistic Knowledge, Postmodern Challenges*, (pp. 138–60). New Brunswick and London: Rutgers University Press.

Ball, S. J., ed. (1990). *Foucault and Education*. London and New York: Routledge.

Bartky, S. L. (1988). "Foucault, Femininity, and the Modernization of Patriarchal Power." In I. Diamond and L. Quinby, eds. *Feminism and Foucault: Reflections on Resistance*, (pp. 61–86). Boston: Northeastern University Press.

Baym, N. (1990). "The Feminist Teacher of Literature: Feminist or Teacher?" In S. L. Gabriel and I. Smithson, eds. *Gender in the classroom:*

Power and pedagogy, (pp. 60–77). Urbana and Chicago: University of Illinois Press.

Bell, L. (1987). "Hearing All Our Voices: Applications of Feminist Pedagogy to Conferences, Speeches and Panel Presentations." *Women's Studies Quarterly*, *15*(3,4): 74–80.

Bernstein, B. (1975). *Class, Codes, and Control: Towards a Theory of Educational Transmission*. London: Routledge and Kegan Paul.

———. (1986). "On Pedagogic Discourse." In J. Richardson, ed. *Handbook of Theory and Research for the Sociology of Education*, (pp. 205–40). New York: Greenwood Press.

———. (1990). *The Structuring of Pedagogic Discourse*. London and New York: Routledge.

Berry, E. and Black, E. (1987). "The Integrative Learning Journal." *Women's Studies Quarterly*, *15*(3,4): 59–64.

Beyer, L. (1988). *Knowing and Acting: Inquiry, Ideology, and Educational Studies*. London: Falmer Press.

Bourdieu, P. (1984). *Distinction*, trans. R. Nice. Cambridge, Massachusetts: Harvard University Press.

———. (1988). *Homo Academicus*, trans. P. Collier. Stanford: Stanford University Press.

Bourdieu, P. and Passeron, J. (1977). *Reproduction in Education, Society and Culture*. London and Beverly Hills: Sage.

Bové, P. (1986). *Intellectuals in Power: A Genealogy of Critical Humanism*. New York: Columbia University Press.

———. (1988). "The Foucault Phenomenon: The Problematics of Style." In G. Deleuze *Foucault*, (pp. vii-xl). Minneapolis: University of Minnesota Press.

———. (1990). "Discourse." In F. Lentricchia and T. McLaughlin, eds. *Critical Terms for Literary Study*, (pp. 50–65). Chicago and London: University of Chicago Press.

Bowers, C. A. (1991a). "Some Questions about the Anachronistic Elements in the Giroux-McLaren Theory of a Critical Pedagogy." *Curriculum Inquiry*, *21*(2): 239–52.

———. (1991b). "Critical Pedagogy and the 'Arch of Social Dreaming': A Response to the Criticisms of Peter McLaren." *Curriculum Inquiry*, *21*(4): 479–87.

Boxer, M. J. (1988). "For and About Women: The Theory and Practice of Women's Studies in the U.S." In E. Minnich, J. O'Barr, and R. Rosenfeld, eds. *Reconstructing the Academy: Women's Education and Women's Studies*, (pp. 69–103). Chicago and London: The University of Chicago Press.

Bright, C. (1987). "Teaching Feminist Pedagogy: An Undergraduate Course." *Women's Studies Quarterly*, *15*(3,4): 96–100.

Britzman, D. (1990). "Reconstituting our Teaching Practices: Relationships among Literary Theory, Pedagogical Practices and Self-Critique." Paper presented at the Annual Meeting of the American Educational Research Association, Boston.

———. (1991). *"Practice makes Practice."* Albany: State University of New York Press.

Bunch, C. and Pollack, S., eds. (1983). *Learning our Ways: Essays in Feminist Education.* New York: Crossing Press.

Butler, J. E. (1985). "Toward a Pedagogy of Everywoman's Studies." In M. Culley and C. Portuges, eds. *Gendered Subjects: The Dynamics of Feminist Teaching,* (pp. 230–39). Boston and London: Routledge and Kegan Paul.

Carr, W. and Kemmis, S. (1986). *Becoming Critical: Knowing through Action Research.* Geelong: Deakin University Press.

Castellano, O. (1990). "Canto, Locura y Poesia." *The Women's Review of Books,* 7(5): 18–20.

Cherryholmes, C. (1988). *Power and Criticism: Poststructural Investigations in Education.* New York: Teachers College Press.

Clark, M. (1989). *The Great Divide: The Construction of Gender in the Primary School.* Canberra: Curriculum Development Centre.

Clarricoates, K. (1981). "The Experience of Patriarchal Schooling. *Interchange, 12*(2,3): 185–205.

Cocks, J. (1985). "Suspicious Pleasures: On Teaching Feminist Theory." In M. Culley and C. Portuges, eds. *Gendered Subjects: The Dynamics of Feminist Teaching,* (pp. 171–82). Boston and London: Routledge and Kegan Paul.

———. (1989). *The Oppositional Imagination: Feminism, Critique and Political Theory.* London and New York: Routledge.

Collins, P. H. (1990). *Black Feminist Thought: Knowledge, Consciousness, and the Politics of Empowerment.* Boston: Unwin Hyman.

Connell, R. W. (1983). *Which Way is Up?* Sydney: George Allen and Unwin.

———. (1985). *Teacher's Work.* Boston and London: George Allen and Unwin.

Corrigan, P. R. (1991). "The Making of the Boy: Meditations on What Grammar School did With, To, and For My Body." In H. A. Giroux, ed. *Postmodernism, Feminism, and Cultural Politics,* (pp. 196–216). Albany: State University of New York Press.

Crumpacker, L. and Vander Haegen, E. (1987). "Pedagogy and Prejudice: Strategies for Confronting Homophobia in the Classroom." *Women's Studies Quarterly, 15*(3,4): 65–73.

Cruickshank, D. (1987). *Reflective Teaching.* Reston: Association of Teacher Educators.

Cuban, L. (1984). *How Teachers Taught: Constancy and Change in American Classrooms, 1890–1980.* New York: Longman.

Culley, M. (1985). "Anger and Authority in the Introductory Women's Studies Classroom." In M. Culley and C. Portuges, eds. *Gendered Subjects: The Dynamics of Feminist Teaching,* (pp. 209–18). Boston and London: Routledge and Kegan Paul.

Culley, M., Diamond, A., Edwards, L., Lennox, S., and Portuges, C. (1985). "The Politics of Nurturance." In M. Culley and C. Portuges, eds. *Gendered*

Subjects: The Dynamics of Feminist Teaching, (pp. 11–20). Boston and London: Routledge and Kegan Paul.

Culley, M. and Portuges, C., eds. (1985). *Gendered Subjects: The Dynamics of Feminist Teaching*. Boston and London: Routledge and Kegan Paul.

Davidson, A. I. (1986). "Archaeology, Genealogy, Ethics." In D. C. Hoy, ed. *Foucault: A Critical Reader*, (pp. 221–34). Oxford and New York: Basil Blackwell.

Davis, B. H. (1985). "Teaching the Feminist Minority." In M. Culley and C. Portuges, eds. *Gendered Subjects: The Dynamics of Feminist Teaching*, (pp. 245–52). Boston and London: Routledge and Kegan Paul.

Deleuze, G. (1988). *Foucault*. Minneapolis: University of Minnesota Press.

DeLone, R. H. (1979). *Small Futures: Children, Inequality and the Limits of Liberal Reform*. New York: Harcourt Brace Jovanovich.

Dewey, J. (1897). "My Pedagogic Creed." *The School Journal, 54*: 77–80.

——. (1933). *How we think*. Chicago: Henry Regnery.

Diamond, I. and Quinby, L., eds. (1988). *Feminism and Foucault: Reflections on Resistance*. Boston: Northeastern University Press.

Dreyfus, H. L. and Rabinow, P., eds. (1983). *Michel Foucault: Beyond Structuralism and Hermeneutics*, 2nd edition. Chicago: University of Chicago Press.

Ducharme, E. and Agne, R. (1989). "Professors of Education: Uneasy Residents of Academe." In R. Wisniewski and E. Ducharme, eds. *The Professors of Teaching*, (pp. 67–86). Albany: State University of New York Press.

Dutton, T. A. and Grant, B. C. (1991). "Campus Design and Critical Pedagogy. *Academe*, July–August: 37–43.

Ellsworth, E. (1989). "Why Doesn't this feel Empowering? Working through the Repressive Myths of Critical Pedagogy." *Harvard Educational Review, 59*(3): 297–324.

——. (1990). "Speaking out of Place: Educational Politics from the Third Wave of Feminism." Paper presented at the Twelfth Conference on Curriculum Theory and Classroom Practice, Dayton, Ohio.

Fay, B. (1987). *Critical Social Science: Liberation and its Limits*. Ithaca: Cornell University Press.

Feher, M. (1987). "On Bodies and Technologies." In H. Foster, ed. *Discussions in Contemporary Culture*, (pp. 159–72). Seattle: Bay Press.

Felman, S. (1982). "Psychoanalysis and Education: Teaching Terminable and Interminable." *Yale French Studies, 63*: 21–44.

——. (1985). *Writing and Madness*, trans. M. N. Evans, S. Felman, and B. Massumi. Ithaca: Cornell University Press.

Fisher, B. (1987). "The Heart has its Reasons: Feeling, Thinking, and Community-Building in Feminist Education." *Women's Studies Quarterly, 15*(3,4): 47–58.

Foucault, M. (1972). *The Archaeology of Knowledge and the Discourse on Language*, trans. A. M. Sheridan Smith. New York: Pantheon Books.

——. (1973). *The Birth of the Clinic: An Archaeology of Medical Perception.* New York: Pantheon Books.

——. (1977a). *Language, Counter-Memory, Practice.* D. F. Bouchard, ed. New York: Cornell University.

——. (1977b). *Discipline and Punish: The Birth of the Prison.* New York: Pantheon Books.

——. (1978). *The History of Sexuality: Volume 1: An Introduction.* New York: Vintage Books.

——. (1979). "Governmentability." *Ideology and Consciousness,* 6: 5–22.

——. (1980a). "Questions on Geography." In C. Gordon, ed. *Power/Knowledge: Selected Interviews and Other Writings 1972–1977,* (pp. 63–77). New York: Pantheon Books.

——. (1980b). Truth and Power. In C. Gordon, ed. *Power/Knowledge: Selected Interviews and Other Writings 1972–1977,* (pp. 109–33). New York: Pantheon Books.

——. (1983a). "Structuralism and Post-Structuralism," interview with G. Raulet, trans. J. Harding. *Telos,* 55: 195–210.

——. (1983b). "Afterword: The Subject and Power." In H. L. Dreyfus and P. Rabinow, eds. *Michel Foucault: Beyond Structuralism and Hermeneutics,* 2nd edition, (pp. 208–26). Chicago: University of Chicago Press.

——. (1983c). "On the Genealogy of Ethics: An Overview of Work in Progress." In H. L. Dreyfus and P. Rabinow, eds. *Michel Foucault: Beyond Structuralism and Hermeneutics,* 2nd edition, (pp. 229–52). Chicago: University of Chicago Press.

——. (1984a). "Nietzsche, Genealogy, History." In P. Rabinow, ed. *The Foucault Reader,* (pp. 76–100). New York: Pantheon Books.

——. (1984b). "What is Enlightenment?" In P. Rabinow, ed. *The Foucault Reader,* (pp. 32–50). New York: Pantheon Books.

——. (1985). *The Use of Pleasure: Volume 2 of The History of Sexuality.* New York: Pantheon Books.

——. (1986). *The Care of the Self: Volume 3 of The History of Sexuality.* New York: Pantheon.

——. (1988a). "The Political Technology of Individuals." In L. H. Martin, H. Gutman, and P. H. Hutton, eds. *Technologies of the Self: A Seminar with Michel Foucault,* (pp. 145–62). Amherst: The University of Massachusetts Press.

——. (1988b). "The Ethic of Care for the Self as a Practice of Freedom." In J. Bernauer and D. Rasmussen, eds. *The Final Foucault,* (pp. 1–20). Cambridge, Massachusetts and London: The Massachusetts Institute of Technology Press.

Fraser, N. (1989). *Unruly Practices: Power, Discourse and Gender in Contemporary Social Theory.* Minneapolis: University of Minnesota Press.

Freire, P. (1968). *Pedagogy of the Oppressed.* New York: Seabury Press.

——. (1973). *Education for Critical Consciousness.* New York: Seabury Press.

———. (1978). *Pedagogy in Process: Letters to Guinea-Bissau*. New York: Seabury Press.

———. (1985). *The Politics of Education: Culture, Power, and Liberation*. Massachusetts: Bergin and Garvey.

Friedman, S. S. (1985). "Authority in the Feminist Classroom: A Contradiction in Terms?" In M. Culley and C. Portuges, eds. *Gendered Subjects: The Dynamics of Feminist Teaching*, (pp. 203–08). Boston and London: Routledge and Kegan Paul.

Fuss, D. (1989). *Essentially Speaking: Feminism, Nature and Difference*. New York and London: Routledge.

Gabriel, S. L. and Smithson, I., eds. (1990). *Gender in the Classroom: Power and Pedagogy*. Urbana and Chicago: University of Illinois Press.

Gardner, S., Dean, C., and McKaig, D. (1989). "Responding to Difference in the Classroom: The Politics of Knowledge, Class, and Sexuality." *Sociology of Education, 62*(Jan): 64–74.

Gentile, J. R. (1988). *Instructional Improvement: Summary and Analysis of Madeleine Hunter's Essential Elements of Instruction and Supervision*. National Staff Development Council, Oxford, Ohio.

Giroux, H. A. (1979). "Paulo Freire's Approach to Radical Educational Reform." *Curriculum Inquiry, 9*(3): 257–72.

———. (1981). "Pedagogy, Pessimism, and the Politics of Conformity: A Reply to Linda McNeil." *Curriculum Inquiry, 11*(3): 211–22.

———. (1983). *Theory and Resistance in Education*. Massachusetts: Bergin and Garvey.

———. (1985). "Teachers as Transformative Intellectuals." *Social Education, 38*(2): 33–39.

———. (1988a). *Schooling and the Struggle for Public Life: Critical Pedagogy in the Modern Age*. Minneapolis: University of Minnesota Press.

———. (1988b). *Teachers as Intellectuals: Toward a Critical Pedagogy of Learning*. Massachusetts: Bergin and Garvey.

———. (1988c). "Schrag Speaks: Spinning the Wheel of Misfortune." *Educational Theory, 38*(1): 145–46.

———. (1988d). "Postmodernism and the Discourse of Educational Criticism." *Journal of Education, 170*(3): 5–30.

———. (1988e). "Border Pedagogy in the Age of Postmodernism." *Journal of Education, 170*(3): 162–81.

Giroux, H. A., ed. (1991). *Postmodernism, Feminism, and Cultural Politics*. Albany: State University of New York Press.

Giroux, H. A. and McLaren, P. (1986). "Teacher Education and the Politics of Engagement: The Case for Democratic Schooling." *Harvard Educational Review, 56*(3): 213–38.

Giroux, H. A. and Penna, A. N. (1981). "Social Education in the Classroom: The Dynamics of the Hidden Curriculum." In H. A. Giroux, A. N. Penna, and W. F. Pinar, eds. *Curriculum and Instruction: Alternatives in Education*, (pp. 209–30). Berkeley: McCutchan.

Giroux, H. A. and Simon, R. (1988). "Ideology, Popular Culture and Pedagogy." *Curriculum and Teaching*, *3*(1,2): 3–8.

Gitlin, A. (1990). "Power and method." Paper presented at the Twelfth Conference on Curriculum Theory and Classroom Practice, Dayton, Ohio.

Gore, J.M. (1987). "Reflecting on Reflective Teaching." *Journal of Teacher Education*, *38*(2): 33–39.

———. (1989). Agency, Structure and the Rhetoric of Teacher Empowerment." Paper presented at the Annual Meeting of the American Educational Research Association, San Francisco, California.

———. (1990a). "Pedagogy as 'Text' in Physical Education Teacher Education: Beyond the Preferred Reading." In D. Kirk and R. Tinning, eds. *Physical Education, Curriculum and Culture: Critical Studies in the Contemporary Crisis*, (pp. 101–38). London, New York, and Philadelphia: Falmer Press.

———. (1990b). "Pedagogy and the Disciplining of Bodies: An Ethnographic Exploration of Disciplinary Power in Three Pedagogical Sites." Proposal submitted to the Australian Research Council for Postdoctoral Research Fellowship.

———. (1990c). "What We can Do for You! What *can* 'We' Do for 'You'?: Struggling over Empowerment in Critical and Feminist Pedagogy." *Educational Foundations*, *4*(3): 5–26.

———. (1991a). "Practicing What We Preach: Action Research and the Supervision of Student Teachers." In B. R. Tabachnick and K. M. Zeichner, eds. *Issues and Practices in Inquiry-Oriented Teacher Education*, (pp. 253–72). Philadelphia: The Falmer Press.

———. (1991b). "On Silent Regulation: Emancipatory Action Research and Preservice Teacher Education." *Curriculum Perspectives*, *11*(4): 47–51.

Gore, J. M. and Bartlett, V. L. (1987). "Pathways and Barriers to Reflective Teaching in an Initial Teacher Education Program." Paper presented at the Australian Curriculum Studies Association National Conference, Sydney, Australia.

Gore, J. M. and Zeichner, K. M. (1991). "Action Research and Reflective Teaching in Preservice Teacher Education: A Case Study from the United States." *Teaching and Teacher Education*, *7*(2): 119–36.

Greene, M. (1978). *Landscapes for Learning*. New York: Teachers College Press.

———. (1988). *The Dialectic of Freedom*. New York: Teachers College Press.

Greenberg, S. (1982). "The Women's Movement: Putting Educational Theory into Practice." *Journal of Curriculum Theorizing*, *4*(2): 193–98.

Grumet, M. R. (1988a). *Bitter Milk*. Amherst: The University of Massachusetts Press.

Grumet, M. R. (1988b). "Women and Teaching: Homeless at Home." In W. F. Pinar, ed. *Contemporary Curriculum Discourses*, (pp. 531–40). Scottsdale, Arizona: Gorsuch Scarisbrick.

Habermas, J. (1986). "The Genealogical Writing of History: On Some Aporias in Foucault's Theory of Power," trans. G. Ostrander. *Canadian Journal of Political and Social Theory, 10*(1–2): 1–9.

——. (1987). *The Philosophic Discourse of Modernity*, trans. F. Lawrence. Cambridge, Massachusetts: The Massachusetts Institute of Technology Press.

Hamilton, D. (1989). *Towards a Theory of Schooling*. London, New York, and Philadelphia: Falmer Press.

Harding, S. (1990). "The Permanent Revolution." *The Women's Review of Books, 7*(5): 17.

Haywoode, T. L. and Scanlon, L. P. (1987). "World of our Mothers: College for Neighborhood Women." *Women's Studies Quarterly, 15*(3,4): 101–09.

Henricksen, B. and Morgan, T. E., eds. (1990). *Reorientations: Critical Theories and Pedagogies*. Urbana and Chicago: University of Illinois Press.

Herbst, J. (1989). *And Sadly Teach: Teacher Education and Professionalization in American Culture*. Madison: University of Wisconsin Press.

Hill, C. E. (1990). *Writing from the Margins: Power and Pedagogy for Teachers of Composition*. New York and Oxford: Oxford University Press.

The Holmes Group. (1990). *Tomorrow's Schools: Principles for the Design of Professional Development Schools*. East Lansing: Michigan State University, School of Education.

hooks, b. (1984). *Feminist Theory: From Margin to Center*. Boston: South End Press.

——. (1990). "From Scepticism to Feminism." *The Women's Review of Books, 7*(5): 29.

Hunter, I. (1988). *Culture and Government: The Emergence of Literary Education*. London: Macmillan Press.

Jardine, A. and Smith, P., eds. (1987). *Men in Feminism*. New York: Methuen.

Jhirad, S. (1990). "Gender Gaps." *The Women's Review of Books, 7*(5): 30.

Jones, K. and Williamson, K. (1979). "The Birth of the Schoolroom: A Study of the Transformation in the Discursive Conditions of English Popular Education in the First-Half of the Nineteenth Century." *Ideology and Consciousness, 5*(1): 59–110.

Journal of Education (1988). "The Hope of Radical Education: A Conversation with Henry Giroux." *170*(2): 91–101.

Keenan, T. (1987). "The 'Paradox' of Knowledge and Power: Reading Foucault on a Bias." *Political Theory, 15*(1): 5–37.

Kelly, G. and Nihlen, A. (1982). "Schooling and the Reproduction of Patriarchy." In M. Apple, ed. *Cultural and Economic Reproduction in Education*, (pp. 162–80). Boston: Routledge and Kegan Paul.

Kemmis, S. and McTaggart, R. (1982). *The Action Research Planner*, 2nd edition. Geelong: Deakin University Press.

Kenway, J. and Modra, H. (1989). "Feminist Pedagogy and Emancipatory Possibilities." *Critical Pedagogy Networker, 2*(2,3): 2–14.

——. (1992). "Feminist Pedagogy and Emancipatory Possibilities." In C. Luke and J. Gore, eds. *Feminisms and Critical Pedagogy*, (pp. 138–166). New York: Routledge.

King, B. (1990). "Disciplining Teachers." Paper presented at the Annual Meeting of the American Educational Research Association, Boston, Massachusetts.

Klein, R. D. (1987). The Dynamics of the Women's Studies Classroom: A Review Essay of the Teaching Practice of Women's Studies in Higher Education." *Women's Studies International Forum*, *10*(2): 187–206.

Knorr-Cetina, K. (1981). "Introduction: The Micro-Sociological Challenge of Macro-Sociology: Towards a Reconstruction of Social Theory and Methodology." In K. Knorr-Cetina and A. N. Cicourel, eds. *Advances in Social Theory and Methodology: Towards an Integration of Micro- and Macro-Sociologies*, (pp. 1–47). Boston and London: Routledge and Kegan Paul.

Kohl, H. (1976). *On Teaching*. New York: Schocken.

Kozol, J. (1968). *Death at an Early Age*. New York: Bantam Books.

——. (1975). *The Night is Dark and I am far from Home*. New York: Bantam Books.

Labaree, D. (1990). "Power, Knowledge, and the Science of Teaching: A Genealogy of Teacher Professionalization." Unpublished manuscript, Michigan State University.

Ladwig, J. G. (1990). Preliminary examination. Unpublished paper, University of Wisconsin-Madison.

——. (1992). *A Theory of Methodology for the Sociology of School Knowledge*. Unpublished Ph.D. thesis, University of Wisconsin-Madison.

Laird, S. (1988). "Reforming 'Woman's True Profession': A Case for 'Feminist Pedagogy' in Teacher Education?" *Harvard Educational Review*, *58*(4): 449–63.

Lather, P. (1990). "Staying Dumb? Student Resistance to Liberatory Curriculum." Paper presented at the Annual Meeting of the American Educational Research Association, Boston, Massachusetts.

——. (1991). *Getting Smart: Feminist Research and Pedagogy with/in the Postmodern*. New York: Routledge.

Lewis, M. (1988). *Without a Word: Sources and Themes for a Feminist Pedagogy*. Unpublished Ph.D. thesis, University of Toronto.

——. (1989). "The Challenge of Feminist Pedagogy." *Queen's Quarterly*, *96*(1): 117–30.

——. (1990a). "Framing: Women and Silence: Disrupting the Hierarchy of Discursive Practices." Paper presented at the American Educational Research Association Annual Conference, Boston.

——. (1990b). "Interrupting Patriarchy: Politics, Resistance, and Transformation in the Feminist Classroom." *Harvard Educational Review*, *60*(4): 467–88.

Lewis, M. and Simon, R. (1986). "A Discourse not Intended for Her: Learning and Teaching within Patriarchy." *Harvard Educational Review*, *56*(4): 457–72.

Liston, D. P. and Zeichner, K. M. (1991). *Teacher Education and the Social Conditions of Schooling*. London and New York: Routledge, Chapman and Hall.

Lorde, A. (1984). *Sister Outsider*. Trumansburg, New York: Crossing Press.

Luke, C. (1989a). *Pedagogy, Printing and Protestantism*. Albany: State University of New York Press.

———. (1989b). "Feminist Politics in Radical Pedagogy." In C. Luke and J. Gore, eds. *Feminisms and Critical Pedagogy*, (pp. 25–53). New York: Routledge.

Luke, C. and Gore, J., eds. (1992). *Feminisms and Critical Pedagogy*. New York: Routledge.

Lusted, D. (1986). "Why Pedagogy?" *Screen*, *27*(5): 2–14.

Maas, J. (1991). "Writing and Reflection in Teacher Education." In B. R. Tabachnick and K. M. Zeichner, eds. *Issues and Practices in Inquiry-Oriented Teacher Education*, (pp. 211–25). Philadelphia: Falmer Press.

Maglin, N. B. (1987). "A Review of Margo Culley and Catherine Portuges, 'Gendered Subjects: The Dynamics of Feminist Teaching.' " *Radical Teacher*: 15–16.

Maher, F. A. (1985a). "Pedagogies for the Gender-Balanced Classroom." *Journal of Thought: Special Issue: Feminist Education*, *20*(3): 48–64.

———. (1985b). "Classroom Pedagogy and the New Scholarship on Women." In M. Culley and C. Portuges, eds. *Gendered Subjects: The Dynamics of Feminist Teaching*, (pp. 29–48). Boston and London: Routledge and Kegan Paul.

———. (1987). "Inquiry Teaching and Feminist Pedagogy." *Social Education*, *51*(3): 186–92.

———. (1991). "Gender, Reflexivity and Teacher Education." In B. R. Tabachnick and K. M. Zeichner, eds. *Issues and Practices in Inquiry-Oriented Teacher Education*, (pp. 22–34). Philadelphia: Falmer Press.

Maher, F. A. and Rathbone, C. H. (1986). "Teacher Education and Feminist Theory: Some Implications for Practice." *American Journal of Education*, *94*(2): 214–35.

Mahony, P. (1988). "Oppressive Pedagogy: The Importance of Process in Women's Studies." *Women's Studies International Forum*, *11*(2): 103–08.

Martin, J. R. (1981). *Reclaiming a Conversation: The Ideal of the Educated Woman*. New Haven: Yale University Press.

———. (1984). "Bringing Women into Educational Thought." *Educational Theory*, *34*(4): 341–53.

Martin, L. H., Gutman, H. and Hutton, P. H., eds. (1988). *Technologies of the Self: A Seminar with Michel Foucault*. Amherst: The University of Massachusetts Press.

Mazza, K. A. (1981). "Reconceptual Inquiry as an Alternative Mode of Curriculum Theory and Practice: A Critical Study." *Journal of Curriculum Theorizing*, *2*(1): 1–89.

McCarthy, C. (1986). "Teacher Training Contradictions." *Education and Society*, *4*(2): 3–15.

McLaren, P. (1988a). "Language, Social Structure and the Production of Subjectivity." *Critical Pedagogy Networker*, *1*(2–3): 1–10.

——. (1988b). "Schooling the Postmodern Body: Critical Pedagogy and the Politics of Enfleshment." *Journal of Education*, *170*(3): 53–83.

——. (1989). *Life in Schools: An Introduction to Critical Pedagogy in the Foundations of Education*. New York and London: Longman.

——. (1991). "Schooling the Postmodern Body: Critical Pedagogy and the Politics of Enfleshment." In H. A. Giroux, ed. *Postmodernism, Feminism, and Cultural Politics*, (pp. 144–73). Albany: State University of New York Press.

McTaggart, R. and Singh, M. G. (1986). "New Directions in Action Research." *Curriculum Perspectives*, *8*(2): 42–46.

Miedema, S. (1987). "The Theory-Practice Relation in Critical Pedagogy." *Phenomenology + Pedagogy*, *5*(3): 221–29.

Miller, J. L. (1990). *Creating Spaces and Finding Voices: Teachers Collaborating for Empowerment*. Albany: State University of New York Press.

Moore, M. C. (1987). "Ethical Discourse and Foucault's Conception of Ethics." *Human Studies*, *10*: 81–95.

Morris, M. (1988). "The Pirate's Fiancée: Feminists and Philosophers, or Maybe Tonight it'll Happen." In I. Diamond and L. Quinby, eds. *Feminism and Foucault: Reflections on Resistance*, (pp. 21–42). Boston: Northeastern University Press.

Morgan, K. P. (n.d.). "The Paradox of the Bearded Mother: The Role of Authority in Feminist Pedagogy." University of Toronto.

——. (1987). "The Perils and Paradoxes of Feminist Pedagogy." *Resources for Feminist Teaching*, *16*: 49–52.

Morton, D. and Zavarzadeh, M., eds. (1991). *Theory/Pedagogy/Politics: Texts for Change*. Urbana and Chicago: University of Illinois Press.

Mumford, L. S. (1985). "Why Do We Have to Do all this Old Stuff? Conflict in the Feminist Theory Classroom." *Journal of Thought: Special Issue: Feminist Education*, *20*(2): 88–98.

Noddings, N. (1984). *Caring*. Berkeley: University of California Press.

Noffke, S. (1989). "The Social Context of Action Research: A Comparative and Historical Analysis." Paper presented at the Annual Meeting of the American Educational Research Association, San Francisco, California.

Noffke, S. and Brennan, M. (1991). "Action Research and Reflective Student Teaching at the University of Wisconsin-Madison: Issues and Examples." In B. R. Tabachnick and K. M. Zeichner, eds. *Issues and Practices in Inquiry-Oriented Teacher Education*, (pp. 186–201). Philadelphia: Falmer Press.

Norton, T. M. and Ollman, B. (1978). *Studies in Socialist Pedagogy*. New York and London: Monthly Review Press.

Omolade, B. (1985). "Black Women and Feminism." In H. Eisenstein and A. Jardine, eds. *The Future of Difference*. New Brunswick: Rutgers University Press.

Omolade, B. (1987). "A Black Feminist Pedagogy." *Women's Studies Quarterly*, *15*(3,4): 32–39.

Orner, M. (1989). "Sit Up and Speak: Exploring the Meanings of Student Voice and Silence." Paper presented at the American Educational Studies Association Convention, Chicago.

———. (1990). "Con/textual Critiques in the Classroom: Interpretation and the Politics of Identity." Paper presented at the Annual Meeting of the American Educational Research Association, Boston.

Pagano, J. (1990). *Exiles and Communities: Teaching in the Patriarchal Wilderness*. Albany: State University of New York Press.

Pinar, W. F., ed. (1981). *Curriculum Theorizing: The Reconceptualists*. Berkeley: McCutchan.

Popkewitz, T. S. (1988). "Culture, Pedagogy, and Power: Issues in the Production of Values and Colonialization." *Journal of Education, 170*(2): 77–90.

———. (1991). *A Political Sociology of Educational Reform*. New York: Teachers College Press.

Rabinow, P., ed. (1984). *The Foucault Reader*. New York: Pantheon Books.

Rajchman, J. (1985). *Michel Foucault: The Freedom of Philosophy*. New York: Columbia University Press.

Rich, A. (1979). "Taking Women Students Seriously." In *On Lies, Secrets, and Silence*, (pp. 237–246). New York: W. W. Norton and Co.

Robottom, I. (1988). "A Research-Based Course in Science Education." In J. Nias and S. Groundwater-Smith, eds. *The Enquiring Teacher: Supporting and Sustaining Teacher Research*. London: Falmer Press.

Rose, N. (1990). *Governing the Soul: The Shaping of the Private Self*. London and New York: Routledge.

Roy, P. A. and Schen, M. (1987). "Feminist Pedagogy: Transforming the High School Classroom." *Women's Studies Quarterly, 15*(3,4): 110–15.

Russell, M. (1985). "Black-Eyed Blues Connection: Teaching Black Women." In M. Culley and C. Portuges, eds. *Gendered Subjects: The Dynamics of Feminist Teaching*, (pp. 155–68). Boston and London: Routledge and Kegan Paul.

Sarason, S. B. (1982). *The Culture of the School and the Problem of Change*, 2nd edition. Boston: Allyn and Bacon.

Sawicki, J. (1988a). "Feminism and the Power of Foucauldian Discourse. In J. Arac, ed. *After Foucault: Humanistic Knowledge, Postmodern Challenges*, (pp. 161–78). New Brunswick and London: Rutgers University Press.

———. (1988b). "Identity Politics and Sexual Freedom: Foucault and Feminism. In I. Diamond and L. Quinby, eds. *Feminism and Foucault: Reflections on Resistance*, (pp. 177–92). Boston: Northeastern University Press.

Schilb, J. (1985). "Pedagogy of the Oppressors?" In M. Culley and C. Portuges, eds. *Gendered Subjects: The Dynamics of Feminist Teaching*, (pp. 253–64). Boston and London: Routledge and Kegan Paul.

Schneider, B. (1987). "Tracing the Provenance of Teacher Education." In T. S. Popkewitz, ed. *Critical Studies in Teacher Education: Its Folklore, Theory and Practice*, (pp. 211–41). London, New York and Philadelphia: Falmer Press.

Schniedewind, N. (1985). "Cooperatively Structured Learning: Implications for Feminist Pedagogy." *Journal of Thought: Special Issue: Feminist Education*, *20*(3): 65–73.

——. (1987). "Teaching Feminist Process." *Women's Studies Quarterly*, *15*(3,4): 15–31.

Schniedewind, N. and Maher, F., eds. (1987) "Special Feature: Feminist Pedagogy." *Women's Studies Quarterly*, *15*(3,4).

Scholes, R. (1989). *Protocols of Reading*. New Haven and London: Yale University Press.

Schon, D. (1983). *The Reflective Practitioner*. New York: Basic Books.

——. (1987). *Educating the Reflective Practitioner*. San Francisco: Jossey Bass.

Schorr, L. (1988). *Within our Reach: Breaking the Cycle of Disadvantage*. New York: Anchor Books.

Schrag, F. (1988). "Response to Giroux." *Educational Theory*, *38*(1): 143–44.

Scott, C. E. (1990). *The Question of Ethics*. Bloomington and Indianapolis: Indiana University Press.

Sennett, R. (1980). "Destructive *Gemeinschaft*." In A. Soble, ed. *The Philosophy of Sex and Love*, (pp. 291–321). Totawa: Rowman and Allanheld.

Shapiro, J. P. and Smith-Rosenberg, C. (1989). "The 'Other Voices' in Contemporary Ethical Dilemmas: The Value of the New Scholarship on Women in the Teaching of Ethics." *Women's Studies International Forum*, *12*(2): 199–211.

Shor, I. (1980). *Critical Teaching and Everyday Life*. Boston: South End Press.

——. (1987). "Equality is Excellence: Transforming Teacher Education and the Labor Process." In M. Okazawa-Rey, J. Anderson, and R. Traver, eds. *Teaching, Teachers and Teacher Education*, (pp. 183–203). Cambridge, Massachusetts: Harvard Educational Review.

——. (1988). *Freire for the Classroom: A Sourcebook for Liberatory Teaching*. Portsmouth: Boynton/Cook.

Shor, I. and Freire, P. (1987). *A Pedagogy for Liberation: Dialogues on Transforming Education*. Massachusetts: Bergin and Garvey.

Shrewsbury, C. M. (1987a). "What is Feminist Pedagogy?" *Women's Studies Quarterly*, *15*(3,4): 6–14.

——. (1987b). "Feminist Pedagogy: A Bibliography." *Women's Studies Quarterly*, *15*(3,4): 116–24.

Simon, R. I. (1984). Signposts for a Critical Pedagogy: A Review of Henry Giroux's 'Theory and Resistance in Education.'" *Educational Theory*, *34*(4): 379–88.

Simon, R. I. (1987). "Empowerment as a Pedagogy of Possibility." *Language Arts*, *64*(4): 370–82.

——. (1988). "For a Pedagogy of Possibility." *Critical Pedagogy Networker*, *1*(1): 1–4.

Smart, B. (1986). "The Politics of Truth and the Problem of Hegemony." In D. C. Hoy, ed. *Foucault: A Critical Reader*, (pp. 157–74). Oxford and New York: Basil Blackwell.

Smithson, I. (1990). "Introduction: Investigating Gender, Power, and Pedagogy." In S. L. Gabriel and I. Smithson, eds. *Gender in the Classroom: Power and Pedagogy*, (pp. 1–27). Urbana and Chicago: University of Illinois Press.

Spelman, E. V. (1985). "Combating the Marginalization of Black Women in the Classroom." In M. Culley and C. Portuges, eds. *Gendered Subjects: The Dynamics of Feminist Teaching*, (pp. 240–44). Boston and London: Routledge and Kegan Paul.

——. (1988). *Inessential Woman: Problems of Exclusion in Feminist Thought*. Boston: Beacon Press.

Spender, D. (1981). "Education: The Patriarchal Paradigm and the Response to Feminism." In *Men's Studies Modified*. Oxford and New York: Pergamon.

Spivak, G. C. (1992). *Outside in the Teaching Machine*. New York: Routledge.

Stanage, S. M. (n.d.). "Freire and Phenomenology: Person, Praxis, and Education for Infinite Tasks." Unpublished paper, Northern Illinois University.

Stow, D. (1850). *The Training System, the Moral Training School, and the Normal Seminary*. London: Longman, Brown, Green.

Tabachnick, B. R. and Zeichner, K. M., eds. (1991). *Issues and Practices in Inquiry-Oriented Teacher Education*. Philadelphia: Falmer Press.

Taubman, P. (1986). "Review article, 'Gendered Subjects: The Dynamics of Feminist Teaching,' Margaret [*sic*] Culley and Catherine Portuges, Editors." *Phenomenology + Pedagogy*, *4*(2): 89–94.

Taylor, C. (1986). "Foucault on Freedom and Truth." In D. C. Hoy, ed. *Foucault: A Critical Reader*, (pp. 69–102). Oxford and New York: Basil Blackwell.

Telos (1981–82). "Symposium: The Role of the Intellectual in the 1980s," *50*: 115–60.

Tetreault, M. K. (1987). "The Scholarship on Women and Teacher Education." *Teacher Education Quarterly*, *14*(2): 77–83.

Valli, L. (1983). "Becoming Clerical Workers: Business Education and the Culture of Femininity." In M. W. Apple and L. Weis, eds. *Ideology and Practice in Schooling* (pp. 213–34). Philadelphia: Temple University Press.

van Manen, M. (1977). "Linking Ways of Knowing with Ways of Being Practical." *Curriculum Inquiry*, *6*: 205–28.

Walker, J. (1980). "The End of Dialogue: Paulo Freire on Politics and Education." In R. Mackie, ed. *Literacy and Revolution*, (pp. 120–50). London: Pluto Press.

Walkerdine, V. (1985). "On the Regulation of Speaking and Silence: Subjectivity, Class and Gender in Contemporary Schooling." In C. Steedman,

C. Unwin and V. Walkerdine, eds. *Language, Gender and Childhood*, (pp. 203–41). London, Boston and Henley: Routledge and Kegan Paul.

——. (1986). "Progressive Pedagogy and Political Struggle." *Screen*, 27(5): 54–60.

——. (1988). *The Mastery of Reason*. New York: Routledge.

Weedon, C. (1987). *Feminist Practice and Poststructuralist Theory*. Oxford: Basil Blackwell.

Weiler, K. (1988). *Women Teaching for Change*. Massachusetts: Bergin and Garvey.

——. (1991). Freire and a Feminist Pedagogy of Difference." *Harvard Educational Review*, 61(4): 449–74.

Weiner, G. (1988). *Just a Bunch of Girls*. Milton Keynes: Open University Press.

Wexler, P. (1987). *Social Analysis of Education: After the New Sociology*. London and New York: Routledge and Kegan Paul.

Williams, R. (1976). "Base and Superstructure in Marxist Cultural Theory." In R. Dale, G. Esland and M. Macdonald, eds. *Schooling and Capitalism: A Sociological Reader*, (pp. 202–10). London: Routledge and Kegan Paul.

Williamson, J. (1988). "Is There Anyone here from a Classroom? And Other Questions of Education." *Screen*, 26(1): 90–95.

Willis, P. (1977). *Learning to Labour*. Westmead: Saxon House.

The Women's Review of Books (1990). "Entering the Nineties." 7(5): 17–32.

Zeichner, K. M. (1987). "Preparing Reflective Teachers." *International Journal of Educational Research*, 11(5): 565–76.

——. (1990a). "Issues of Control in Research on Teacher Education." Paper presented at the Journal of Education for Teaching International Colloquium on Teacher Education, Birmingham, England.

——. (1990b). "When you've said Reflection you Haven't said it all." In T. Stoddard, ed. *Guided Practice in Teacher Education*, (pp. 59–67). National Center for Research on Teacher Education, East Lansing, Michigan.

Zeichner, K. M. and Teitelbaum, K. (1982). "Personalized and Inquiry-Oriented Teacher Education." *Journal of Education for Teaching*, 8(2): 95–117.

Index